"Tyler Merritt had me laughing, crying, and learning throughout *I Take My Coffee Black*. His writing and humor are brilliant, but his authenticity shines through above all. We really are beautiful in the broken places, and I'm better because he shared that beauty so transparently."

—Jud Wilhite, senior pastor, Central Church, Las Vegas, Nevada, and author of *Pursued*

"I've never been schooled in such a charming way! Relevant, funny, poignant, and powerful, Tyler takes us on a deeply personal journey as he recounts his coming-of-age experiences and the devastating impact of America's harsh realities. With delightful prose and meaningful intention, Tyler skillfully guides us toward our shared humanity yet doesn't pull any punches discussing the historic facts about systemic racism. His deft and accessible storytelling offers us fresh perspective, allowing us to see with our eyes and hearts wide open, like his, and we leave feeling inspired and knowing, without a doubt, that we are all kindred."

—Moira Walley-Beckett, Emmy Award–winning writer/executive producer, *Breaking Bad, Anne with an E*

"Listen. I don't know what I expected when I picked up this book, but I know what I didn't expect. I didn't expect to laugh out loud multiple times, cry real tears, learn complete history lessons, and truly feel seen as a black person. If I'm being honest, it was more than feeling seen, it was feeling explained to the point of others being able to see me. Tyler does this in the most charming and disarming way. I will give this book to everyone I know who truly wants to understand the depth and breadth of what it is to be black."

—Melinda Doolittle, recording artist, actress, and author

"Tyler Merritt invites us into his life with genuine, vulnerable humor that reveals deep truths. *I Take My Coffee Black* begs readers to consider the stereotypes and assumptions we all carry about one another and push against them for a higher chance at deep, lasting relationships with those who don't look like us or live like us. As a Black man, this book speaks to the inner self that society, stigma, and stereotypes often push into the dark. A must-read."

—Albert Tate, lead pastor of Fellowship Church and author

"I could not be more honored to be writing this endorsement. I am not only endorsing this book but also a man who has held a sacred and special place in my life over the last year and a half of knowing him. Tyler has used his life as a testimony to love others well and to encourage us to be more loving, kind, empathetic, and authentic humans. *I Take My Coffee Black* is a work that flows with truth, story, and conviction. Over the last few years, I have recognized just how uninformed I am. Tyler has been a voice of reason, truth, belief, and love to me and now we all get to hear from him in this book. If you are human, you should read this book. Take a seat and allow Tyler to speak into you like he has done to many. I am excited for you to read this book."

—Benjamin Higgins, television personality, entrepreneur, and former *Bachelor*

"To know someone is to love them, and Tyler Merritt reveals himself completely in this poignant and vulnerable memoir laced with Black history, the personal effects of systemic racism, show tunes, Jesus, and his brilliant sense of humor. The antidote to our nation's current divide is understanding…and the intimacy at which Tyler shares his life experience as a Black man in the US makes you understand. You have no other choice but to love him…and this book."

—Laura Bell Bundy, Broadway actress and singer

"*I Take My Coffee Black* is equal parts endearing, eye-opening, and insightful. It makes me, as a white woman who has had a vastly different upbringing and experiences (I grew up in the suburbs of Minneapolis), thirsty to do better in my expansion and interactions with more people around me—especially those who I wouldn't normally pass walking down the street in said small-town Minnesota. Tyler has a way to grab ahold of the reader to push them to genuinely want to connect with others, all races, religions, ethnicities, socio-economic statuses encompassed, and to get to know them for who they are to their core. Because if everybody did this a little bit more, our country—and world—would look like a much different place. Hopefully a more peaceful, accepting one. He incorporated the perfect combo of wit, realness, growth, and openness that I don't often have the privilege of receiving in many books. It was a real treat for me to spend my time reading through these pages. Maybe one day I'll be so lucky as to sit down face-to-face with Tyler, share a cup of joe, and dive deeper into all things life (of course, black for him and a splash of oat milk for me)."

—Rebecca Kufrin, television personality, *The Bachelor* and *The Bachelorette*

I TAKE MY COFFEE BLACK

REFLECTIONS ON TUPAC, MUSICAL THEATER, FAITH, AND BEING BLACK IN AMERICA

TYLER MERRITT

WITH DAVID TIECHE
FOREWORD BY JIMMY KIMMEL

WORTHY
PUBLISHING

New York • Nashville

Worthy
Hachette Book Group
1290 Avenue of the Americas, New York, NY 10104
worthypublishing.com
twitter.com/worthypub

First Edition: September 2021

Worthy is a division of Hachette Book Group, Inc. The Worthy name and
logo are trademarks of Hachette Book Group, Inc.

The publisher is not responsible for websites (or their content) that are not
owned by the publisher.

Library of Congress Cataloging-in-Publication Data
Names: Merritt, Tyler, author. | Tieche, David, author. | Kimmel, Jimmy,
    1967- author of foreword
Title: I take my coffee black : reflections on Tupac, musical theater, faith, and
    being black in America / Tyler Merritt with David Tieche ; with a foreword
    by Jimmy Kimmel.
Description: First edition. | New York : Worthy, 2021. | Includes
    bibliographical references.
Identifiers: LCCN 2021019943 | ISBN 9781546029410 (hardcover) | ISBN
    9781546029403 (ebook)
Subjects: LCSH: African American actors--Biography. | Actors--United
    States--Biography.
Classification: LCC PN2287.M623 A3 2021 | DDC 791.4302/8092 [B]--
    dc23
LC record available at https://lccn.loc.gov/2021019943

ISBNs: 978-1-5460-2941-0 (hardcover), 978-1-5460-0149-2 (signed
    edition), 978-1-5460-0148-5 (B&N.com signed edition),
    978-1-5460-2940-3 (ebook)

Printed in the United States of America

LSC-C

Printing 1, 2021

We are not monolithic.
This book is dedicated to the beautifully diverse people
that we are and to the stories that have made us.

CONTENTS

FOREWORD

In June 2020, in the days following the murder of George Floyd, the Black Lives Matter protests awakened the country to inequities and injustice we'd turned a blind eye to for too long. I thought hard about what I might say on television, about how I'd benefited from being born pink, about the systemic racism I had ignored and how I could share my thoughts in simple terms with those who reject and/or simply don't understand what has come to be known as "white privilege."

That night, my wife, Molly, texted me a video titled "Before You Call the Cops." In that video, a man named Tyler spoke about himself, sharing his likes, dislikes, habits, quirks, upbringing, and fears. Tyler spoke directly to the camera, shattering stereotypes with small details and encouraging us to look harder at one another, beyond skin color. Tyler told us that he enjoys basketball *and* hockey, NWA *and* Bon Jovi. He subtly and kindly reminded us of how much we have in common and that assumptions are made by fools.

Moved by Tyler's words, I reached out to ask permission to air his video on television. Tyler agreed, his work was exceptionally well received, and here I am opening for him again. Tyler and I have a lot in common. We are of similar age and were both raised in our beloved Las Vegas. In our correspondence, we bonded over Vegas things: our rival high schools, our neighborhoods, hotel buffets, the lizards every Clark County kid calls "horny toads"… the usual subjects children raised in a very adult city share. Over the next several months, Tyler shared the rest of his story with me—a sad, happy, moving, troubling, inspirational, humorous, and brutal account of the people and experiences that formed this exceptionally well-formed man.

Now he shares it with you. I am very fond of Tyler Merritt. I hope and expect that you will be as captivated by the stories and thoughts on the pages to follow as I was. The man has been through a lot and somehow remains funny, optimistic, and strong. I feel lucky to know him.

—*Jimmy Kimmel*

AUTHOR'S NOTE

People! If you're reading this, then you done chose well!
Congratulations!
So...first, I want to thank you.
Second, I want to warn you that as you get deeper into the pages
of this book, things are about to get real, REAL.
So as a courtesy, I have changed the names and identifying details
of a few people who appear in this book.
Got it? We cool? Dope. Let's go.

CHAPTER 1

IF SHE ONLY KNEW
(PART 1)

Every single day, I try to exercise.

I have a five-mile route that takes me down my block, through some city streets, and then out to the J. Percy Priest Dam, where I can look out over the lake and the water. There's a bench along that route that is my bench.

I even call it that.

When I see it, I say to myself, "That's my bench."

Sometimes, when I see people sitting on it, I get a bit indignant. "Yo. Why are you sitting on my bench?"

But I digress.

I have done some of my deepest thinking on that bench, and though it's a common bench, I've had some uncommon moments on that bench.

Also, it's a place to rest my tired black butt and drink a swig of Smartwater.

It was a fall day in Nashville, and the air was crisp. I put on my Alabama sweatshirt, because my family is from the South and if I don't Roll Tide, they will disown me. I put on my bandana to keep the sweat out of my eyes and my sunglasses to keep the sun out of my eyes. I put on my wireless Bluetooth Beats by Dre headphones because I am an audiophile, and stereophonic sound while exercising keeps me going.

You think I'm going to listen to Bon Jovi on crappy-ass, low-end Walmart headphones?

1

Please.

Now, some geography. On my walk, I go down some busy Nashville streets, and then I cross a fairly busy intersection on my way to the trails and quieter side streets that lead to the dam and the lake. As I was walking down the street this day, I approached the crosswalk.

And there…

On the other side of the street…

Parked at the curb right in front of the crosswalk…

Was an older white woman…

In a blue-and-white older-model Ford truck.

She had her driver's-side window down, which meant that I would be passing by her open window, and at some point, I would be less than a few feet away from her.

And I knew. I knew in that instant. Because…well, life. When you live in the South, and you're six foot two and black with dreadlocks, you know how some people perceive you. I have had a lifetime of white women reacting to me in fear, not because of my size, or because of my clothing, but because of my blackness.

But—let me be clear—I have also had a lot of white women react to me because of the complete and utter magnitude of my sexiness.

But in this moment, I was keenly aware that my blackness was going to be a problem. As the light was getting ready to change, I realized that I was going to have to pass right by her. And at some point, she was going to see me walking toward her. And I knew that she was going to be scared. That I was going to frighten her.

I decided, at that moment (like I do in most moments), that I was going to do everything I possibly could to keep an old white lady from freaking out. Everything I could. I took off the hood to my sweatshirt to expose my face. I wanted to appear like a black Mister Rogers, just taking a stroll through the neighborhood. I took off my sunglasses so that she could see my eyes. I took off my headphones so she would know I could hear her. I put on a smile. A big one. A bright one. Have you seen my smile? It's pretty dope.

I was trying to say to her, "I am not menacing."

"I am not a thief."

"I am not a thug."

"I am just me. It's me! Tyler!"

The light changed. And as I walked toward her car, I slowed down. I was saying to myself, in hushed tones, "Black Mister Rogers, black Mister Rogers." I figured that would be less threatening. And as I got within a few feet of her, she saw me. And her reaction was not at all what I thought it was going to be. It was worse. Her reaction was like something out of a Bugs Bunny cartoon. I thought I was in a *Key & Peele* sketch.

This. Woman. Lost. It. For. Real.

First, this woman practically jumped out of her seat, her gray hair nearly touching the roof of the cab.

"Oh my GAAAWWWD," she said, terrified like she'd just seen a veloci-raptor attack Betty White. I am sorry for that visual. Betty White is a national treasure. This woman grabbed her purse from the passenger seat and then frantically rolled up her window. I heard the *click* of her automatic door locks activating. And then she stared straight ahead at the stoplight. She wouldn't look at me. She tried to pretend I didn't exist.

And as I crossed in front of her truck, in that crosswalk, I stopped. I looked at this poor woman, and I laughed.

I was not laughing at her.

I was laughing because I wanted to say, "Lady. If you only knew."

Lady, if you only knew how much work I just put into trying to make sure what just happened didn't just happen.

Lady, if you only knew my purposeful, intentional effort to disarm myself of all aggressive black man ish, anything that might be misconstrued as frightening.

Lady, if you only knew that I taught Sunday school every week at church, to kids, because I want kids of all colors and backgrounds to know the universe-changing reality of the love of God.

Lady, if you only knew that I love my mother more than my own life and that just the sound of her voice is like cocoa butter to the skin of my soul.

Lady, if you only knew that mere seconds ago I was listening to the soundtrack of the Broadway show *Bring It On: The Musical*.

But she did not know. Instead, this woman saw me as a threat, clear and present, and clutched her pearls and locked her doors.

That moment ruined my walk. As I walked back home, I began trying to process this. And the thought came to me.

If she knew me, maybe she wouldn't be afraid. But even more than that, if this woman knew me, I mean, if she really knew me, I bet she might even like me. Oh, but more than that! I bet I could make her smile. I bet I'd make her feel valued. I bet I'd make her feel joy at just being alive. I bet I'd be one of her favorite people. If she knew me, I bet she would love me.

But she didn't.

She gasped in fright and locked her doors.

That moment was seared in my mind.

I walked through the first stage of grief: denial. "It's not her fault," I said to myself as I sat on my front porch, weary from so much more than the walk. I reasoned with myself. "We know from biology that humans like things they are familiar with, and I don't look like someone that she's familiar with. She doesn't have anyone in her life who I look like, so I'm alien, foreign, different. Her unfamiliarity with people who look like me is what the issue is. It's basic biology," I said to myself, trying to sound convincing.

I sipped my water and felt the second stage of grief descend. Anger.

Nah.

Nah.

What just happened was some *bullshit*.

It is not my job to make sure that some older white lady isn't scared when I am walking on a public street in broad daylight. Listen, lady, the fact that you're scared is YOUR problem, not mine.

Why should I have to diminish myself because you feel uncomfortable with who I am?

Why should I have to edit all my behavior and hide and shrink and apologize because your preference is that I don't exist?

Why should I have to make myself smaller?

If you knew everything I had to go through in my entire life to get here to this moment—all the failures and heartbreaks and triumphs and tragedies that have made me who I am in this moment in this instant—if you knew my heart, and all the love I have tried to give to this world, then you would leap out of the cab of your car and run to me and say, "Who is that brilliant, beautiful, kind, loving man?"

And I would say, "You forgot 'sexy as Denzel.'" And we'd laugh.

But you didn't.

Hey, white lady. I am in front of you. And yes, I am a black man. I am from a proud heritage of beautiful black people whose impact on this planet and on this nation cannot be understated. How I see it, you wouldn't have barbecue if it weren't for my people. And your sports would be boring. For real, sports would suck without black people. Except for hockey—that would stay the same. And let's keep it real, most of the good music—the really good music—that's ours too, homie. I am a proud black man from a proud black heritage.

But more than that, the same Bible we both probably read declares that I am created by God Himself. As a person of color, I am not less, I could NEVER be less because I am made in the very Image of God. In the very beginning, in Genesis, when the Almighty Creator forged the heavenly bodies, He made them to reflect His glory and goodness, and He placed them in the night sky, and in the same way, God Almighty placed me on this earth to shine. I am the reflection of the Image of God, and I wear that as a royal robe, bright as starlight.

But none of that matters to you.

Does it?

Because you don't see that. All you see is a no-good n*gg*r.

And then the third stage: depression. I tossed my empty water bottle against the wooden railing of my porch.

"I give up," I said, to no one in particular, and I sank into my chair, and even deeper into helplessness.

This wasn't fair.

The point was not that my desperate attempts to make this woman feel at ease failed. The point was that—had I been white—this NEVER WOULD HAVE BEEN AN ISSUE. If I had been white, this woman wouldn't have noticed. This situation was not because I was tall. Or big. This situation happened because the color of my skin is black.

And in this moment, I knew this was true.

Because when I first saw this lady, walking up the street, toward the crosswalk, a white guy—roughly my size and roughly my build—walked right across the exact path I was going to take. He didn't think about this woman. He didn't have to, because his skin color was not a threat to her. I have no idea who that man was, but I guarantee no one has ever said to him, "Listen, have you ever tried changing your hairstyle, you know, just so that you're a bit less threatening?" I guarantee no one has said to him, "Be sure not to wear a hat and sunglasses, because if people can't see your eyes, they'll think maybe you're up to something."

This was because I was born with black skin and no other reason. This was not fair.

It's not my job to try to make every human with fearful or racist thoughts feel comfortable.

I did not cause this mess.

I am tired of trying to clean it up.

I sat on my porch, wrapped in sweat and sorrow.

I think maybe the reason so many people in our world cannot lament well is that it requires us to be brave enough to be truly honest about our hurts. About the brokenness. About the pain. About reality. It's tough to face that. I don't care what color you are.

Lord, I am tired of making myself less. It's not fair.

Why did I tell you all this?

Well, I tell you all this because, for me, it's not just a story. For me, it could very well be a matter of life and death. I want to remind you, my friend, that there are a lot of people who won't give me—or people who look like me—the benefit of the doubt. And I don't have the privilege to guess who those people will be. Even when I try my absolute HARDEST, there is still nothing I can do to make some people feel safe.

I was thinking that maybe walking together in this book might be a start.

I'm going to tell you some of my stories in this book. My guess is that you'll relate to some of them. Especially if you think that banana-flavored any-thing is straight-up disgusting OR that spiders are mini-Satans—teeny-tiny little Lords of Darkness just crawling all over the earth.

I was thinking that maybe if you got to know me, you wouldn't be fright-ened. Or better yet, maybe you'd see that we have more in common than you thought. Or better yet, at the end of this book, you would think to yourself, "Man, that Tyler Merritt. We could kick it. For real."

Or at the very least, the next time a six-foot-two black man comes near, you might think to yourself: "Maybe he's listening to *Bring It On: The Musical*."

And maybe we'd grab a cup of coffee, and you and I could laugh about it. Because I think you'd like me if you took some time to get to know me.

CHAPTER 2

LAS VEGAS IS A TERRIBLE PLACE TO RAISE A RACIST

Wow.

Okay.

I think we can all agree: That first chapter was fantastic. In fact, I think I just cured racism. You're welcome.

For real, though, before we move on, I want to go back—all the way back to my childhood. I grew up in Las Vegas, Nevada.

That's right.

Vegas, baby.

And—let's be honest here—Las Vegas is a supremely unique city.

We moved to Las Vegas when I was six because my father was a world-renowned zoologist specializing as a behaviorist for large felines. He went to work with Siegfried and Roy to train their tigers for their live shows at the Mirage.

Y'all know that ain't true.

Black folks ain't trying to kick it with tigers.

Did you hear about that time in Vegas when that black dude was mauled by a tiger? No. No, you didn't. Because it never happened. That's some white

people nonsense. Black people look at that stuff and say, "Nah, bro. I'm good."
My father is a black man born in Alabama during the 1940s, and in general,
his motto is "My people did not survive slavery and Jim Crow by being stupid, so no, I will not voluntarily get into a cage with a tiger."

The *real* reason we moved to Las Vegas was because my father was a military man. Air Force, in fact. I was born in an Air Force hospital in Albuquerque, New Mexico, then my father was sent to Fairbanks, Alaska. He was
transferred to Nellis Air Force Base in June of 1982. I turned six years old
somewhere in the middle of Canada, as my family drove from Fairbanks to
Las Vegas, with only my mom and dad and some moose around to sing me
"Happy Birthday."

What I did not understand at the time, but what I know now, is that Las
Vegas is an *uncommon* place.

In fact, I'd wager that Las Vegas has one of the strangest, most bizarre, and
most unique stories of any major American city.

Every city has a past, a history, and a character to it, so let me tell you a
little bit about my hometown. Kids, this is the time to sit back and grab some
popcorn, because I'm about to get all History Channel on you. Prepare to
learn you something.

Civilization always follows water, and Las Vegas is no different. Because
it's surrounded by mountains, the Las Vegas valley is a basin that collects every
drop of rainwater and snowmelt, storing that water in aquifers that lead out to
small springs. The Mojave Desert, which was legit known for killing people,
because you know, it's a giant desert, was a barrier for people trying to make
their way west. So Las Vegas became a key stopover in the 1800s for settlers
heading west, because what's better than fresh water in the middle of a desert?
Later, it became a pivotal place for trains and railways going to LA.

Then, when the Hoover Dam was built in the middle of the Great Depression, the small town of 5,000 swelled to 25,000, mostly unemployed males
wanting a steady job. Because hardly any of these migratory job-hunting
young men had any family ties to the community, they got bored. And quick.
So theaters, showgirls, and gambling venues popped up, largely built by the
Mafia. Because it was Prohibition, and the Mafia had alcohol, and young men

like alcohol—let's just say that's when Vegas as a city started having a drinking problem.

After Pearl Harbor, the US entered into World War II, and Las Vegas became a military area. The war effort needed raw materials, and what do you know, the desert around Vegas was filled with copper and silver, leading to a boom in mining and the building of several military bases. The US Atomic Energy Commission also reserved an area outside of Las Vegas as its official atomic testing site. Vegas was the bomb.

(I'm sorry. I couldn't resist.)

So. To recap:

Settlers.
Railroads.
Military.
Tons of young men.
Gambling.
Showgirls.
Mafia.
Atomic bombs.

That's all kinds of crazy, right? What other city has that kind of story?

Because Las Vegas's financial interests have always been so diverse, its citizens have always been diverse, too. Devout Mormons made their way west through Vegas. Chinese and Irish immigrants working on the railroads settled down. Black folk, unable to find jobs in the South after the Civil War, moved out to be cowboys and seasonal ranchers. Did you just imagine Will Smith in *Wild Wild West*? I did. All sorts of first-generation immigrants made their way out during the Depression to work on the Hoover Dam. Jewish and Italian Mafia families moved out from the East Coast to run business and entertainment ventures. In fact, the 1870 census found that 44.2 percent of the new state's population was foreign-born.

That's insane.

I guess it's true.

Immigrants. They get the job done.

Las Vegas has *always* been friendly to people from a wide range of backgrounds. So growing up in Las Vegas meant, by definition, I was part of an incredibly diverse community. With that in mind, let me introduce you to my seven closest friends who I hung out with at J. E. Manch Elementary School.

Keep in mind, this is in the middle of the 1980s in the United States.

Sandra Padilla. Sandra was Spanish and Mexican and Native American. And she is also the entire reason that—to this day—I am still obsessed with Bon Jovi. In fifth grade, she was standing by her locker and asked me, "Hey. Tyler. Do you like Bon Jovi?" I had no idea what a Bon Jovi was. But Sandra was super pretty, and I wanted to impress her. So I said, "Of course! Who doesn't?" To which she said, "Oh! What is your favorite song?" I had no idea, so I responded, "Ohh, yeah, that's tough, I think I'd have to say ALL OF THEM."

After school, I went to the Base Exchange (BX) and bought the cassette tape of *Slippery When Wet*. That night, I listened to that whole damn album. I did this mostly because I wanted to impress Sandra Padilla, but also because it was dope. Now I had a conversation topic for Sandra the next day. I had a line in my head: "I play for keeps 'cause I might not make it back." That blew me away. Those New Jersey white boys are some gangstas. Those lines? That's some Run DMC shit, right there. And that's how I became a black kid with an LL Cool J poster—with his bright red Kangol hat and ghetto blaster on his shoulder—on one side of my room and a Bon Jovi poster—with them looking like eyeliner-wearing white women—on the other. All because of Sandra Padilla.

Jennifer Smith. She was a white girl, as if you couldn't tell by her name. Her family was military, like mine. Here's what I remember about Jennifer Smith. One time, I was at her house, and her mother told us that her dad was out golfing. And in that moment, because I wanted to impress Jennifer, I said to her mother, "That's awesome. I like golf." But I didn't know *anything* about golf. Jennifer's mom said, "Oh, you golf." But, instead of saying no, I said, "Yes." Because did I mention Jennifer was cute? And Jennifer's mom said,

"Oh, that's great. So, what's your best score?" She might as well have asked me how many points a hit wicket is worth in cricket. I had no idea how golf scores worked. This is before Tiger Woods and therefore before black people liked golf. So, I just said, "It's tough to say." Then I quickly left the room and ran my lying black butt back home.

Bridget Rodriguez. She was Filipino and Chinese. The first time I met her was in first grade. We were in the sandbox, and Bridget said, "You're going to mess up your nice brown pants." And in that moment, it was as if the world had stopped turning on its axis. I thought to myself, "Wait. She likes my nice brown pants." For the next four to five minutes, I was in love with Bridget Rodriguez. I planned our life together. As I was thinking about what we'd name our twins (Luke and Leia, obvs), Brian Garrett walked up, and Bridget said to him, "Oh my gosh, I like your shirt." I was devastated. She didn't have a crush on me—she was just really nice. Dammit.

Robby Longbrake. Robby was Vietnamese. Las Vegas is what's called a "secondary hub" for immigration, but that's not why Robby was there. Robby was there because his dad was a white man in the military who just happened to like Asian women. Anyway. Robby was really into baseball and was easily the most athletic person I knew. One time, I made the mistake of not immediately knowing that the Orioles were in the American League. And he never really stopped making fun of me about it.

Todd Thompson. You could probably tell by the name that he was a white kid. His dad was in the Air Force, too, and he had also lived in Alaska and had also been recently transferred to Las Vegas. So he got that whole "Throw out your ice skates and go buy some flip-flops." Our parents sort of knew each other, so they thought we should get together, and as I walked into his house, Todd said to me, "Do you want to play Star Wars?" And I was like, "Hell to the yes, I want to play Star Wars." And that was that.

Rudy Reyes. Rudy was a little Hispanic dude who had double dimples in his cheeks that made the girls go crazy over him, like he was A.C. Slater or something. I remember being so jealous of him that I went home and tried to make dimples in the mirror. I was like, "Screw this kid, I can make myself have dimples." Turns out, I could not.

Brian Moana. So Brian was from Hawaii. Did you know Vegas is called the "Ninth Island" because of all the Hawaiian people who move here? Well, it is. The main thing you need to know about Brian is that he had great hand-writing. This dude's handwriting was so epic that girls would ASK him to write them notes. I looked at this and was like, "Whaaaaaaaat? This dude is pulling ladies with his *penmanship*?" All summer, I worked on my handwrit-ing for several hours a day. To this day, my handwriting is off-the-charts good. But here's the truth—I don't exactly remember what Brian's ethnicity was. And honestly, I am not sure if Moana was really Brian's last name. I don't even know where I got that from. Oh. Wait. I do. My bad.

The point is, my friends in elementary school were as varied as the general population of Las Vegas, which is to say ALL OVER the place. Now, don't get it twisted: I knew I was black. I was fully aware of my blackness. But because I was in the middle of it in Vegas, a place with so many different sorts and colors and kinds of people and ethnicities, I had come to believe that a difference in ethnicity didn't really mean that much.

Then came the summer of 1984.

In the summer of 1984, in between third and fourth grade, my mother decided that it would be a good idea for me to spend a big chunk of my sum-mer break with my grandparents. So my folks put me on a plane and flew me out to their hometown of Eutaw, Alabama.

Eutaw, Alabama, is in the middle of nowhere. At the time, it was a tiny town of 2,000 people. It did not have an Air Force base. It did not have a giant, thriving economy of lavish hotels. It did not have a built-up downtown.

It had dirt.

Also, humidity.

And if you think they had air conditioning, you would be wrong. My grandmama still doesn't have air conditioning.

This town was off the freeway, down a few dirt roads framed by vast per-pendicular groves of southern yellow pine trees. It wasn't just off the freeway. It was off the grid.

I remember two main things from that summer.

First, I remember the dirt.

Every morning, while it was only eighty degrees with 80 percent humidity, my aunt Net would give me a chore to do.

"Go rake the dirt," she said.

"Rake the dirt?" I asked.

"Yes."

The area around my grandparents' house wasn't grass. It was just dirt. And so I came to find out this is just what people did in that area, I guess. It's a cross between mowing your lawn and sweeping your front porch. You get rid of all the pine needles, leaves, debris, and footprints. At first I thought, "Why am I doing this? It's dirt." But then I realized it was a way of showing you have pride in your home and in your community. You take care of what you have, because what you have is yours, and that's all you got.

Second, I remember the black people.

But the most dominant thing I remember is that even though this city's name was the same phonetically as Utah—a state famous for having only beautiful blue-eyed Mormons—this Eutaw had only black people.

That's it.

No Filipino-Chinese people, like my friend Bridget.

No white people, like my friend Todd.

No Vietnamese people, like my friend Robby.

No Latinos, like my friends Sandra and Rudy.

No (probable) Hawaiians, like my friend Brian.

Just. Black. People.

At the time, I didn't realize it, but technically, the city of Eutaw does have white people. I just never saw them. They lived in a completely different part of the town, and it was a part where we never went. Black kids just didn't go over to the white people part of the town.

At one point, my cousin Shon and I were playing baseball outside, and this neighborhood boy came over and just looked at me for a bit.

"Are you kin?" he asked me, in a deep Southern drawl.

"What?" I asked.

"Are you kin?" he asked again.

"No, I'm Tyler," I said.

"He's asking if we're family," Shon said. "He's my cousin."

The boy then smiled a big smile and joined us on the field.

This story is important, because it ties to the story of Eutaw, Alabama.

<Cue History Channel theme music; refill popcorn.>

You see, Eutaw was a cotton-farming town laid out on the banks of the Black Warrior River. The cotton crop was wildly lucrative for a few families who built incredible plantation homes—many of which are still registered landmarks.

It's a strange thing, now, to drive through this area, seeing giant mansions of white, with their wraparound porches, knowing these were built off the backs of enslaved African Americans, many of whom share my DNA. That's crazy to me.

After the Civil War, the newly freed slaves started thinking, "What if we run for office and determine our future politically?" After all, freed slaves made up the vast majority of people in the county. Makes sense, right? You'd think that would work. But it didn't.

One example: on October 25, 1870, a few days before the national congressional election, thousands of black people showed up on the steps of the Greene County Courthouse in Eutaw to proclaim, "We're going to vote, and we're not scared."

Scared of what, you might ask. Well, buckle up. The South is about to South.

You see, in the 1868 election, the county, which was a majority black, had voted overwhelmingly for Ulysses S. Grant, the former head of the Union Army. This did not go over well with the white folk in the region. In addition, local black men started running for office. To the remaining Confederate sympathizers, any sort of political action by black people was akin to violence against "the Southern way of life."

So, in March of 1870, members of the KKK killed James Martin, a local black politician running for office. Then, in September of 1870, the highest-ranking black politician in the area, a former slave turned political activist named Gilford Coleman, was lynched by members of the KKK. They dragged him out of his house into the forest and literally hacked his entire body apart until he was unrecognizable. They even left someone to guard his wife so she couldn't run to get help.

You could say they were trying to send a message.

Message received.

Then, a few days before election day, more than 2,000 black voters gathered on the steps of the county courthouse to say, "You cannot terrorize us out of our Constitutional right to vote." When they did, more than 170 armed members of the Ku Klux Klan showed up, firing weapons on the mostly black crowd, injuring 50-plus people and killing 4 people in what historians now call the Eutaw Massacre.

The Klan made the choice crystal clear:

You could vote.

Or you could live.

Black folks took the hint and stayed home on election day. The tactic worked: the party of Lincoln and Grant (which had won in a landslide just two years earlier) lost by forty-three votes.

Violent terror has a way of dissuading one from voting. Yeah. Dead men don't vote.

This is the history of Eutaw, Alabama. And this is why, in essence, the neighborhood kid asked me if I was kin.

Because a black kid in Eutaw, Alabama, learns early on that the only safe people are black people and family.

For black folk in this area, both before AND after the Civil War, the message was clear: this place is dangerous if you're black. Being black will get you killed. This was the history. This was the environment in Eutaw, Alabama. In Eutaw, Alabama, black people stick near black folks. Because that's the only safe place for you.

So starkly different than Las Vegas, where the only really dangerous place for a black kid was inside a tiger cage.

So that was part one of nine-year-old me discovering some hard truths about being black in America. But it was nothing compared to what happened the next summer.

THE NEXT SUMMER—JUNE 1985

The following summer, my mother took me to South Wales, New York, which is located in upstate New York. A military family that my parents had met in Fairbanks had retired from active service and moved back to the father's childhood home to take care of his aging parents. My mother and I flew out to visit them. They had a son named Scotty who was my age, so it was perfect.

Now, I don't know if you know much about upstate New York, beyond the fact that it's the setting for *Dirty Dancing* (a cinematic masterpiece), but it's pretty amazing when you're a ten-year-old kid who has never lived near trees.

We got in pretty late in the evening, and when we arrived, Scotty was outside in the backyard with a flashlight.

"Come on," he said, excitedly, handing me a flashlight.

"What…uh…what are we doing, exactly?" I asked.

"Hunting nightcrawlers," Scotty said.

We stayed out there hunting these large worms until our mason jars were full. The next day, Scotty and I just walked out the back door, down to a raging creek that ran through his backyard, and we fished all day, using those nightcrawlers.

I was astonished. In Las Vegas, we didn't have forests like this, or freshwater rivers and creeks, or, you know, seasons. And as a ten-year-old kid, this was the coolest thing I had ever done. It wasn't even close.

After a few days, I don't mean to brag, but your boy learned to catch some fish. One day was particularly good, and we both caught a bunch. We felt like superheroes. Blaquaman.

"Come on," Scotty said to me. "Let's go show my friends."

And so we walked around this tiny upstate community, going from door to door to invite his friends out to see what a haul of fish we'd caught. The first door we went to, the parents didn't let us in and wouldn't let their kid come out.

The second door, the parents said the same thing, that so-and-so couldn't come out right now.

It was a small town, so I figured, "Huh. Maybe they don't like visitors, or people from out of town."

The third house, we stood on the front porch, excited, holding our fish and grinning like idiots. The mother stood at the front door, looking at us through the screen door. "Well, Scotty, you can come in," she said calmly. "But we can't let your Negro friend in."

And those words hit me. I still feel them.

"We can't let your Negro friend in."

And in half a second, I realized that these families weren't letting me inside to hang out with their kids because I was black.

Now again, I want to make it clear: My dad was black. My mom was black. I knew I was black.

But what I *didn't* know yet was that my being black was a problem for some people.

That.

That was brand-new.

And it hurt. It was the most hurtful thing I'd experienced up until this point in my life.

Sometimes, when I tell my white friends this story, they try to connect and say, "That's crazy that woman hated you for *no reason.*"

But this woman on the front porch in South Wales, New York, didn't hate me for no reason.

She hated me for a very specific and known reason.

She hated me because I'm black.

And the problem with *that* is that being black is something that I cannot change.

So I'm done.

I'm rejected.

And there's no way to ever be accepted.

Not if I get better at fishing.

Or become more polite.

There's no chance.

And even though I didn't know this woman from Eve, and even though her abject rejection of me based upon my skin color shouldn't matter at all, I can still feel the sting.

I can still feel it.

Because it's what she was saying.

"There's something wrong with you. And it will always be wrong."

That's a hell of a thing to tell a ten-year-old.

That's something a Disney villain says.

That kind of venom doesn't just affect little kids of color. That can poison *any* kid. Some of you have been there. And if me telling this story is a trigger for you, I'm sorry.

You didn't deserve that.

Not then. Not now.

The black poet Countee Cullen, often associated with the Harlem Renaissance of the 1920s, once penned a poem about the first time he was made aware that the color of his skin was an issue.

INCIDENT

Once riding in old Baltimore,
Heart-filled, head-filled with glee,
I saw a Baltimorean
Keep looking straight at me.
Now I was eight and very small,
And he was no whit bigger,
And so I smiled, but he poked out
*His tongue, and called me, "N****r"*
I saw the whole of Baltimore
From May until December:
Of all the things that happened there
That's all that I remember.

I feel you, Countee. Because of all the time I spent in South Wales, New York, that moment on the porch is the one that's seared into my memory.

"We can't let your Negro friend in."

I remember thinking in that moment, "I want to go home. I just want to go home."

Not home to where my mom was, in Scotty's house. I wanted to go home to Vegas. Where I was safe. Where my friends were.

We all need a home.

Look, I'm not saying that messed-up racial stuff never ever happened in Las Vegas. I'm sure it did. But I was generally protected from it.

It says something that it took until I was ten years old to realize that my being black was a problem for some people. It took me until I was ten years old to discover that not everybody feels the way about me that my friends do.

When I was growing up, Las Vegas was a place where our family lived in close proximity to folks of all sorts of different ethnic backgrounds. And our community determined (however imperfectly) that we were going to try to get along despite the fact that we looked different.

In Eutaw, Alabama, and South Wales, New York, I learned that Vegas is not like the rest of the world.

Not.

Even.

Close.

So here's what I want to say. I want to say, "Thank you" to Las Vegas. Yeah, you're a whore of a city. But you're my mother. I was lucky to grow up in Las Vegas. I had no idea. Really. Thank you. I could have been stuck in Alaska, where my only friend would have been a moose.

But instead, I grew up in a perfectly weird city that had a perfectly weird history that provided me a glimpse of America that Countee Cullen never had. A place where my skin color wasn't an issue. A place where I was accepted and loved for me. Having this kind of home helped give me the psychological strength and the emotional endurance to deal with that rejection.

So.

If you plan on raising a racist, I wouldn't do it in Las Vegas.

CHAPTER 3

DEATH BY GANG? OR DEATH BY MY MOTHER?

Living life like a firecracker, quick is my fuse
Then dead as a deathpack the colors I choose
—Ice T (1988)

Boy. Roll your eyes at me one more time. Try me.
—My mama (Sometime last week)

Little known fact about me: rap music saved my life. But we'll get to that in a minute.

First, let's talk about gangs in Las Vegas.

It's important to understand that my hometown during my most formative years had a gang problem. Ready for this? Vegas, right now, has more than 20,000 gang members inside its city limits.

So. How did we get here?

As we talked about in the last chapter, drugs, alcohol, prostitution, and gambling have always had a part of the fabric of Vegas. First it was the Mafia running alcohol during Prohibition. That was just the start. Growing up, I remember going downtown and seeing bright pink birds in front of this huge hotel. Little did I know that in 1946, it was East Coast Mafia money from the famed mobster Bugsy Siegel who built those Flamingos.

But then the colors changed from bright pink to red and blue. In the eighties, Vegas began attracting the gangs of LA, especially the powerful and influential Crips and the Bloods.

Gangs have been a problem ever since. Remember when Tupac got shot? I do. Because it happened in Vegas on September 7, 1996, at 11:15 p.m. at a red light at East Flamingo Road.

Yep.

Same Flamingo.

And who did it?

No one is exactly sure, but anyone with any knowledge of what went down at that time would most likely tell you that it all sounded a bit gangy. In fact, I'd say it's one of the most famous modern gang killings of my lifetime. It all went down like this.

- Tupac went to Las Vegas to see Mike Tyson fight some chump named Bruce Seldon.
- The winner of this fight got to fight heavyweight champion Evander Holyfield.
- Tyson knocks out the dude in 1:49.
- The match was over so fast the crowd started chanting, "Fix fix fix fix."
- Whatever. If Mike Tyson hit me in the face, I'd fall down in less than two minutes, too. I ain't mad at you, Bruce.
- The rowdy crowd is released and starts walking through the lobby of the MGM Grand.[1]
- Tupac is rolling with his boys, including a dude from LA who is a Blood.
- We'll call that member of Tupac's entourage Red Skittle.

- In the teeming sea of people in the lobby, Red Skittle spots a member of the rival Southside Crips gang.
- We'll call that dude Blue Skittle. Are there Blue Skittles? There should be. Anyway.
- Earlier that year, Blue Skittle had tried to rob Red Skittle at a Foot Locker.
- No, I am not making that up.
- Yes, this is in the official police reports.
- No, they are not junior high school boys.
- Red Skittle tells his friend Tupac this information and points out Blue Skittle.
- Tupac is hyped. He just watched Tyson, after all.
- Tupac goes over and levels Blue Skittle with his fists.
- That fight also lasts less than two minutes. Why? Cuz thug life.
- Blue Skittle didn't like being embarrassed like that.
- Blue Skittle gets his friends, the Crips.[2]
- They roll up next to Tupac on the Strip and shoot him.
- Tupac is hit four times, twice in the chest.
- Six days later, Tupac dies of ballistic injuries.[3]

Well, that's the "official" story from the police and the FBI investigations. I mean, for all we know, Tupac could be living with Elvis and Alf at Area 51.

The point is, growing up, we were HIGHLY AWARE of our home city's gang problem. And the single most powerful gang in Las Vegas when I was growing up were the Donna Street Crips.

The Donna Street Crips came to North Las Vegas when one of the earliest members of the Crips, an original gangsta named Ramont "Pap" Williams moved out from Compton.[4] From the time he was eleven years old, Williams had been a personal disciple of Stanley "Tookie" Williams, who literally started the Crips. Ramont's mother wasn't down and wanted to pull a Fresh Prince of Bel-Air* to get her teenage son away from the gang life.[5] Let's just say that didn't work. What's that saying? "You can take the boy out of the gang,

---

* He got in one little fight, and his mom got scared.

but then he'll single-handedly create a near-exact replica of that gang, down to the colors and creeds, and all in less than four years." Is that the expression? Well, with Pap Williams that's exactly what went down.

Williams (nearly) single-handedly started the Donna Street Crips, an offshoot of the Compton Crips gang, and before long, the entirety of LA's color-coded, genocidal gang culture was imported, too. I don't know how they measure this, but it's said that more deaths by gunshot have occurred on Donna Street than in any other street in all of Nevada.[6] And remember, a guy named Bugsy Siegel lived here at one point.

What I'm getting at is this. As a reasonable person, would you or would you not conclude with me the following:

If you live in Las Vegas, and you have half a mind, then you stay the HELL away from Donna Street.

Which leads me to the next chapter of my life.

Middle school.

Right away, I knew this was going to be a different beast. For starters, my new middle school was not going to be a quiet, small community school, like J. E. Manch Elementary had been. My friends and I got on a bus and were driven fifteen minutes down the highway to Jim Bridger Middle School. This school was much bigger, with multiple elementary schools feeding into it.

Before we go any further, can we all just admit that junior high sucks eggs? I have never met a person who said, "Man. Seventh grade was the best." And if I did, I would not want them in my life. Like a person who wears Crocs on purpose, or prefers Pepsi over Coke, I don't need that kind of delusional idiocy in my life.

First of all, in junior high, *everything* is constantly changing on you. Your body is changing. Your face is changing. Your voice is changing (sometimes in mid-sentence). Your emotions are more volatile than a tired toddler's. And because all of those things are happening in everyone, even your most stable friends are not stable.

But as bad as middle school is for every human, it was about to get a lot worse for me.

All because of a matter of geography.

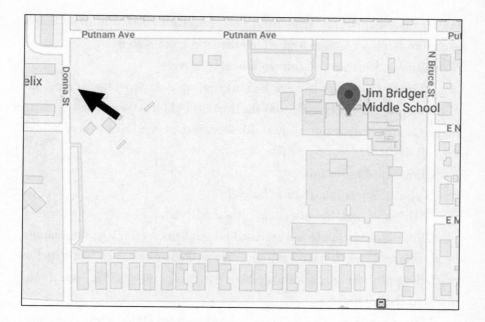

My junior high school was on Donna Street.

And let me tell you, the experience that all my old elementary school friends—Bridget, Todd, Robby—had at Jim Bridger was vastly different than mine. Here are three examples from my first week of junior high.

MOMENT 1: THE FIRST DAY OF SCHOOL

On my very first day of junior high school, this black kid named Chris approached me. He had a tight Jheri curl peeking out of his LA Raiders hat, looking like a miniature Eazy-E.[†] He was wearing black Nike Cortez shoes with white tube socks, and blue Dickey shorts with a black t-shirt. I didn't know it then, but that was the school uniform for people claiming DSC. "That's a nice chain," he said.

He was pointing to the gold chain that I was wearing around my sixth grade neck. It had been a Christmas present from my mom and dad the previous December. Now, when I say "gold chain," please don't think I was sporting some giant thirty-six-inch-long rope dookie chain. I'm talking "barely

---

† You know how difficult it is to be a miniature Eazy-E? He was already miniature.

thicker than dental floss" gold chain here. Less Run DMC and more Ralph Macchio. But it was mine. And my mother had given it to me.

"Gimme that chain," Chris said, looking at me.

"What?" I said, not because I didn't understand the words coming out of his mouth, but because I was in shock at his boldness. Was I really getting mugged in the hallway outside Mrs. Rhodes's fifth period history class? Where the hell was I?

Chris stepped forward.

"I said, 'Gimme that chain,'" he said.

"Uh. No." I said. Because…uh…it was MINE.

Chris didn't blink. He just snatched my gold chain off my neck as though he was borrowing a pencil off my desk. He walked away like he had to get to math class. And the only arithmetic I knew at that point was that I was minus one gold chain.

I found out later that Chris's older brothers were DSC. While I was busy begging my mom to buy me some Bon Jovi tapes down at the Air Force Base Exchange, Chris was rolling with some brothas that looked like Full Force.

Brothas who didn't play.

As he walked away with my Christmas present in his balled fist, I leaned back against the locker. And although I hadn't fully processed what had happened, one thing was crystal clear: this was a different breed of black kid.

Fast-forward two days, to the third day of junior high school.

MOMENT 2: THIRD DAY, PE CLASS

During PE, our brigade of sixth grade boys was outside, being forced to run/walk around the school track. We heard the sound of tires screeching to a stop, which arrested our attention. We pulled our chins out of our chests as we jogged. Out past the chain-link fence that ran along the western boundary of the school, we watched as four cars slammed to a stop on Donna Street and a whole mess of people poured out. A guy in a white tank top was walking and dropped whatever he was carrying. The group surrounded this guy, like a pack of orcas circling a lone seal. They rushed in, and even from far away, I could see the fury of flashing fists.

"Damn," someone whispered.

"He just got jumped in," someone else said, in a hushed tone. "He's a DSC now."

Getting "jumped" into a gang is an initiation where practically the whole gang surrounds you and everyone tries to beat your ass to a pulp, and you try to fight your way out of it. You basically fight everyone all at the same time, like Bruce Lee in *Fist of Fury*, only without the benefit of nunchucks. And his world-class elite martial arts training. And his chiseled six-pack. Man, Bruce really knew where the gym was. Getting "jumped in" is baptism by fisticuffs. Once you get past that, you're in the gang. But I didn't need to be told this. I was watching it happen right in front of me.

Our collective pace slowed to a walk, as we watched the group finally relent. We heard whooping and hollering, vaguely, floating on the air. The man, broken on the ground, bleeding, had fought valiantly against impossible odds.

He was now in.

Family.

They picked him up, and the cars sped away almost as quickly as they had come.

I remember everything about that moment. I remember my Latino and white friends (who had just watched what I had watched) shrug a little and continue on around the track. This brutal fact of nature didn't concern them.

And I remember looking around and seeing that all the black kids like me had stopped walking. We were frozen to the track in ninety-three-degree heat. We knew. This was coming for us.

MOMENT 3: FRIDAY NIGHT

That Friday night, at the end of my first week of middle school, my mom took me out to the BX. It was back-to-school shopping time. I didn't tell her why, but I didn't buy a single item of clothing that had any color on it at all that day. For the next seven years, I would not—I could not—wear any color other than white or black. Certainly nothing blue or red. Just black and white.

I had less color than the cast of *Les Misérables* before the most recent revival, where they wised up and black people could finally hear the people sing.

Robby did not have to do this.

Neither did Rudy.

Todd didn't.

Nor did Brian.

They wore whatever the heck they wanted. I could not. Why? Because I was black, and the rules were different for me there in North Las Vegas.

In my first week, the profound and heavy realization set in. Being black wasn't value-neutral at Jim Bridger Middle School. Those of us who were black were immediately targeted, pressured, recruited, and threatened to join the Donna Street Crips.

It was a thing.

It was real.

And it was coming for me.

The only question left was what I was going to do about it.

A: Don Corleone. Highways. Parts of the Nile during hippo mating season. Black mamas.
Q: What are "Things you don't cross for $300, Alex."

I want to talk now about something that some folks don't understand, but which you need to understand.

Look, I don't have the right or the authority to make sweeping statements explaining all the toils of being black in the United States. But I know a little something. And that first week in junior high, I felt the pressure of my blackness for the first time. I knew, at age twelve, that I was dealing with something much larger than myself here. Joining a gang would in some ways solidify my blackness, and it would cast my lot into something Much Bigger Than Myself, which every middle schooler is longing for.

And so NOT joining a gang could feel, to a good number of black boys, like shirking your blackness. There was a war against us, from the outside world, which was hostile to our skin color, or so the narrative went. There was a war, and the gangs were the way to make it out alive. And the draft was ubiquitous for every young black man. And there was no such thing as a conscientious objector. Just like in Vietnam in 1969, you couldn't just say, "Uh, no thanks. I'd prefer not to go to war."

And yet, it was crystal clear to me, almost immediately, that joining a gang was NOT an option for me.

And the reason why it was NOT an option for me was because I was afraid of dying.

I wasn't afraid I'd be shot by a rival gang member. No.

No, I was afraid of getting killed by my mama.

Because that's what would happen if she ever found out I joined a gang.

The threat of getting my ass beat on the daily by some dude wearing blue did not compare to the corporal fear I held thinking about my mama. My mother was not dealing with ANY of this gang nonsense. That was a moot point.

My mother wasn't a gangsta. She was the whole damn gang. She was an entity unto herself. You think she couldn't mount up and regulate? Child, please.

So, joining a gang was NOT an option for me because of my mama.

Which brings me to black men and their moms.

Let's go back to Tupac. Tupac has the twenty-fourth and twenty-fifth most played albums on the entirety of Spotify, which is saying something. And the fourth most played Tupac song is "Dear Mama." It's got 128 million spins. Why? Because even gangstas revere their mamas. It's a thing.

Black mamas are it. Now, every race and every creed gets this. I am told that in World War II, as men were dying on the battlefield, they would cry out for their mothers. Mother is safety. Mother heals. Mother is home.

And I'm no sociologist or anthropologist or meteorologist, but I think this Mama Effect is even more pronounced when the world is generally hostile toward you. In a dangerous world, the safety of mom becomes even more critical. She's the protector you always come back to.

And for black folk—and other minorities—sometimes it was the only safety we had in a harsh world.

Now without being rude, I gotta say this: white folks—by and large—don't get this. One time, when I was in fifth grade, I went to my friend Jimmy's house after school. We went into his living room and plopped in front of his Nintendo to play some Teenage Mutant Ninja Turtles.

As we picked up our controllers, Jimmy called out, "Hey, mom, can I have some milk?"

I looked at Jimmy sideways.

"Something wrong with your legs, boy?" I said, almost preemptively. Because that's what my mom would have said if I had asked her to do something I was perfectly capable of doing myself. I might as well have asked my mother to brush my teeth for me.

"Sure, honey," I heard Jimmy's mother call sweetly from the other room.

I looked around.

What.

Was.

Happening.

We played video games for a few moments, and I got lost in the action, when all of a sudden, Jimmy erupted next to me.

"Mom!" he yelled. "Where's my milk!!"

I looked at Jimmy, with sadness in my eyes.

"I'm going to miss you," I said. "You were a good friend."

I dropped the controller and instinctively rolled away from Jimmy behind a chair. That's what you do when you know that someone is about to die. And I knew Jimmy was going to die because he had just talked to his mother like that.

"Sorry, honey," his mother called from the kitchen. "Just one minute."

And in that moment, one thought went through my mind.

??????Da FuQ?????

If I had spoken to my mother that way, she would have ripped my arms off and beaten me with them. And then yelled at me for getting blood on the carpet. And then I would have had to clean up the mess. With no arms.

You just DO NOT speak to your mother that way when you're black. You just do not.

Another example. Do you remember that gold chain I had, which was stolen by Chris on the first day of junior high? When that happened, I wasn't worried about which gang Chris was in—I was worried about having to tell my mother that I lost the gold chain she'd given me for Christmas.

When I told her that night what had happened, her face tightened.

"I see," she said, calmly and coldly.

She stood up and went into the other room. She called the school the next day and talked to whoever she talked to. The school administrator helped her identify the student, and conversations were had.

About a day later, Chris came up to me. "Here," he said, handing me my gold chain. "Sorry." He walked away like a scolded puppy.

He didn't have to tell me anything. Because I knew EXACTLY what that was—that was "I got in trouble with my mama, and I don't want to die, so here."

The black mother structure is the same with this kid as it was for any other black kid. It doesn't matter how gangsta a kid is, or how juicy their Jheri curl is, if they have to deal with their mom, it's going to go down the exact same way. The scariest-ass gangsta still has to answer to his mother.

It just so happened that my mother was scarier than any gangsta.

And to understand why, you have to understand my mother.

THE BAD-ASSERY OF JERRIE ELAINE MERRITT

My mother was born in rural Alabama in 1955, during Jim Crow, before the Civil Rights Voting Act of 1964. She was born Jerrie Elaine Hicks, and was the oldest of eight children.

And in that poor, rural town, two things were birthed within my mother. First, competence. She was in charge of running things from the time she was ten years old. She was indispensable at a critical task that was deeply important—making sure none of her siblings died.

Second, my mom developed ambition. Eutaw hasn't changed that much in a hundred years. The very first job my mom had when she was eighteen was at the truck stop off Interstate 20 and Alabama State Route 14. She was a waitress in a segregated diner—she served the side of the room that was reserved for white people. One day, her family came in to visit her, and she was forced to seat them on the other side. She realized that she couldn't even eat in the section where she worked. That's when she decided she had to leave town. She married my father, Milton Merritt, when she was nineteen.

My father's escape pod was the US military. The military's offer of a steady job, educational training, and a legitimate chance for advancement was a dream for a rural black man. He took my mother with him.

Their first stop was Albuquerque, where my mom made jeans in the Levi Strauss factory by day and took classes at the University of New Mexico at night, studying business. Then they were transferred to Alaska.

One day my mother saw an ad in the paper that a local bank was hiring tellers. There were not a lot of employable people around, so she took her half-finished degree in business from UNM into that branch and they hired her. As a black woman. During those four years in Alaska, my mother became a big fish in a small pond, and with her natural skill and business mind, my mother went from teller to the manager of the entire branch of that bank. In the early eighties, bank managers were men. They certainly were not women. And they for damn sure weren't black women. My mother gained years of bank management experience in perhaps the only place in the country that would allow for such a thing.

Four years later, though, my father was transferred to Las Vegas. And when my mother applied to be a bank manager in this new city, she discovered the cold facts: there was not a single non-male branch manager in any bank in Las Vegas. She was forced to go back to being a teller. It would take my mother an entire decade to climb her way back into being a manager.

But in Vegas in the 1980s, banks kept failing for being stupid, so they were bought by other banks, who were then bought by other, bigger banks, who poached the other bank's best employees.

So my mom kept getting poached, and each time, she'd move up a step on that ladder. She moved from teller to head teller, and then to bank operations manager, and finally to manager. But it wasn't easy. Women didn't go after leadership roles in banking during that time.

So my mom had to do a better job than anyone around her, because she was held to an impossible standard, representing all women and all black people. Mistakes could not be tolerated. And she had about four seconds to win people over with her competence before she lost them.

At one point while she was working at Wells Fargo, a rival bank called First Security approached my mom and tried to steal her away. With her job secure at Wells Fargo and with literally nothing to lose, my mom had the stone-cold audacity to ask to move from bank management to be a private banking officer who dealt with high-net-worth clients. My mom thought she'd be good at this, so she'd quietly gotten all the training and certificates she needed.

This was quite the request. But First Security gave her a shot. Now, high-net-worth clients don't tend to be female. Or black. And this is where my mother's name came into play.

My mother's name is Jerrie. Which phonetically sounds identical to a man's name. So, when Las Vegas's high rollers called into the bank, requesting a private meeting with a private banker, my mom gave her assistant sharp orders.

Never use pronouns.

Ever.

Never say, "She will meet with you." Or "I'll put you down on her calendar." This allows these good old boys to hedge, leaving a crack in the door that might allow any dormant sexism to rear its ugly head.

Instead, her assistants were to say, "Jerrie will meet with you" or "I have you down on Jerrie's calendar."

"Let them think I'm a man," my mom said. My mom wanted a shot and figured if these men already came in to meet, if they'd already made the drive, then perhaps sunk-cost theory would buy her a minute. And about a minute was all my mom needed to convince these men that she was competent, understood their business positions, and had something helpful to say from one brilliant business mind to another.

You don't get rich being stupid, and my mom put these men on notice: I don't suffer fools any more than you do. Now let's get down to business.

A little while later, my mom's previous bank, Wells Fargo, bought First Security. And because she was *already* a private banker with First Security, my mom retained her title and position at one of the largest banks in the US, even though there were *no other black women* in any sort of positions like that in any banks in Las Vegas.

And that's how my mom became a VP at a bank.

To this day my mom is still in banking in Las Vegas. She is the executive in charge of ensuring that her bank has fair lending practices for low-income segments of the state and helps funnel money for economic and community development. I think of my mother as the Oprah Winfrey of Las Vegas.

YOU get a loan.
And YOU get a loan!
Everybody gets a loan!
As long as it's in line with solid banking processes!

And that, my friend, is what you call some gangsta shit.

So you see, I was not going to mess with my mama.

And it is why, when I was grounded and I was not allowed to watch TV after school, I did not watch TV. Even though I was home alone, I knew that somehow, if I watched TV, my mom would be able to smell the warmth of the cathode ray tubes or something, and she'd rip my arms off.

"You want to watch TV when I tell you not to? Try to change the channels without any arms," she'd say, ripping my arms off. "Now clean up this mess."

So joining a gang was absolutely not on the table.

But *not* joining a gang was going to be a real problem for me.

So as a twelve-year-old boy, I had to use all my ingenuity and social skill to try to figure out a way to escape gang culture at my school. Luckily, I had a plan.

REMEMBER WHEN I SAID RAP MUSIC SAVED MY LIFE?

I had to find a way to balance out my life. And there was only one way to do that: talent. In the black community, solidarity is everything, but transcendent talent always trumps everything else. If you're truly gifted at something—I mean, truly exceptional—the black community will let you opt out of traditional roles and responsibilities, because, intrinsically, everyone knows, "Well, you have to work on that craft for the betterment of the world."

If you're an incredible singer.

Or a truly gifted athlete.

Or maybe even a brilliant speller at the Scripps National Spelling Bee.

The black community will recognize true greatness and release you, with the implicit agreement that you won't forget from whence you came. So, if talent wins, then I was going to win with talent. I decided that I was going to be a rapper. I was pretty good with iambic pentameter and end rhyme, so I went home, and just like I worked all summer on my handwriting, I started working on rhymes.

During lunch, some of the kids would rap. They'd get in a circle and freestyle battle to see who had the best flow. This was my chance to battle Crips and win, in a way that both gained their respect and kept all my bones unbroken. I could gain some social clout and buy protection because of my fire bars all while allowing me to NOT JOIN THEIR GANG.

I still remember my first rhyme, which I penned on a piece of loose-leaf notebook paper that I kept in my Trapper Keeper. Wanna read it? You know you do. My rap name was Tyler T. What did the T. stand for? I don't know. "Terrible" probably. I chose it because more words rhyme with T than M. Look, I was in junior high, people. Anyway, here was my first rap battle.

Yo, I'm Tyler T, that's who I be,
and on the M-I-C.
You know you can't beat me.
Because I am fly,
Do you want to know why
Try to battle me,
and you will surely die

Oh snap! I had bars. That flow had everything.

✓ Bombastic bragging about proficiency at my skill. (You can't beat me.)
✓ Overt implication of sexual prowess AND material prosperity. (I am fly.)
✓ Taunting and threat of punishment against any opponents. (Try to battle me.)
✓ Annihilationist warrior exultation. (Surely you will die.)

Wow. I just now realized how much my sixth grade recess rhymes and Kim Jong-un's political speeches have in common, rhetorically.

And BY THE WAY: a lot of people—and I mean a LOT of people—say things like, "I like all kinds of music…except rap."

This is maddening to me because it's so immediately dismissive. It's like someone going to France and saying, "Listen, I don't know what all the fuss is about French cooking, but I take my hamburger medium rare." It's like, "Shut up, sit down at the table, and let the chef do his work. I guarantee you'll learn something, and your mouth will thank me later."

If you try it and don't like the sound, that's cool, but be respectful. I don't like mid-century modern architecture, but I'm not going to say Frank Lloyd Wright's buildings aren't "real buildings" and that the Guggenheim is just "too repetitive. It's the same curves, over and over. Ugh."

When someone says, "I don't like rap music" you're not just saying, "I don't like this genre of music." You're also saying, "I don't like the way black people have traditionally told their stories and expressed themselves." Because for black folk, rap is bigger than merely music. Hip-hop is life. It's our life. This isn't just music to black people. And if you don't know, now you know. <END RANT>

Anyway, about that rap battle. I won. And the crowd went NUTS. Every other day or so, at lunch, all I had to do was get some of my friends to hype me up, and then I'd break out a rhyme I'd written using fourth-grade-level rhyme schemes. I was using my talent to navigate safely through the dangerous racial and social landmines of middle school.

So that, my friends, is how I avoided gangs in junior high. Incredible, high-performing creativity necessitated by sheer fear of one Jerrie Elaine Merritt.

CHAPTER 4

BOY, GO HIT A HOME RUN RIGHT NOW

*A father is a man who expects his son to be as good a
man as he meant to be.*
—Frank A. Clark

*There is a way I laugh,
when I pick up on things fast
I get it from someone
There is something about this drive
That's keeping this whole thing alive
I get it from someone
I get it from my dad*
—"Best Part of Me" by Broken Frame

My father hardly ever called me by my name, but almost always called me "boy."

Okay, it's important to understand that there are two facts about my family of origin that must be accounted for. These facts cast a shadow over the entirety of my life. And you already know both of these facts, because you is smart, you is kind, you is important. What I'm trying to say is that you have been paying attention up until this point, and I appreciate it. These facts are:

1. My father was in the military—in the Air Force, to be exact.
2. Both of my parents are from the poor, rural town of Eutaw, Alabama.

But we have not yet answered the question as to how those two facts became reality. And the second fact has a lot to do with the first.

The year was 1969. It was the year Bryan Adams got his first real six-string and it was also the year my father, Milton Merritt, was a senior in high school. He was the oldest of five kids, two minutes older than his twin brother, Wilton. That's right—my father and his twin brother were named Milton and Wilton. What can I say? They were from the South, and names like that happen in the South. Is this the appropriate time to tell you that I also have an uncle named Junebug? And that nobody in Alabama thinks that's weird?

My father's first job was picking cotton as a sharecropper in Alabama. He was eleven years old. Now, at this point, I have to explain what sharecropping is, because most people reading this probably aren't familiar with the agricultural practices in rural Alabama.

I don't blame you. I grew up in Vegas. I don't know this stuff, either. I had to call my folks. It's not like I was picking cotton at age eleven.

Sharecropping developed in the South right after the Civil War. Here's why: as it became increasingly clear that the North was going to win the Civil War, Union General William Tecumseh Sherman, who was marching through the South like LeBron James took care of the Warriors in 2016, said, "What are we going to do with all these newly freed black folk?" He met with a whole slew of black ministers and leaders who advised him.

"LAND," they all said, unanimously. "We need land. Then we will have the means to grow food, determine our own destiny, and build wealth." Sherman was like, "That sounds right."[1]

So, Sherman—at the advice of black ministers and with the blessing of

Lincoln's secretary of war, Edwin Stanton—confiscated more than 400,000 acres of Southern farmland from white plantation owners and ordered it to be divided up and given to freed slaves to work. Historically this is known as Special Field Order 15, but it came to be known by recently freed slaves as "forty acres and a mule"—which in theory would have provided freed slaves with a means to provide food and shelter for their families in perpetuity.*

Enter John Wilkes Booth, screwing the whole thing up and killing our boy Abraham Lincoln.

Ugh.

Out-of-work actors are the worst. Am I right?

The new president, Andrew "Jackass" Johnson, was a Southerner and promised to give back all the land to the white Southerners if they took a loyalty pledge to the US. Surprisingly, all the white people said, "No. Give these black people the land they deserve. Also, a mule!"

Naw, they all white-folked up and took the pledge to get their land back. So Andrew Johnson gave all the land back to the people who—just a few years earlier—had declared war on the US.

Hooray.

I can't stress how devastating the death of Lincoln was. It meant the death of Special Order 15, and with it, the promise of financial independence for freed black slaves died, too. So now these Southern white plantation owners had their land back, but they had no labor force.

Now, the white landowners could have, in theory, rented out this land to the freed black slaves. But these slaves had no money and no collateral because for the past 197 years they had been someone else's property.

Enter sharecropping, which became the most common way to farm in the South.

Here's how it worked: my father's parents lived on land that was owned by a white man, who allowed my dad's family to live on the land and grow cotton on it. After the cotton was harvested, 50 percent of the proceeds went to the landowner, with another 15 to 25 percent paid to the landowner for the

---

* Fun fact: Spike Lee's production company is called 40 Acres and a Mule.

farming equipment, farm animals, seeds, etc. So my dad and his family raised a whole crop and got to keep as little as a quarter of the profits.

Not a great deal. But when you don't have options, you don't have options.

The problem was leverage. As in, the landowner had it, and the sharecroppers did not. The white landowners could threaten not to renew the terms unless the sharecroppers gave them more money. Or the landowners could demand an unreasonably high interest rate for money lent out for seeds. There were all sorts of ways that poor sharecroppers got screwed by the system.

When I learned about this, I said to my dad, "So, Dad, growing up, you were basically a slave?"

"No!" my mom interjected. "He wasn't in shackles!"

My dad paused and said, "Yep, you get it, son. I was basically a slave. Don't listen to your mom."

My mom likes to downplay some of the crappy things in her past. To this day, she thinks my middle school on Donna Street was a Blue-Ribbon School.

Either way, this was NOT a great deal. And as a result of this, most sharecroppers were trapped in a cycle of poverty. This went on for generations—and the same basic system was in place from 1880 to the time my father was born. Sure, his family earned enough money to eat and have a place to live, but they were no closer to owning the land, nor could they save enough money to achieve fiscal independence.

My dad saw this clearly. He knew that if he was going to have any shot at life, he was going to have to get out of Eutaw.

But my dad wasn't the only one who noticed this. You know who else saw this trend? One of the most powerful men in the entire world: the secretary of defense for the United States, Robert McNamara.

McNamara was the architect of the Vietnam War, and one of the most influential men in the world in the 1960s. He firmly believed that military service could be used to "rehabilitate" men caught in the cycle of poverty.

He also needed about 500,000 men every year to fight the Vietnam War, and he was having trouble getting people to voluntarily sign up. So, in August 1966, McNamara announced Project 100,000—a plan to bring up 100,000 previously ineligible men into the military every year to "rescue" and "salvage" poor—and especially poor minority—men. Forty percent of these new draftees were black—at a time when the general US population was only about 9 percent black.

I'll pause here for a second and let you read that last sentence again.

Meanwhile the number of wealthy white kids given deferments for being in college went up 650 percent during the Vietnam War era. But you had to have money to be in college—something my dad and his brother certainly did NOT have. McNamara targeted and drafted more than 340,000 poor people—again, a large number of whom were minorities, the vast majority of whom were assigned to be infantrymen in Vietnam.

Fun fact: of the 2.5 million enlisted men who served during Vietnam, 80 percent came from poor or working-class families, and the same ratio had only a high school education. As historian Christian Appy wrote in his book *Working-Class War*, "Most of the Americans who fought in Vietnam were powerless, working-class teenagers sent to fight an undeclared war by presidents for whom they were not even eligible to vote."[2]

In the fall of 1968, my father and his twin brother both received a letter that started out:

Greeting:
You are hereby ordered for induction in the Armed Forces of the United States.

My father was seventeen. Seventeen!!! He had not even graduated high school yet. But my father was told by the United States government that one month after graduating high school in June, he would have to report for active duty in the US Army.

Where he would (most likely) be placed as an infantryman.

And be (most likely) sent to the front lines of the Vietnam War.

And then (most likely) return home in a body bag, like the 58,000 other young men who died in the war.

In the words of our great black patriarch Marvin Gaye:

Father, father
We don't need to escalate
You see, war is not the answer[3]

At the end of 1968, as my father was about to graduate, the world must have seemed like it was coming apart at the seams. Earlier that same year, MLK and RFK had both been assassinated. LBJ had sent more than 536,000 young men over to Vietnam. And it had been the deadliest year of the war, with more than 16,000 young men coming home in coffins draped with the American flag. That's more than five September 11ths. Things were *not* looking good.

My dad realized that he had about six months until graduation. To quote Marvin, he had six months to "find a way."

STANDARDIZED TESTS SAVED MY LIFE

This is where I want to brag on my dad a bit. Obviously, he was a hard worker. If you harvest cotton in the Alabama summer before you're a teenager, you automatically get to be called a "hard worker" for the rest of your life.

But my dad was more than a hard worker. He was smart. He had common sense, and a good mind for school, so when that draft letter came, he devised a plan.

"I looked into the casualty statistics and realized that the branch I was least likely to die in was the Air Force," my dad told me. "So, I signed up for the Air Force. Ain't nobody trying to die today."

My dad was not about to be a statistic.

But first he had to be admitted into the Air Force. And to do that, he had to pass the Armed Forces Qualification Test (AFQT).[4] If he failed this test, or did poorly, he would not be invited to be in the Air Force. They would have just sent him to the Army and made him an infantryman.

My dad took the test, and he tested so high in the areas of math and science that he was assigned to be an "aerospace ground equipment mechanic." I can barely spell math, and here my dad was calculating his future. He was given his assignment, grabbed my mom by the waist, and said, "Let's get the hell out of here." Mom threw her apron on the counter of that segregated diner, and that was that.

My dad never saw even a hint of the humid tropics of Vietnam. Ironically, he spent most of his career in Vegas, which, meteorologically speaking, is the exact opposite of Vietnam.

You could make the case that the only reason I exist is because of a government-issued standardized test. For Marty McFly in *Back to the Future*, it was a single bolt of lightning hitting the town's clock tower that saved his life.[†] But for me? It was a single military test. With a different result, it's not only possible, but highly likely, that I would fade out of existence, like Marty disappearing from that Polaroid of his family.

Talk about high-stakes testing.

STEALTH BOMBS

When you're a kid, Vegas isn't that much different than any other midsize metro area, I imagine. I loved sports, mainly because there wasn't a whole lot to do in Sin City when you're eleven years old. After all, the high-stakes poker tables were out, and you already know how my dad felt about me playing around with Siegfried and Roy's tigers. So seasonal sports leagues for Air Force kids were the *business* when I was growing up.

This was multiplied by the fact that I was a latchkey kid who didn't have a whole lot going on in my social life. Sports were a chance for me to see my friends.

It was also multiplied—no, amplified exponentially—by the fact that my father was incredibly involved in my youth sports career. I don't think this was a black thing. I think it was more of a "my dad used to be pretty athletic and enjoyed sports, so this was a really easy way to connect with his son" thing. So, my dad was *always* at my games, or coaching my Pop Warner football team, or helping out with my Little League team.

Having him be this involved in my sports was a big deal for me and was

---

† Well, that and Doc Brown's ziplining ability.

multiplied—no, amplified exponentially—by the fact that for five days of the week, my father wasn't even home. My dad was assigned to be a part of a top-secret classified team that worked on the F-117A, otherwise known as the Stealth Fighter. Growing up, he couldn't tell us what he did, so he told us he worked on air conditioners for the Air Force. I should have known something was up when our AC unit at our house would break and he would say, "Jerrie. Call the AC people." And I was like, "Bro, I thought you were the AC people."

My dad's team would get on a plane on Monday morning and fly 200 miles north to the literal middle of nowhere in the Nevada desert and come back early on Friday afternoon. There, they had all the room they needed to work on this top-secret weapon system, away from prying eyes who didn't have a classified badge. Gone before it was light on Monday, back on Friday. He did this for years.

But he was always at my Friday games or weekend practices. Always.

Which communicated something to me. It meant that I could connect with my dad by performing athletically. There was nothing more I wanted to do with the limited time that I had my dad at home than make my dad proud. And more than that, to let my dad know that I was great at something.

I think this is at the heart of every boy. Heck, every kid.

One time, during a Pop Warner season, we were playing a team that was undefeated. My dad, who was the coach, said to us, "These guys aren't better than you. They just work harder. If you beat them, I'll take the whole team to McDonald's afterwards."

"For real?" one kid asked, because that was almost too good to be true.

"Yes," my father said.

"And will you...buy us food?" one kid asked, timidly. A valid question. Always clarify the terms and conditions of contracts, I say.

"Yes," my father said. "Anything you want."

The team looked around at one another.

LEGGO!!!!

We kicked the ever-loving shit out of that team. Hamburglars Mount Up! The opposing coach didn't see that one coming. The amount of pain we unleashed upon him, destroying his perfect season, was courtesy of Ronald McDonald.

As our team sat on the hard red plastic benches of McDonald's, that bunch of kids was elated. And my dad was like Russell Crowe in *Gladiator*, riding through the fields of wheat, having inspired men to defeat the lumbering Germanic tribes. He walked up to the counter and yelled, "Are you not entertained! We'll take twenty-eight Happy Meals."

My dad told the team how proud he was of us, and I realized in that moment that I was hooked. Hooked, like an addict. I was hooked on my dad's approval. I was hooked on my dad's affirmation. It was better than McDonald's french fries in the eighties, and that is saying something.

But here's the problem: my love language is so clearly words of affirmation, and I came from a family where encouragement wasn't really a thing. Being recognized for the extraordinary things that you do just didn't happen. I don't come from an "attaboy" family. There was no cheering from the metal bleachers, "Good job, Tyler, we love you!" That's just not how my family is set up. Affirmation didn't happen. It was more like, "Look, we obviously love you and if that changes, you'll be the first to know."

My dad could affirm his team. But not me. Not me individually. Not his son.

My closest friend in college was a guy named Mike. That dude's family was affirming as heck. (More on my brother Mike and his family and their impact on me later.) I once ate dinner at his house, and after sitting down, the family basically showered each other with compliments for like ten minutes.

"These hamburgers are just terrific, honey."

"Thanks, babe. I tried a new seasoning on them."

"Well, whatever you did, it's fantastic."

"And the corn is so sweet, isn't it."

"So sweet."

"Done perfectly."

I just sat there, watching them, thinking I was in an *SNL* sketch. Who talks like this? But it wasn't fake. It was REAL. I was super jealous. I wanted, more than anything, for my father to say those kinds of things to me. And if

I'm honest, I was a little mad at God for giving Mike such a wildly supportive family structure, while mine was so un-gushing and stoic.

I'm not really blaming my father for this, though. Affirmation is about truly seeing people, and when you are from poor, rural Alabama and you're black, you're not used to people truly seeing you.

Oh, sure. They might see your skin.

Or, like Bob McNamara, they might see your situation.

But they don't see you.

If my father had waited for someone to truly see him—to recognize his latent intelligence and encourage it—he'd still be sitting in Eutaw to this day. He had to score high enough on a government test for someone to notice him. Nobody groomed his gifts. Nobody affirmed him. His family was too busy trying to make the profit from 30 percent of a cotton crop last the whole year. When life is hard, and you're the working poor, survival is the name of the game, not affirmation.

And, let's be honest, military culture isn't exactly warm and fuzzy, either.

The military doesn't care about your self-actualization. Boot camp isn't focused on helping every recruit reach level five of Maslow's hierarchy. There are wars to fight. You have a job to do, and you best not mess up. No errors. Do your damn job. That's the baseline.

That's just where my dad was.

But for an insecure little black kid craving his dad's affirmation, this was not great.

TWO FINAL STORIES

Let me wrap this up, because this is getting a bit therapy-y. The first happened when I was in fourth grade. We had been in Vegas for about four years at that point, and one night we went out to dinner as a family at the NCO Club, which was not a common occurrence. We were dressed up more than normal. There was a white tablecloth, and waiters with crisp white shirts and black ties. And over the course of dinner, my dad began talking about what might be next. When you're in the military, you're always wondering about what's next. You sign up for this lifestyle. He mentioned to my mother, casually, that they might transfer us to Germany.

I started to cry.

For the first time in my life, I had real friends. I was playing sports. For as much as a fourth grader can have "his people"—I had "my people." We listened to BON JOVI TOGETHER. If that doesn't mean something, then what is the point of life? In short, Vegas, in a very real way, was becoming home.

It was the first time I remember crying when I wasn't in trouble.

My father and mother looked at me.

"Boy, what's wrong?" my father asked. He had not made the connection from his conversation topic to my tears.

"Are you okay? What is wrong?" my mother asked.

I looked at my dad.

"I don't want to move," I said. It was all I could manage.

There was a pause.

He put down his napkin. He nodded and breathed in deeply. "I'll look into putting in for an extension," he said. I felt the world pivot, and I knew in that moment that he saw me.

I felt seen and protected. Even though I didn't know how the US military worked, I could tell that my father was telling me something to comfort me in that moment.

My father finished out his career with the Air Force in Vegas. Twenty-three years. To this day, they still live there. He did that for me.

He saw me clearly in that moment.

Which is why what happened later was always confusing to me. My father raised me to play sports. He was actively in my life while I was playing sports. But—and we will get into this in depth later—during my ninth grade year, I discovered music. I discovered drama and theater. And my focus shifted.

As my focus shifted away from sports, things started to change between us.

In fact, I started a band in 1995, and he didn't come see me play live music in person until 2008. That's thirteen years. I had been playing in my band for most of my adult life. But music just wasn't something he valued. Not like baseball.

That kinda sucks.

It sucks when your own father can't quite see you for who you are and can't quite affirm what you're good at.

When it came to things outside of my father's wheelhouse, or things that he saw as not as valuable, my dad just withdrew into disinterest. Which hurt.

God, it hurt.

Here's what I learned, though. Father issues will drive you to WORK. When you're desperate for affirmation, that ignites a live volcano inside you. When you have two incredibly driven and ambitious parents who expected you to be great but never handed out attaboys or recognized your greatness, it keeps you continually running.

I have a tattoo on my forearm that says "Driven."

And for years, my license plate said the same.

It's unclear to me if I could project my issues any more clearly to the outside world.

A ROYAL MESS

I have one more memory blazed in my mind. This one is from my eighth grade year. My dad was the third-base coach for my Little League baseball team. We were the Royals, with uniforms featuring the same logo and colors as Kansas City, which for some reason was not a blatant trademark violation.

Now, growing up, my dad's best sport had always been baseball. And my best sport was baseball, too. Also, it was the sport that required the least amount of energy output for the maximum impact. Basketball was a crap-ton of running. Soccer was even worse. Football required pads and heavy equipment, which was never fun in the Vegas sun. But baseball? You sit in the dugout with your friends and chew gum and sunflower seeds roughly half the time. That's my kind of sport.

Oh, yeah, and I was good. I was always bigger than most of the kids my age, and I was strong and fast, too. I'm not bragging. I'm just giving you a reality check on how awesome I was in eighth grade, as a general athletic specimen. I played first base because I was tall and had fantastic hand-eye coordination. My favorite player was Tony Gwynn, partially because I was a West Coast kid, and he played in San Diego, and also because he was the best hitter in the entire game of baseball for years and years and years, and he was black. I also loved Darryl Strawberry, because his last name was Strawberry. And that's pimp.

Back to the Royals. Our copyright-infringing team was down two runs in the ninth inning. It was the top of the order, and I was batting cleanup. Because, not to belabor this point, I was really awesome at baseball.

Being down two runs in the bottom of the ninth is never ideal. The winning percentage on that one is pretty low. But two of my teammates managed to coax singles out of the opposing team's pitcher.

As I walked from the dugout to go to the batter's box, I passed by my dad, who was the third-base coach.

"Boy," he said. "Go hit a home run, right now."

I didn't even blink.

"Yessir," I said.

The guy who was pitching was Robert Matson, who I knew from school. He was a big, thick white dude. Like me, he was a little too big for his age. Like if this were the Little League World Series, they'd be checking both our birth certificates. Robert settled in on the mound. He threw hard. He was their best pitcher.

But it didn't matter. My dad had given me an order.

It was not a question of "if" I was going to hit a home run. The question was "how" and "when." This was not about the game. This was not about my teammates, the joy of victory, or that clown Ronald McDonald. This was not about me driving in a run, or possibly two, and helping us get closer to a win. This was about NONE of that.

This was about my dad.

This was about doing what my father said.

This was about me communicating through an aluminum bat that I had heard my father, and that I was able to do what he'd said.

This was about my manhood.

The first pitch came in a bit outside. I took it as a strike.

The second pitch was a ball, high. I laid off. Ball one.

The third pitch, Robert threw inside for a strike. One ball, two strikes.

Robert adjusted his hat and smirked to himself. He was firmly ahead in the count.

He had me.

But what Robert didn't know is that he absolutely did NOT have me. I'd deliberately taken all three of those pitches to let him get two strikes on me. Because I knew what Robert did when he was ahead in the count, and the pressure was on. I'd seen him do it before.

When he was ahead in the count like that, he had an off-speed pitch he'd throw. It was almost like a lob. It came in slow, and it was confusing, and most batters would get nervous, and swing too early...and Robert would strike you out.

But I knew that pitch was coming. Robert was big and strong, but he wasn't going to be scoring 1600 on his SATs. You know? Sure enough, Robert threw his off-speed lob, and I waited on it. I shifted all my weight to my back leg, and I hit that ball. Oh, boy, did I hit that ball. I hit it like a four-year-old beats a piñata.

It was a line drive that screamed about three feet over Robert Matson's head, and kept traveling until it cleared the four-foot fence in center field.

My team was probably cheering. I don't remember. I don't remember rounding the bases, either. I only remember walking to the dugout. The team was swarming me, patting me on the back, giving me high-fives. But I didn't give two cents about them.

The coach said something to me. I have no idea what he said. There was only one opinion on the planet that mattered to me. I walked into the dugout, and as I did, I passed my dad.

He didn't give me a high-five.

He didn't say, "Good job."

He didn't say, "That's my boy."

He didn't say anything.

He just stood there.

I still remember his expression. No joy. No smiles. It was as if his eyes said, "What do you want from me? You did what you were supposed to do."

A three-run, game-winning home run was the starting point—that kind of performance was simply the baseline of expectations.

If I am being honest with myself, that moment affected me a lot more than I can even say out loud.

And if I am being really honest, all of this has probably messed me up way more than I would like to admit.

Damn. Yeah, I'm done with this chapter.

CHAPTER 5

I GOT 99 PROBLEMS AND PRETTY MUCH ALL OF THEM ARE WOMEN

The course of true love never did run smooth.
—William Shakespeare, *A Midsummer Night's Dream*
(Act 1, Scene 1)

Never trust a big butt and a smile.
—Bell Biv DeVoe, "Poison"

There's one track on the *Hamilton* soundtrack that is super difficult for me to listen to.

I *hate* listening to it.

But that melody, though. So I pretty much play it every time.

It's the song "Say No to This," which is the moment in the musical biography of Alexander Hamilton where a defect in his character nearly destroys his entire life. Hamilton succumbs to his lust and has an affair with a married woman, nearly destroying his political career and his marriage in one moment of tragic weakness.

The ancient Greeks called this fatal flaw *hamartia*, and it was a central theme in their dramas. *Hamartia* means a transgression against the gods—and for the Greeks, it was the kind of thing from which no mortal can recover. It's Icarus flying too close to the sun.

In the Bible, the Greek word *hamartia* is translated into the word "sin." The destructive power of *hamartia* is likened to a deadly disease, a stain, and a forest fire. This is probably why I don't like listening to that song from *Hamilton*. I don't like watching a man's life unravel because of his weaknesses. Who wants to watch someone pour gasoline on themselves and then light the match?

For me, it's too painful, because I've been there.

I've watched my own life unravel in my hands because of my own failings. And to be reminded of those moments still stings a bit. Who am I kidding? Sometimes it stings a lot.

And yet.

And yet.

I am also of two minds about this.

Maybe it's because I'm in my forties and I am much less interested in someone else's victories and triumphs—how you killed it at this or were a stone-cold playa at that. I am more interested in how life has beaten you up, and how you managed to get back up and keep going. Stories of people's strength and triumph matter less to me. I think they tell me less about you than the stories of moments when life fell apart. Or when you fell apart.

Because those are the moments when you are forged. Not in victory. But in pain and suffering. I'm interested in those moments. What you learned. Why you are still standing. How you are still standing.

Now, I was honestly trying to keep this book as light, fluffy, laughy as possible—about being beautifully and unapologetically black as possible—up until this point.

But I truly believe that the best way to get to know someone is to understand their brokenness—and that when someone is brave enough to be vulnerable, that vulnerability begets vulnerability. It helps other people open up. And then you have a connection. So I thought I'd talk about my own *hamartia*.

My dysfunction.

My failures.

My fatal flaw.

If Superman has his kryptonite, and Othello his jealous rage, and cats have that little red laser-pointer thingy, then my fatal flaw is women. Let's be completely honest: the opening chapters in the micro-biography of my life thus far are filled with examples that pointed to this dysfunction. If you recall:

- I memorized an entire Bon Jovi album in one night because of a girl.
- As a teenager, I locked myself in my room and practiced penmanship over summer vacation because I thought it would help me catch the attention of girls.
- I lied to a grown-up and pretended to have a deep and abiding passion for golf (!) because of a girl. Golf!
- I pledged my heart to a girl because while playing in a sandbox because she said that she liked my khakis.

Obviously, I have some issues. So, let's take this break to talk about women.

Now before we get going, the feminist side of me needs to explain this a bit. I discovered at a very young age that I just loved women. I'm not sure what age boys are supposed to start noticing girls, but I was born ready.

Part of this is because of my own incredible, badass mother. As I talked about in previous chapters, I had a deep respect—and at times all-consuming fear—for my mother. This led, I think, to a general respect for and interest in women. I just liked being around them. Have you met women? They're great.

But even in elementary school, I realized there is nothing like the attention of the opposite sex.

I'll share with you three quick anecdotes that will illustrate how deeply this dysfunction ran for me.

STORY NUMBER 1:
THE OLD JESSICA AND PATRICIA SWITCHEROO

One of the first times I realized that girls were going to be a problem for me was in fourth grade. My best friend, Robby, and I lived in the same neighborhood as two girls named Jessica and Patricia. We all lived near each other and we were all latchkey kids (unsupervised kids is never a good idea). So we'd all walk home from elementary school together.

Robby and I were best friends.

Jessica and Patricia were best friends.

So it only made sense that we would become boyfriend and girlfriend. I got Patricia, and he got Jessica. These girls were in fifth grade, so it was a big deal. Looking back on it, it felt like Patricia was my girlfriend for months and months, but in reality, it was probably more like four days. Time in fourth grade is like time to Kiefer Sutherland in *24*. Anyway, after those four days of complete and total bliss, for reasons that even the most brilliant philosophers couldn't decipher, Jessica decided to break up with Robby, and on the same day, Patricia decided to break up with me.

Robby and I were devastated. Hurricane Patricia had destroyed the infrastructure of my heart, flooding me with a storm surge of loneliness, wreaking havoc with 100-mile-an-hour winds of rejection. Robby and I walked home together, broken. We swore off women. We knew, at that moment, that the pain was so intense, that we would never, ever date again. For the rest of our lives. There was only one thing we could do…sit in my room as I sang New Edition's "Lost in Love" over and over again, out loud until I no longer felt the pain. *"I'm lost in love. Can't live without you."*

As we were drowning our sorrows in a Capri Sun, the doorbell rang. It was Jessica and Patricia. They stood before us, visions of beauty. Visions of pain.

They explained that Jessica decided she wanted to date me instead of

Robby, and Patricia decided she wanted to date Robby instead of me. They said this as if this behavior were completely normal.

Our response was "Okay, that works."

The point is, I realized pretty quickly that "having a girlfriend" was a drug to my ego, and I was an addict. When you "have a girlfriend" it's a ratification that you're good enough to get someone awesome to pay attention to you and like you. Which brings me to a core flaw in me. A core insecurity.

- I was awesome at sports, so I wasn't insecure there.
- I was outgoing and could make friends, so I wasn't insecure there.
- My parents loved me, so I wasn't insecure there.

But I was insecure about one thing: the color of my skin. More specifically, the tone of my skin.

I was always a really dark-skinned kid. Being in Vegas and the heat and the sun didn't help, because I always got darker. And yes, dark people can get a suntan. White people—I just saved you from several awkward conversations with black people because I know you have definitely wanted to ask that. You're welcome.

There's a stigma that goes along with dark-skinned black men and black women that we are less attractive. Light-skinned is seen as beautiful, but dark skin is not. In the eighties, DeBarge messed it up for all of us dark-skinned brothers. Drake continues to mess it up for us. Him and Lenny Kravitz. And Rick Fox. And Shemar Moore. And The Rock.

Yo, skip those dudes. Looking like I put too much creamer in my coffee. Yeah, I said it.

Nowadays, finally, us dark-skinned people have Idris Elba. I did not have this growing up: a super dark brother who could finally win the title of *People*'s Sexiest Man Alive.

Oh, oh, and wait. Taye Diggs! When Stella got her groove back, all us dark-chocolaty boys got our swagger back. Thank you, Taye.

But this was not always the case. And being honest, it took a toll on me.

You remember late elementary and junior high school, right? Adolescence is a merciless minefield of savage insecurity, and to counteract that, young boys cap on each other with an endless barrage of put-downs and insults. If someone else is put down, then at least for a few seconds, you're safe.

And nine times out of ten, any cap on me had to do with my black skin. Physical appearance is the easiest target, anyway, and my dark skin got all the focus. Stuff like, "Smile so that we can see you, Tyler!"

I'm not going to lie to you: this wasn't easy for me. It's tough getting made fun of regardless, but it hits different when you're mocked for an immutable characteristic over which you literally have no control—like the pigmentation of your skin.

(I can't even imagine how this made black girls feel.)

So, to compensate and save my fragile ego, I realized that if I could get a cute girl to like me, that meant I was okay.

Now I had two things going for me in this endeavor to save my ego. First, I was talented, and talent has always attracted girls. I already talked about my freestyling rapping ability in previous chapters, and in junior high, I used this skill to not only escape gang culture but get the attention of honeys. Because, again, talent attracts girls. Here is some historical proof of that thesis:

- Billy Bob Thornton—who kinda looked like a meth addict from Arkansas got a coupon for nineteen free tattoos—well, this *Slingblade*-drawl brother married Angelina Jolie.
- Lyle Lovett—a musician who looked like a drunk Muppet— married Julia Roberts.
- Arthur Miller—the first nerd in American history, complete with thick black glasses—married Marilyn Monroe. Marilyn Mon-f*cking-roe!

So yeah. Talent attracts girls. But that was only part one of my secret weapon. Part two was that I genuinely liked women. I was always a really good listener. I loved to listen to women tell their stories. I'm legitimately interested in the relational dynamics of people's lives and what makes people tick. This is a giant advantage. A lot of dudes are not only emotionally unaware, they're emotionally incapacitated. I'm not saying I had a hyper-realized ability to access emotions at a young age, but here are some facts:

- I've seen *Titanic* twenty-seven times.
- I can tell you the plot to every Lifetime Christmas movie ever made. Which means I can tell you the plot of one Lifetime Christmas movie. Heck, I was even in one.
- One of my favorite movies is *Love Actually*. And it should be yours, too.

So, when you are a male, and you can listen well and understand emotional, relational dynamics, you are LIGHT-YEARS AHEAD OF ALL THE OTHER BOYS.

I used those two skills to get the attention of Jessica, whose attention made me feel good about myself, and the fear that my dark skin made me unlovable subsided.

Of course, Jessica broke up with me when summer started, which I think was a few weeks later. After all, she was going on to middle school. I was hurt, but it was summertime, so it's not like I was seeing her every day in math class.

I didn't see Jessica for an entire year, until the opening days of sixth grade at a back-to-school assembly. They had invited all sixth graders to come forward to sign up for extracurriculars, and as I looked around, I saw her, across the crowded gymnasium, high in the bleachers, standing with her new boyfriend, who was in the eighth grade.

I felt my heart sink, that strange feeling of rejection and shame.

And in that moment, I decided that I needed to do something that would not only grab Jessica's attention, but also grab her heart. To show Jessica that she made a mistake when she left me. My sixth grade brain decided that the way to do this was to show her my incredible speed. So I started running back to my seat on the other side of the gym. I was not running—I was at a full sprint, like Dash in *The Incredibles*. This was my moment. I was going to prove to Jessica (and her stupid eighth grade boyfriend) that I was fast. Very fast. Very, very fast. That would show them.

What would this accomplish? It's unclear. Don't judge me. Again, I was in sixth grade.

As I was bolting across the gym floor, my mind suddenly kicked in: "Uh... hey guys...Why are we running so fast?" But my body was in full adrenaline flight. It would not let me stop. And I think my mind confused my body. Because right after that moment, I tripped. Just fell down, while running full speed.

I slid across the floor like I was sliding into second base. In front of God and everybody in the entire school.

To this day, I have no idea what possessed me to do that. Why in the name of Tom Cruise did I do that? Why did my mind turn into Jenny from *Forrest Gump*? "Run Forrest! RUN!"

Again, I argue that this temporary insanity was caused by the desperate need to gain Jessica's attention. Because, as I've said before and I'll say again:

There is nothing like the attention of the opposite sex.

STORY NUMBER 2:
STACEY'S TRAPPER KEEPER

If the episode with Jessica proved that sometimes trying to get the attention of the opposite sex can lead you to do stupid things that hurt you, then sixth grade taught me the reverse lesson: sometimes, in seeking the attention of a girl, you can wind up doing something stupid that will hurt someone else.

In my sixth grade social studies class, there was a girl named Stacey, a white girl with pretty brown hair. Stacey was not only the smartest person in the class, she might have been the smartest person I had ever encountered. This girl could free-draw a map of the entire world, complete with major bodies of water. She knew *exactly* where the Gobi Desert was. Damn, Stacey. She had it going on.

I wrote her a note, and passed it to her, asking her to be my girlfriend. She checked the box that said "yes."

But this relationship had real obstacles. She lived very far away from me. We didn't ride a bus home together. We didn't even have any other classes together. The only thing that made her my "girlfriend" is that we passed notes in ONE CLASS. Also, Jim Bridger Middle School was Gang Central, and I could NOT be seen holding the nerdy raise-your-hand-first-in-class girl's hand.

I knew what I had to do.

I had to write a note and break up with Stacey. I wrote the note out in math class the period before. I proofread it carefully, making sure there were no spelling errors. I had crafted every word with nuance and care. I was Michelangelo and that college-ruled lined notebook paper was my Sistine Chapel.

Stacey
I'm going to have to break up with you.
Tyler

I watched her eyes read it. Then she reached into her desk, and pulled out her Trapper Keeper. She slowly pulled out a white piece of paper, which was filled with doodles. I could see some of them. They read:

Mrs. Stacey Merritt
T + S = Forever
And there were hearts drawn everywhere. And I mean *everywhere*.

But the centerpiece of this work of tributary art was a great, white unicorn, galloping across a rainbow, with cartoon caricatures of her and me riding off into a sunset.

I had no idea she felt this way about me.

Stacey took out this piece of paper and took a black Sharpie out of her bag, and with her eyes locked on me, she proceeded to scribble over the paper, blacking it out, as her eyes breathed fire at me.

I was shocked. I just sat there and watched. What did I just do? I didn't know we were riding a unicorn across a rainbow bridge into forever. And this was the first time I realized that male-female relationships are actually complicated, and people really can get their feelings hurt because of something you do.

STORY NUMBER 3:
THE ICE CREAM STORY

Up until now, this chapter has been light and fun and PG, but it's important for you to understand that pretty quickly in my life, it stopped being that.

I lost my virginity at a young age.

Not young enough to call the cops, but certainly not old enough to make a morally acceptable John Hughes movie about it. At a very young age, I came to believe that the act of sex was not that big of a deal. Like I mentioned before, I was a latchkey kid, with untold hours of unsupervised time at home. Some kids smoked. Some kids sneaked alcohol. Me? I fooled around with girls.

It's important to state that at this age, sexuality was not connected to disrespect. I wasn't trying to "take" something from these girls. We were showing each other mutual attention. I didn't understand or know any better. It's very different than when you get older. For me, it was just a simple formula:

Boy + Girl + Not a whole lot to do + Empty houses = Lots of Sexual Encounters

The bottom line is this: the feeling of being attracted to someone who is attracted to you is magical. Defining myself by which girl liked me and who was on my arm would become an important aspect of my life and dramatically influence my decision-making.

If you attempt to compartmentalize sex as only a physical act—if you start to do that and practice doing that—that can be a dangerous thing. This is not the way a normal, healthy person should look at something so powerful and so intimate. And this would cause me real problems in life.

It would cause me to be fired from a job.

It would cause me to be kicked out of my church.

It would cause me to nearly lose my career.

It would cause me untold pain, and to inflict untold pain on others, too.

I started down that road in junior high. That part of me—my sexuality and sexual expression—got twisted. And going forward, I need you to know that, like Alexander Hamilton, my character flaw would come back to hurt me.

So how did that all happen? Well, that brings me to my final story, which would become a defining moment in my psyche for years. It's a story I simply call:

The Ice Cream Story.

It happened to me in tenth grade.

You know what?

I thought I could tell that story now.

I thought I was ready to get into this.

But I'm not.

But stick with me. We'll get there.

CHAPTER 6

MORMONS AND GANGSTERS AND THESPIANS. OH MY!

I will tell you that these next few paragraphs put me at high risk of getting my black card revoked. What's a black card, you might ask?

BLACK CARD

An imaginary card that all black people are born with, constantly under threat of being revoked if said black person does not act black enough or in a proper black way.

EX:

Black Person 1: I'm not feeling that Nas *Illmatic* album, but that Vanilla Ice song "Ice Ice Baby" is my jam.

Black Person 2: Bro. Imma need you to come up off that black card.

The reason I'm at risk here is because I'm about to go *all in* on Gwyneth Paltrow. No six-foot-two black man should know as much as I'm about to tell you about Gwyneth Paltrow. But before you yank my black card, trust me, I'm going somewhere with this.

Gwyneth Paltrow is a fantastic, award-winning actress. But yo, she is white. Like white, white. I'm not mad about it. Yeah, she did steal Iron Man's heart, but the fact remains, she is super white, and she needs to stop with all that kale propaganda.

For ten years, she was married to Chris Martin, the lead singer of Coldplay. Gwyneth once referred to her divorce from Chris Martin as an "conscious uncoupling," which is just about the whitest white woman thing ever. Actually, no. The whitest thing Gwyneth Paltrow ever did was write a weekly "lifestyle newsletter" which promoted things like Bee Venom Therapy. That's right. Get stung by bees on purpose. I'm not saying that is some white people nonsense, but let's just say that my uncle Junebug—he wasn't spending his money on that. She also once extolled the virtues of "vaginal steaming." No commentary needed for that. I'm just going to leave that right there for you.

But I'm not here to cap on Gwyneth Paltrow. I'm actually a pretty big fan. But the reason I am bringing her up in all of her fantastical whiteness is because in 1998, she was in a film titled *Sliding Doors*. It is a fascinating film that follows two storylines, showing two vastly different trajectories of a woman's life based upon whether she caught her train on the London Underground or not.

Paltrow's character misses the train in one plot arc, and catches it in another—and we watch as the outcomes of her day and life diverge in stark ways. The point of the film, I think, is to get us to see that seemingly small details sometimes have nearly indescribably important consequences on our lives.

Do you have moments like this? Think about your own life. What are your *Sliding Doors* moments? Stuff like:

- What if you hadn't been accepted to that college?
- What if you hadn't gone to that get-together or party and you'd never met so-and-so?
- What if you hadn't read a book that forced you to grapple with the concept of vaginal steaming?

What if?

In previous chapters, I've already talked about some of the critical *Sliding Doors* moments in my own life. What if my father hadn't passed that Air Force AFQT exam? What if my mom hadn't seen the stark reality of segregated life in Alabama in that diner that one day and determined to get out? What if my dad had taken that assignment and moved our family to Germany? So many questions. So many different outcomes. I think about this a lot.

Sliding doors.

The philosophical question this movie is subtly asking through the sliding doors of that London Underground train is this—is life random, or do things happen on purpose? Is there any rhyme or reason to the way that life unfolds? Is there a bigger story that somehow my life fits into? And finally, why are these cosmic, theological questions prompted by a Gwyneth Paltrow movie?

I say all this to point to the central focus of this chapter—which is my own *Sliding Doors* moment in which my history and destiny were forever shaped.

And it all happened because of a class scheduling glitch my freshman year of high school.

PEOPLE BUFFET

After I left the gang-riddled halls of Jim Bridger Middle School, I started high school at Rancho High in North Las Vegas, which was a gargantuan school with more than 3,000 students. And my, if it wasn't a strange buffet of humanity. Taste the smorgasbord of students with me, won't you?

FLAVOR 1: *Gangs*

First, you had the same gang presence that we experienced at Jim Bridger, only instead of it only being the Donna Street Crips, there were brand-new gangs that we'd never experienced before.

FLAVOR 2: *Military Kids*

We were also a military town with a massive number of kids who came from Nellis Air Force Base, so we had a junior ROTC on campus run by actual Air Force personnel to train high school students who were interested in going into the military.

FLAVOR 3: *Mormons*

Rancho High School also had a cosmic crap-ton of Mormons. Historically, Las Vegas was part of a small cluster of cities that were settled by Mormon pioneers, led by Brigham Young. There was a huge Mormon church right off our campus, and the Mormon kids would go off-campus for lunch and the church would serve free pizza. I went because the Mormon girls were CUTE. Yo. Mormon girls are always cute. If you're a Mormon girl reading this right now, go on. Take a look at yourself in the mirror. Jump back and kiss yoself.

So on Fridays our school hallways were just plain...bizarre. We looked like a bad Halloween episode of *Saved by the Bell*. What a weird slice of one city.

The point was, I didn't fit into any of those three groups. A lot of kids didn't. So where was my group? Where was my tribe? Well, I'd soon find out, through a mathematical accident of scheduling.

IT'S ELECTIVE. BOOGY WOOGY-WOOGY.

Like every other state, Nevada's mandated educational requirements pretty much filled up our academic schedules. Every incoming freshman had to select one elective course.

Every student was handed a simple form with two blanks: your primary elective and your secondary elective in case your first choice was filled up. Well, I knew for sure what I was putting for my primary elective.

Spanish.

I thought learning to speak another language would be DOPE. Also, and I know this is going to come as a major source of surprise for all of you, I figured that speaking Spanish might help me spit some game at some of the finer Latina ladies at my school. Rico Suave.

So I wrote down Spanish for my first choice.

However, I made one crucial error. I dramatically underestimated the craftiness of my classmates. I think every single Hispanic kid in the entire school put Spanish as their primary elective because it was literally a language THEY ALREADY KNEW. Talk about an easy A. Every Intro to Spanish class was full of students who already knew Spanish.

I was so mad. And I got bumped. I didn't get my first elective. I got my secondary elective, which I had chosen using the same formula that every other student did: which class seemed like an easy A?

- I looked at pottery, but that seemed messy. Also, it reminded me of the film *Ghost*, and I was uncomfortable if that was the teaching technique.
- Badminton I assumed would get me hot and sweaty during the middle of the day. Also, I was very uncomfortable with the word "shuttlecock." Moving on.
- School newspaper seemed easy, but probably a ton of work.

So I put down "Drama 1."
"How hard can that be?" I said to myself as I wrote it onto the form.
And that's how my black butt ended up in a theater class.
Sliding doors.

DRAMA MAMA

Drama 1 was taught by Mrs. Sandra Seaton, a woman who had her work cut out for her.

First, this class was largely filled with misfits who were in the class only because their primary elective had been filled up, too. This was not a class filled with a bunch of aspiring Anthony Hopkinses dying to play the role of King Lear. Sure, there were a handful of very excited theater-loving kids in the class, but we all looked at them the same way we look at those kids who voluntarily sign up for the chess club after school.

"Yo. What the hell is wrong with you?"

But this woman was up to the challenge. Mrs. Seaton had one goal: to expose a bunch of reluctant learners to theater and show them its complexity and beauty. And like the Mormon missionaries who rode their bikes around town, she truly believed in this message. Also like those Mormons, Mrs. Seaton would be undeterred in sharing it. And like so many people who answer the door and find Mormon missionaries standing there, we felt trapped, but knew we just had to let this happen or we'd never get on with our lives.

Midway through first semester, Mrs. Seaton urged all of us to go to the school play, which was being performed by members of her advanced drama classes. I remember thinking, "There's no way I'm going to do that."

I would have rather watched televised bowling. But then she said, "And if you go, I'll give you extra credit." Grades were pretty important to me, and this seemed like a very easy way to ensure an A. The play was called *Murder on Center Stage*, and it was about the cast of a production of *Romeo and Juliet* who get trapped in the theater with a murderer, which didn't sound terrible.

I ended up sitting in the back row of the theater watching this production. The house lights went down, the lights went up on the stage, and let me tell you, these upperclassmen killed this play. For the next hour I was gone. I mean, I stopped existing. I had never seen anything like this before. These upperclassmen were transformed from people I didn't even know into superstars in my mind. They were untouchable giants of otherworldly talent to me. It was the coolest thing I had ever seen. For those two hours, there were no gangs outside, there were no dad issues at home, there was no homework, there was nothing. Nothing existed except that play. The escapism was intoxicating.

Now, I know what you're probably thinking. "Wait, Tyler, why was this moment so transformative to you? After all, you'd seen acting before. You'd watched television, right?"

Yes, but the reason this live theater experience was so impactful to me—and this is critical to understand—is because I was an idiot.

As an idiot, it had never occurred to me that acting was a profession. I had no idea that TV shows like *Diff'rent Strokes* were actually a group of actors playing fictitious roles—I thought they just turned the camera on a family in New York's Upper East Side. *Silver Spoons* wasn't a performance—it was more like a documentary where we saw this rich kid ride around his house on a choo-choo train. I didn't know there were lines, and a script, and acting.

Shut up. You were dumb in high school, too. My friend Eric thought that the vacuum cleaner was an indoor lawn mower, meaning that the carpet kept growing and that he was trimming it by running the vacuum cleaner. His dad still makes fun of him to this day for that. My other friend, Kate, thought that Hawaii just floated around the ocean, like a giant inflatable raft. "On maps, Hawaii was always in those boxes, always in a different location," she once told me, defending herself. So I don't want to hear anything about this, okay?

Needless to say, that experience with live theater was magical, but never for one millisecond did I ever consider that theater might be something that I would want to do. When you watch Cirque du Soleil, you don't think, "Man, I really want to put on some tights and swing from a gold hoop by my ankles." No. You just leave with your jaw on the floor and say, "That was awesome." Little did I know, my mother's stubborn pride would change all that.

MY MOTHER'S DUMBEST PARENTING DECISION

A few weeks later, our school held a back-to-school night, where parents would come with their students and walk around from class to class and meet the teachers. My mother was vaguely aware that I was in Drama 1, and that I was enjoying it. But that's as far as it went. To participate in theater, you had to stay after school and take the late bus home. All the other buses left at three p.m., but the late bus left at six p.m. There is not a scenario in this world in which I could go to my mother and say, "Hey, Mom. I would like to come home three hours after school is over and stay out until dark. Are you good with that?"

There's not a world that exists where that would go down. So I didn't audition for anything.

But during back-to-school night, my mother was walking out of my theater class, and Mrs. Seaton was standing by the door, saying goodbye to the line of parents filing out.

"Hello, Mrs. Seaton," my mother said. "Nice to meet you. Thank you for being my son Tyler's teacher."

"Oh, Tyler is so talented," Mrs. Seaton gushed. "Why did he not audition for the recent school play?"

"Whaaaaaaat?" my mother said, with the tone of someone who thinks they're in trouble and very much wants to get out of it. "Tyler, why didn't you tell me about this play?"

I already told you about the late bus. That's why I hadn't auditioned. But I couldn't say this to my mama, who was obviously trying to impress Mrs. Seaton.

So I said the first thing that came to mind.

"I just…didn't," I said.

At this point, there's a line of parents behind us, we all have to get to the next class, and my mom is under real pressure to try to save face with this teacher. She turned to me with fire in her voice.

"Well, Mrs. Seaton, I will guarantee you this," she said. "He *will* be auditioning for the next play."

At that moment I realized that I was going to be auditioning for the next play. Whatever that meant.

A number of weeks later, Mrs. Seaton announced the next school play, which was called *The Interview*. Believe me, I signed up. I had been given very clear instructions, and I was not about to cross my mother.

I auditioned. I was cast in the play, which meant that I would have to stay after school for rehearsals. That night I went home and told my mother.

"I auditioned for the play," I told her.

She looked up from the mail she was sorting at the counter. "What?" she said.

"The play that you told me to audition for," I said.

She put down the mail and looked at me as if I just told her I liked wearing my grandmother's underwear.

"Now what are you talking about, son?" she said.

I was genuinely confused.

"The play you told me to audition for, or you would end my life on this earth," I said. How did she not remember this?

"Oh," she said. I was still not sure she remembered. "Okay."

"And I got cast," I said. "So, I have to stay after school and take the late bus home. I'll be getting home around six p.m."

I watched my mom start to get angry, but then she stopped. After all, she had painted herself into a corner. I had done exactly what she had wanted.

So, to recap, a scheduling gaffe was responsible for me being enrolled in a drama class.

And my mother's unique blend of Southern strength and pride basically forced me into auditioning for theater, against both of our wills.

Sliding doors.

HIGH SCHOOL MUSICAL
(BEFORE THAT CUTIE ZAC EFRON)

Now at this point in my high school career, I was suddenly dumped into a strange new world that I knew absolutely nothing about. Now I was surrounded by theater kids, which is like being surrounded by a whole bunch of dangerous drug addicts, only instead of meth, their drug of choice is Andrew Lloyd Webber.

And these kids started pushing this theater drug hard.

The upperclassmen, who earlier that year I'd instantly idolized in the fall play, were now my co-actors. They took me under their wing. I discovered that I really liked this stuff. And that I was pretty good at it. I might have gotten Drama 1 by accident, but I signed up for Advanced Drama because I loved it.

The very next year, Mrs. Seaton left the school, and a new drama teacher was hired, whose name was Mrs. Joy Demain. Now, if Mrs. Seaton was a great educator who happened to teach theater, then Joy Demain was a great actress who happened to teach theater. This woman wasn't merely a teacher—she was an actress, a dancer, a performer, and a fantastic singer. She also liked to eat vegan hot dogs during rehearsal. I only remember this because… vegan hot dogs.

With her first show of the year, Mrs. Demain decided to do a musical. This created a problem, because I didn't even know what a musical was. I had never even seen a musical. I didn't even know what that was. I'd like to remind you again that I'm black. And this was before *Hamilton*.

Lucky for me, I had Kai. Kai was a girl in my class who lived near my house, so we rode the bus home together, and then would walk part of the way home together. I admitted to her one day that I didn't even really know what a musical was. She looked at me as though I had just told her that I didn't know what toilet paper was. Her eyes looked at me with a mixture of horror, deep sadness, and compassion.

She reached into her backpack and pulled out a thick, dual-disc CD case. The front cover featured a yellow sun rising against a red backdrop, with what appeared to be characters from an Asian language. I read the front.

Miss Saigon
Original London Cast Recording
Deluxe 2-CD Edition

"Take this," Kai said, as she put the case in my hands, and then closed her hands around mine, as though she were passing on a family heirloom to her only daughter on the day of her wedding.

Kai then launched into a speech for a solid hour. Was it a speech? A lecture? A sermon? I'm unclear. It was a journey through the history of music. And story. And human civilization. I don't remember much about what Kai said, but I do remember that she spoke with more passion than anyone I had ever heard. She spoke with the urgency of a time-traveler who had gone back to 1937 and now had to convince the world that Hitler was bad. It was intense.

"Kai, Kai," I said. "I get it. I'll listen to it when I get home."

I went home, and went into my dad's den, which had a legitimately excellent stereo system in it that I was allowed to use. I opened the maroon CD case and popped in the first disc. I sat down in front of the two towering speakers covered with black felt, and since no one was home, I turned up the volume. From the moment the first note hit, I was stuck to the ground. For the next two hours, even though I couldn't move, I felt like I was floating.

To this day when someone asks me what my favorite musical is, I'll tell them *Miss Saigon*.

First of all, if you know anything about the London cast of *Miss Saigon*, you'll know that the lead female role of Kim was played by a then-seventeen-year-old Filipino phenom named Lea Salonga, whose voice box was hand-crafted by God Himself. Most people know Lea Salonga because she's the voice of Jasmine in *Aladdin* and Mulan in *Mulan*, but her work in this musical is otherworldly. I'd never heard a voice so crisp, or so beautiful.

And the music!

This photograph appeared in *France Soir Magazine*, October 1985, and was Claude-Michel Schönberg and Alain Boublil's original inspiration for "Miss Saigon."

The *Playbill* from the 1991 production of *Miss Saigon* with the photograph that inspired the show that, in turn, inspired me.

The music was written by Claude-Michel Schönberg and Alain Boublil, who nine years earlier had written the music for the musical *Les Misérables*. Maybe you've heard of it? Yeah.

The story, which is loosely based on the classic work *Madama Butterfly* by Puccini, was inspired when Claude-Michel Schönberg saw a photograph showing a Vietnamese mother saying goodbye to her eleven-year-old daughter, before sending her off to live with her father, who was an American soldier.

Schönberg was emotionally devastated by this photo, realizing this was the height of love and sacrifice: to send one's own child away in order to give them a better life.

I sat in my dad's den, without moving, in front of those two speakers, spellbound, for the whole show. And that was a black brother's gateway drug into Broadway musicals.

THE HEART LOVES WHAT THE HEART LOVES

I want to pause here for a second. I want to talk about passion.

You've heard the expression "The heart loves what the heart loves." But why? Why do some people love what they do? It's a mystery. They just do. For example, why are some kids so good at piano? Do you know how hard it is to get good at piano? The piano is a complex, difficult instrument. It takes years of practice to get good. You have to actually love the piano deep in your heart to practice enough to be good.

The heart loves what the heart loves.

During the Middle Ages, the monks had a word for this idea. They used the term "calling." In fact, our word "vocation" comes from their Latin word *vocare*, which means "calling" or "to call." The idea of "*vocare*" or "calling" is that there is important work to be done in this world, and that God assigns this work to His sons and daughters to do, specifically for them. The monks believed that once you found your "calling," then two things would happen:

1. You'd find joy, because you were made for this work.
2. You'd find meaning, because you'd be doing something important.

And there, in my dad's den, early in the first semester of my sophomore year of high school, in front of those stereo speakers, I think I first heard the "calling." Art called out to me. Music called out to me.

All because I told a girl named Kai that I didn't know what a musical was. Sliding doors.

Let's stop for a minute. I just want to say this to you. Perhaps some of you are reading this, and you remember that feeling of finding something you truly loved, but life has beaten you down. And if you're honest, you've given up a little bit on your dream.

I want to encourage you. I don't think the monks were wrong here. There is something for you, something that the world really needs, and that only you can do. Only you. And it's not too late to do it.

Life can get so crazy, and there are so many different voices saying so many different things to us. But in this moment, I want you to hear my voice. I believe in you. I need you to bring that thing into the world that only you can. Please. For your sake. And for the sake of all of us.

THE AUDITION

A few weeks later, Mrs. Joy Demain held auditions for the fall school musical. Everyone had to choose a song to sing. I wasn't quite sure what to do. I knew rap songs. And I knew R & B songs. But somehow I figured that singing "Iesha" by Another Bad Creation wasn't a good choice. So I chose a song I knew from church, a famous old hymn, "His Eye Is on the Sparrow." I was getting comfortable enough as an actor to be confident with drama, but singing was a whole new game. I'd never sung in front of anyone in my entire life, unless you count my parents in the car. I walked across the stage and took the mic.

I started to sing. Now, I had not been trained. My parents can't sing a lick. Nobody in my family ever sang or was musical.

But I was pretty good at singing. I mean, I had been singing along to Bon Jovi for several years at that point. So I sang at that audition.

Now, let's be clear—this was an amateur high school production, so Mrs.

Demain was scratching the bottom of the barrel to fill out her cast. But I was cast. And with that, I was given my first role in a musical. The musical was called *Working* by Stephen Schwartz. And this would set my trajectory as a theater kid and musician for not only the rest of high school, but pretty much the rest of my life.

ONE FINAL THOUGHT

As I look back on this part of my life, I still wonder how it happened. Most of the general social forces at work were moving against me making this kind of choice. It's not like young black men are groomed by society to do musical theater.

So how did I get into theater? Were the monks from the Middle Ages right? Was this my calling? Did this "call out" to me? Or did it call out to something inside me? Whatever it was, I was hooked. And over the course of the next few months, my entire friend group changed.

Robby. Todd. Those guys faded away. I discovered a new community, and these people were folks who I felt like I might know for the rest of my life.

I had not only found a calling, but I'd found my people. I even lettered in theater. That's right, you can letter in theater. I had a dope black-and-green letter jacket, and I got a giant felt R with the drama masks woven into it to put on the right breast. Haha! Your boy got his letterman jacket. Just not exactly the way my dad was hoping.

I'm not saying that the drama department at Rancho High School saved my life, but for the rest of my time in high school, I didn't think for two seconds about gangs. My free time was all taken. I was laser focused with my extracurricular time and my energy.

And all of this was because a computer logarithm determined that my first-choice elective was filled, so I was given my second choice.

Sliding doors.

Or, as my Latino friends say, "puertas corredizas."

Not that I would know. Because I didn't get into that Spanish class.

CHAPTER 7

I WAS DOING PERFECTLY FINE AND DAMMIT, HERE COMES JESUS,

AKA SUMMER CAMP IN VEGAS IS NO PLACE FOR A GOOSE DOWN JACKET

Now I know what you're thinking.

"Tyler, I just now got the image of 'vaginal steaming' out of my head."

So had I, my friend. So had I. But don't worry, it's time to move on to much less controversial topics.

Religion and race!

At some point when I was a toddler, while my family was stationed in Alaska, my mother decided that she needed to find a church. After all, this was a black woman from Alabama who grew up in the 1960s, where the concept of "church" was baked into the black experience. Also, this was Alaska, and churches were centers of community life. Without them, you're just hanging out in the frozen tundra. Just you and Chilly Willy.

Now, alphabetically, Alabama and Alaska are very close to each other, but culturally, they are very far apart. My mom wasn't going to find a roaring black church to attend, so she just picked a church that was pretty close to our house.

Once we moved to Las Vegas, she did the same thing. She picked Mountain View Assembly of God, a small brown building on the corner of Lamb Boulevard and Cheyenne Avenue. I never really considered my mom as "overly religious." I always considered her "religious enough"—whatever that means. My dad was "not religious," and he didn't go with us. But my mom made me go to church with her on Sunday, which was a miserable experience most of the time. I remember sitting next to her, falling asleep in the pew and literally snoring. She would dig her elbow into my side to wake me up.

On the way home from church, my mom would turn on the car radio to 88.1 KCEP, the black radio station in town, which played gospel music all day on Sunday until six p.m. Right after dinnertime, the station switched formats, back to R & B. So all day long, up until 5:59 p.m., you'd hear gospel music and perhaps Prophetess Amanda Irving speaking about living in the power of the Spirit, and then at 6:01 p.m., it would switch and play the new hit song by Silk, provocatively titled "Freak Me," whose lyrics were not exactly an exercise in subtlety:

Let me lick you up and down
'Til you say stop.

I guess in a way, both were about tongues of fire. Boom! My mom's gonna kill me for that joke.

Before services at eleven a.m., there was Sunday school, and let me tell you, that was a weird collection of kids. About half of the kids were happy to be there, and the other half had a drug problem: their parents had "drug" them to church.

I am so sorry. Yes, that joke was low-hanging fruit, but look, people, I'm here for the picking.

The point is my mom loved her some Jesus on Sunday. Me? Not so much. I also hated that my mom made me dress up in church clothes, which were tight and uncomfortable. And she made me wear church shoes, which were even more tight and even less comfortable. As a junior high schooler, that summed up church for me—dressing up in ways that you didn't normally dress, trying not to die of boredom, and being super uncomfortable for two hours. I could not wait to get home so I could just get back to normal.

DITCHING THE YOUTH PASTOR

More than anything, I just wanted to forget about church and go on with my life. But things kept happening to me that made that very difficult.

One thing that was a particular thorn in my black side was the youth pastor, who we'll call Pastor Scott. Every Sunday, he'd see me and invite me to come to the youth group. I had no interest in that. I wasn't about to hang out in church. That wasn't going to help my game.

But then one day, this dude came up to my mom and me and said, "Hey, Mrs. Merritt. Would it be okay if I swung by Tyler's school to take him out to lunch at McDonald's?"

I knew this trick. Church folk using delicious food to lure teens in so they could talk about God. Like some sort of religious Venus flytrap. The Mormons did this, only they used pizza. Also, cute girls.

"I'll see you tomorrow for lunch?" Pastor Scott said. I nodded. But in that moment, I knew something that Pastor Scott didn't know—I was NOT going to lunch with this dude. The next day, as the bell rang for lunch, I walked out in the hallway and saw him parked outside the school.

"Oh, hell naw," I said to myself and went on with my life.

I don't know how long Pastor Scott waited for me. I literally didn't care. And I thought that ditching him would be the end of Pastor Scott. It would be for most people. But I was wrong. Very wrong. The very next Sunday, Pastor Scott tried again. "Hey, Tyler, I guess I missed you this Monday. You want to try again tomorrow?"

"Sure thing!" I said, feigning excitement.

I ditched him again on Monday. No joke, people, I did this probably ten times. Now two things about this:

1. I know this was a crappy way to treat this guy. But I was a self-absorbed eighth grader trying to protect my rep.
2. To this day, I cannot believe that Pastor Scott didn't call me out in front of my mom. "Yo, dude, why'd you ditch me on Monday, bro?" But he never did.

I finally agreed to meet him for lunch, mostly to get him to leave me alone. And those fries. And Pastor Scott didn't scold me at all. And we didn't even talk about Jesus once. He just asked me about my life. What I was doing. What I liked. What I was excited about. And he was way nicer to me than he should have been.

Years later, I was reading a book by C. S. Lewis, who said that of all the character traits of Jesus, one of the most revolutionary and important was His attribute of humility. Lewis described the trait of humility like this:

To even get near [humility], even for a moment, is like a drink of cold water to a man in a desert. Do not imagine that if you meet a really humble man, he will be what most people call "humble" nowadays: he will not be a sort of greasy, smarmy person, who is always telling you that, of course, he is nobody. Probably all you will think about him is that he seemed a cheerful, intelligent chap who took a real interest in what you said to him. If you do dislike him it will be because you feel a little envious of anyone who seems to enjoy life so easily. He will not be thinking about humility: he will not be thinking about himself at all.[1]

As I read that, years later, I realized this exactly described Pastor Scott. That's how I felt. And it was a drink of cold water, or in this case, orange soda. This dude didn't seem to have an agenda. He just seemed to like...me. That lunch at McDonald's changed something. Pastor Scott went from being Annoyingly Persistent to Pretty Chill Dude.

But if getting me to go to McDonald's was lucky, then what he pulled off next was a downright miracle.

SHOOTING FISH IN A BARREL

At the beginning of summer between my ninth and tenth grade years, Pastor Scott asked me, in front of my mother, if I wanted to go to church camp with the youth group.

This was ridiculous. First of all, my newfound theater friends would not be there. Second of all, what do you do for a whole week at church camp? Make friendship bracelets for Jesus? There was NO WAY I was doing this. I politely said, "Thanks, but no thanks." Later that day, I was emptying the dishwasher, and my mother came into the kitchen. She put her hand on the counter and cocked her head to the side. Now, I'd like to remind you that my mother is a brilliant businesswoman. I didn't realize at the time I was being played. But I was being played.

"Tyler," she said. "You do realize that if you go to camp, there will be girls there."

I stopped, mid-dish.

"Of course!" my brain screamed at me. "There are going to be girls there! Why didn't you think of that?"

And then I realized that at church camp, the only competition I would have for the undivided attention of the ladies would be nerdy white kids. This would be like fishing with dynamite! From that point on, I was practically begging my mother to let me go to church camp.

Well played, Mom. Well played.

CAMP SWAGGER

In the days leading up to camp, I began to pack. Now, I had never been to Christian summer camp, but I knew one thing: I was going to dress to make an impression. I went through my entire wardrobe and decided to bring anything that would make me stand out stylistically.

Now, the dopest thing I owned was a black-and-white Triple F.A.T. Goose jacket. That was the brand—Triple F.A.T. Goose. It made me look like I belonged on *Yo! MTV Raps*. I could have been an extra for Bell Biv DeVoe in their "Poison" video. It looked a little like this:

The dope Triple F.A.T. Goose jacket that I brought to church camp.

So of course, I packed that for summer camp. Is it practical to bring a parka to a summer camp in Vegas? No. But I wasn't thinking about the heat. Well, actually I was. I was thinking about how I could bring the heat for the ladies. I ended up NOT bringing a single pair of shorts, but I *did* bring a black-and-white Triple F.A.T. Goose down-filled winter jacket.

We arrived at the camp on a Monday. The camp was an old Girl Scout camp in Lee Spring Mountains, and as we pulled in, I saw the other buses from all the other churches. Literally busloads of girls. So many girls! And a very minimal number of cool dudes. Wimpy white kids wearing windbreakers, giving each other wimpy high-fives and wearing mid-calf yellow-banded athletic socks. This is what I was up against. This was the Harlem Globetrotters versus the Washington Generals.

Game. Over.

Now, there were a few kids out there who clearly had the same mindset as me. There was a little white kid named Jake, a tiny dude, who wore oversize shirts. Or maybe those were normal-size shirts and he was just that small. At any rate, he was the cute, dimpled Zack Morris against my ethnic A.C. Slater.

Pastor Scott told us to go to our cabins, pick our bunks, get situated, and then come back down for dinner. I milled around the dining room like a politician campaigning for votes. The counselors led us in camp dining cheers, and split us into teams, with colors and nicknames and chants. I'm sure it was all fun, but I was concentrating on making a good impression with a number of ladies I had my eye on.

As the meal ended, Pastor Scott made an announcement:

"Okay, so you have thirty minutes to go back to your cabins before chapel," he said.

Wait, what?

Chapel?

I had been so focused on girls that I had forgotten temporarily that I was at a church camp. I grew irritated. I had an agenda, and Jesus Chapel was not part of that agenda. After dinner, I planned on kicking it with the honeys, perhaps at the fire ring. Maybe by the basketball courts. We'd have to see how the evening would go. But this chapel thing was messing with my game.

I did not have time for that.

Also, I had to get ready. Technically, chapel would be my first formal presentation to the ladies. I changed up my outfit. I changed the laces in my shoes. Put on a different watch. But those details aren't important.

All you really need to know was that it was Triple F.A.T. Goose time.

Lead with the atomic bomb.

This was my debutante ball. What I really needed was a grand spiral staircase to come down, like in every single teen movie ever made. Only instead of *She's All That* it would be *He's All That Plus a Triple F.A.T. Goose Jacket*. Alexa? Play "Kiss Me" by Sixpence None the Richer.

I put on my jacket. I popped the fur hood.

"Damn playa, you look good," I said to myself.

And I did, kids. I did.

I walked outside and immediately regretted my fashion choices. But I had to push past the discomfort. Never mind that it was still easily ninety-two degrees outside. Never mind that I would be sweating balls. Never mind that I was wearing a hooded goose-down jacket in the desert in July.

I looked good, though.

I sat in the very back row of the chapel, surrounded by hundreds of other kids, in my Triple F.A.T. Goose jacket. My only thought was "Do I have to wait until this thing is over to hit on these fly honey dips? Or is there perhaps a way to mack on the ladies DURING a church service?"

You see, up until that point, I thought I was there for the girls.

Turns out, I couldn't have been more wrong.

NEVER TALK ABOUT RELIGION
OR POLITICS

Now, before we go any further, let's just put our cards on the table: I'm about to talk about religion. There's a reason that so many people say, "Never talk about religion or politics." I think it's because people understand that these topics often reveal some of the deepest core convictions of people, and conventional wisdom says that if we reveal our core convictions, that will fracture relationships.

"What's that? You're blue? Well, I vote red, so I guess we're pretty far apart."

"What's that? You're religious. Well, I am not, so I guess we're pretty far apart on the basics of reality."

"What's that? You think that the Whopper is better than the Big Mac? I guess you're a heretic and will have to die."

Conventional wisdom says that for the sake of peace, we have to stay on surface topics, like the weather or Chip and Joanna Gaines's use of shiplap.

I don't subscribe to that conventional wisdom.

In fact, I think it's a deep lie.

One of the most widely viewed TED Talks of all time, with 50 million views, is Dr. Brené Brown's talk on vulnerability. Brown is a social researcher out of the University of Houston, and her thesis, born out of her research, is that human beings are made for deep connection with others. And because of that, our deepest fear is that people will reject us. She says, "Shame is really easily understood as the fear of disconnection: Is there something about me that, if other people know it or see it, that I won't be worthy of connection?"[2]

Therefore, the only way forward is not to hide ourselves, but to be as brave and truthful as possible. About our lives. About what hurts. About who we are.

So I'm going to talk about religion now, which might make some of you pretty uncomfortable. I don't know what your experiences with religion, organized or not, have been. I have some friends who are deeply religious people, and for them, religion has been a source of hope and meaning for their lives. And I have had other friends for whom religion was a source of all sorts of pain. Even abuse.

(If that's you, I'm so sorry that happened to you. No one should ever have to go through that.)

It's hard to see eye-to-eye on this when our experiences are so different. But so far, I haven't held back about the experiences that have been true to my story. So, stick with me, because this one is pretty deep waters for me.

I'm not going to get all Bible-thumpy on you.

I'm not going to attempt to "convert" you.

I'm not going to attempt to sell you anything (although I do have a fleet of high-quality vacuum cleaners whose suction power is unparalleled).

I'm just going to share my story. So let's talk about religion. And let's talk about being black and religion.

STRANGE FRUIT

On Wednesday, May 27, 2020, I swiped up on my phone to look at the news. I wish I hadn't.

Just a day earlier, I had watched a cell phone video of a young white woman in New York City being confronted by a local black man for not having her dog on a leash. I watched in astonishment as she opened up her cell phone and called the police, transforming into Meryl Streep, winning the Academy Award for best actress while pretending to be terrified by this black ornithologist's blackness. She was trying to weaponize the police against a black man because she didn't like him telling her to put her dog on a leash.[3]

So that video was bad. But the top news story of this day was significantly worse.

It was a grainy cell phone video of Ahmaud Arbery, a black man who lived in the coastal town of Brunswick, Georgia. He had been jogging through a neighborhood, as he often did for exercise, and two white men, Gregory McMichael, age sixty-four, and his son, Travis McMichael, age thirty-four, decided they wanted to question him.

Why?

They said they thought he might be a burglar.[4] There's no evidence that they saw Arbery commit a crime. But he was black. And he was running through their neighborhood. So he must have done something.

These two white men (and a third man, their friend William Bryan) got into their white pickup truck and chased Arbery, blocking and redirecting him as he attempted to flee on foot. They cornered him. They drew their weapons. After a desperate struggle, Travis McMichael shot Arbery with a shotgun from point-blank range. In the video, you can see Arbery recoil, stumble backward, and collapse facedown in the middle of the road while Travis backs away.[5]

According to grand jury testimony by William Bryan, Travis looked down at Arbery's dying body and said, "F*cking n*gg*r."

God.

There's terror in watching this video for anyone, because you're watching a human be killed. That's horror.

But it's worse if you're black.

It's absolutely traumatizing. If you haven't seen the video, don't.

Here's why: it's way too familiar. Everything about that scenario, I had seen before. Black people have seen this before. It's called lynching. And it's something we need to talk about now, because it goes to the core of the American black experience in a way that I don't think a lot of people fully understand.

As we've talked about before, after the South lost the Civil War, black people were granted freedom, but the problems did not end. As one historian said, "The North won the Civil War, but the South won the narrative war."[6]

And the narrative was this: black people are not as good as white people. They aren't even fully human.

The Southerners who started the Civil War (as we talked about in previous chapters) were never required to express their sorrow or formally apologize to all the people of African descent whom they had enslaved and kidnapped against their will. When Brother 1 does something wrong against Brother 2, a good parent not only makes Brother 1 apologize, but creates a clear culture in the home that "what you did isn't okay in this family." But that never happened. The South was like a kid who got angry, not because they did something wrong, but because they got in trouble. The North just sort of ignored this, and the South pretended that they weren't wrong. I don't know if you know this or not, but the United States didn't even formally apologize for slavery until 2008.[7]

The mindset of the white Southerner immediately after the Civil War was one still deeply infected by the prejudice of white superiority. But now there were newly freed slaves in the South. And something had to be done to ensure that black folk didn't start viewing themselves as having legal rights or as equal participants in white Southern society. There was a caste system in the South, and black people were at the bottom.

An example: in the state where my parents were born, Alabama, the entire state constitution was rewritten in 1901. John B. Knox, a lawyer and the president of this Alabama constitutional convention, opened the proceedings with this statement: "And what is it that we want to do? Why, it is, within the limits imposed by the Federal Constitution, to establish white supremacy in this State."[8]

> And what is it that we do want to do? Why, it is, within the limits imposed by the Federal Constitution, to establish white supremacy in this State.

An excerpt from the *Journal of the Proceedings of the Constitutional Convention of the State of Alabama, Held in the City of Montgomery, Commencing May 21, 1901.*

This is all recorded. Historical documents. Right there in Alabama state history. So how does one establish white supremacy? Well, through laws. Remove access to voting, etc. But the most effective way to ensure that black folks know their place is through violence.

We've hinted at this in previous chapters, but if a black man demanded legal rights to vote, or complained that a local white businessman was charging unfair rates, or did anything that made it seem like he was on equal footing legally as a white man, well, that was seen as a social transgression worthy of murder.

That black man had to be put back in his place. And the most effective way to do this was through violence. That would cause fear to erupt in the heart and mind of the black man, and in doing so, this violent act would remind the entire community who was in charge.

In fact, lynchings were often done in public, with the entire community showing up. Here's a definition for you:

LYNCHING

An extra-legal punishment that is meted out by a group of individuals who are claiming the authority of a community with an expectation of legal impunity.[9]

From the time period at the end of Reconstruction in 1877 to 1950, there were 4,084 documented racial terror lynchings in the South.

That's one lynching.

Every week.

For seventy-three years.

And those are the ones that were documented. There's a photojournalism book called *Without Sanctuary: Lynching Photography in America* that tells some of these stories, but more shockingly shows pictures of some of these lynchings. This book is 209 pages. Every other page is a photograph from a historical lynching.

If you haven't seen this book, don't.

I wondered, "How in the world did all these old black-and-white photographs survive history?" Then I discovered that these photos survived because they were reproduced and circulated as postcards around the South and even sold as souvenirs to the folks in attendance.

Sold.

As.

Souvenirs.

It's worth discussing how attending a public lynching might affect the psychological well-being of a young white person. How it might dehumanize them. Destroy empathy. Warp their character. That's a worthy conversation.

But I want to focus, instead, on what these lynchings did to the souls of black folks. The South, after the Civil War, was a place filled with racial terrorism.

How in the world do community leaders in black areas, especially in the South, help their black family members, friends, and neighbors, process the reality the world is deeply violent and bent toward their unjust, violent death? If you're black in the South during these seventy-three years, how do you survive psychologically? How do you live in a world knowing that if you look the wrong way at a white woman, or are accused of a crime, not only is your life at risk, but you are at risk of being hunted down, tortured, and killed in horrific ways?

Well, one solution is to flee. Lynchings caused the mass migration of millions of black people to the North. Because of terrorism such as lynching, 260,000 blacks—roughly 22 percent of the black population of Georgia—left between 1920 and 1930[10]—and 24 percent of the black population fled South Carolina during that time.

As founder of the National Lynching Memorial, Bryan Stevenson wrote in his academic work called *Lynching in America*:

In a brutal environment of racial subordination and terror, faced with the constant threat of harm, close to six million Black Americans fled the South between 1910 and 1970. Many left behind their homes, families, and employment after a lynching or near-lynching rendered home too unsafe a place to remain.[11]

But even if you move North, you're still living in a world where that happened. So for black folks that moved, and for black folks that didn't, they both were living in the middle of a society like this. How do you maintain hope? How do you get through that? How do you help a person process that?

The black church.

The black church had a formidable task ahead of it: it had to help its members process the ever-present threat of deadly racial violence and the insidious theology of white supremacy. History tells us that it used a tool that just might surprise you.

The Bible.

The teachings of Jesus Christ.

The example of Jesus Christ.

That's what helped.

I find it odd that I sometimes have to remind my white friends that Martin Luther King Jr. was a preacher. The civil rights movement was birthed in black churches. King's writings and speeches are littered with biblical and religious language. King's whole thesis was that segregation was from the pit of Hell, and God Himself wanted it gone.

Even today, black Americans are the most religious demographic in the nation. According to LifeWay Research in 2018,[12] Black Americans are more likely to believe in God, more likely to read the Bible, more likely to pray, and more likely to go to the Bible as their source for theology and ethics than any other demographic in the US. And it's because of the black church.

I recently discovered the writing and work of a man named Malcolm Foley, a PhD candidate at Baylor University whose doctoral dissertation was studying the sermons of black Protestant preachers in the South during the time of lynchings.

I'm fascinated by this idea. Can you imagine the emotional, rhetorical, philosophical, political, and theological creativity these pastors had to utilize to help their congregants just stay afloat?

Think about how difficult that had to have been.

- You had to help black people lament and grieve injustice and pain well.
- You had to help black people remember their dignity as human beings made in the image of God in a world that assaulted that fact daily.
- You had to help black people remember that God had not abandoned them.

- You had to help black people move away from despair.
- You had to help black people move away from violence.
- You had to help black people move toward hope.

Sometimes all in the same damned moment.

And these black preachers had to do this while white preachers in white churches across town used the same Bible to justify segregation and their belief in the inherent inferiority of black people. Talk about a tale of two cities.

Author Chris Nye once called these two versions the "Christianity of the Poor" and the "Christianity of the Powerful." I'm not here to tell you what to believe about the Bible's overarching story. But I'm just going to leave this right here for you:

- God shows up in a burning bush to tell Moses He's seen the Hebrew people's oppression under Egypt.
- God rescues the enslaved Hebrew people.
- God gives these former slaves land, just laws, and Himself.
- Jesus is born not as an earthly King, but as a poor, minority baby in the corner of an oppressive empire.
- The evil king tries to kill Baby Jesus.
- Jesus grows up. He heals and teaches people—often people on the margins.
- The Sorting Hat puts Hermione in Gryffindor. (Sorry. Just checking to see if you're still paying attention.)
- Jesus chooses twelve nobodies to be His disciples.
- Jesus says He will voluntarily sacrifice His own life.
- Jesus is lynched by a mob.
- Jesus is killed by the Empire.
- Jesus beats Death.
- Jesus sends out a ragtag bunch of men and women to live out His teachings in little nonviolent countercultural communities.
- The Empire tries to crush this fragile group.
- The Empire fails.

- Jesus promises to come back one day and set all things right as the Good King.

So again, which story does that sound like?

The Christianity of Power?

Or the Christianity of the Poor?

But all this was way above my pay grade. I was just a ninth grader. And those giant movements of history were still beyond the scope of my experience or knowledge.

I was just a black kid in the back of a church camp in a Triple F.A.T. Goose jacket.

I didn't know.

But I was about to.

THE BACK OF THE CHURCH

So there I am, at the back of the chapel, surrounded by a whole bunch of white kids. A band came out on stage, including some people with guitars and a drummer. They begin singing a couple of songs. I had no idea what they were singing, but everybody else seemed to know every word.

Every other kid was standing on his or her feet.

Every other kid was singing loudly.

Every other kid was excited.

These kids were pumped about something. Now I had seen adults sing in church, but I had never seen kids my age singing like this. The most curious thing to me was that the excitement level of these kids seemed to have NOTHING to do with the band. At concerts I had attended, people went crazy because of the celebrity of the band. But this very band was very clearly not Keith Sweat. Or Al B. Sure! Or Bobby Brown. This was not about the band. The band wasn't even that cool. This was not about the band at all. This is about something else. And I didn't understand it. I started wondering if maybe I'd made a mistake.

Then the band started the fourth song, and it was weird, but I'm telling you, I felt something shift in the atmosphere. As a theater person, I'd had *some* experience with crowds. I'd heard crowds gasp. I'd heard crowds laugh. I'd heard crowds sing along to music. I'd even heard crowds collectively tune out in boredom. I knew a little something about human crowd dynamics. But this was different.

Suddenly, the echoing singing didn't feel rackety. It sounded almost angelic, like these kids weren't a bunch of weirdos, but that perhaps they understood something very important that I was fundamentally missing— like I was the one who wasn't going the right way. It felt like a heavy blanket was suddenly draped over me, which wasn't helpful since I was wearing a GOOSE DOWN JACKET, mind you. What were these kids doing?

Everyone else was standing up, and I didn't want to be the only one sitting down. "Whatever," I said to myself. "I'll stand up."

I looked around, and every kid around me had their eyes closed. So, I figured, "Well, I guess I'll close my eyes."

I closed my eyes. Unknowingly, this allowed me to block out all the other distractions around me. The lights. That kid that wasn't clapping on the right beat four rows ahead of me. My own ego.

The lead singer sang a simple song. It was a sung prayer of sorts, and these kids were asking God to make them whole. I sang along.

And there I was, in the mountains above Las Vegas, in a simple chapel, and these words were pouring over me in a way I couldn't have possibly anticipated. This was affecting me in ways that I was not prepared for.

And I broke down.

It doesn't take much to convince a ninth grader that they're not whole. I really did think I was okay. I thought I had been managing these wounds that I had just fine. Sure, maybe I was doing some things that I had no business doing. But didn't everyone? I didn't need someone to tell me this.

I didn't know, however, that you could just admit all that stuff to God. I thought you had to hide it from Him or He'd get mad at you, maybe punish you. I didn't know you could ask for help. I didn't know that.

What happened next is difficult to put into words. Let me try.

The Irish people speak of "thin places"—sacred places where mankind becomes keenly aware of the Divine. There's an old Celtic saying that Heaven and Earth are only three feet apart, but in the thin places that distance is even shorter.[13] Thin places are places when we're jolted awake. When God breaks through. When even the most hardened agnostic tilts for a moment in doubt of his doubts. When something touches a human's soul and he or she is gripped by Something More.

Thin places. Maybe you've had an experience like that.

At the top of a mountain.
Down on your knees, at the end of yourself.
At the birth of your child.
Or at that wedding.
Or in that hospital room.

A thin place. A sacred place. A place where life changed for you.

Sometimes this moment is fleeting.

But sometimes, for some people, this moment is life-defining, life-opening. Even life-changing.

It's the slave trader John Newton trapped in the middle of a wild storm at sea, hearing God say, "I have called and ye have refused." Newton would relent, repent, and go on to be a strident abolitionist, and the author of the song "Amazing Grace."

It's Dietrich Bonhoeffer, who had fled Nazi Germany upon threat of death, hearing God tell him to "go back to suffer with your Christian brothers and sisters." He went back, joined the resistance, was arrested for helping Jewish people escape, and was later executed in a German concentration camp.

It's Martin Luther King Jr. sitting in the quiet of his house as his wife and newborn daughter slept, in the middle of the night after receiving a phone call telling him that "in three days, we're going to blow your brains out and blow up your house." King prayed, asking God for help. "I tell you," he would write, "I heard the voice of Jesus saying still to fight on." King would fight on.

Thin places.

Well, let me say, the back of that chapel, in the mountains of the high desert outside Las Vegas, was a thin place for Tyler Merritt. I don't know what else to tell you, and I know that even typing this as I sit here growing emotional as I think about this, I might sound to you like a crazy person. But I'm telling you, in that moment, I had an encounter with God.

Not the same as Newton, or Bonhoeffer, or King. But not too different, either.

A Breakthrough. God entering into history. Here and now. Communicating with me.

In that moment, there was no doubt in my mind that there was a God of the Universe who loved me, even though I was so deeply flawed. This was Grace—undeserved love.

Some of you reading this know *exactly* what I'm talking about. And others of you are really trying hard not to put down this book forever, because if I had said I'd been kidnapped and probed by aliens, that would be easier for you to believe. To which I say, "Why are aliens always probing people? Hey, Alf, leave my ass alone."

But look. I can only tell you what happened to me.

The camp speaker's name was Bob Cooke, and he talked about how God will love you just the way you are, and that He will come to you just how you are, but that He loves you too much to leave you there—and He'll change you, slowly, sometimes without you even knowing it.

Bob Cooke asked this teeming mass of teenagers if anyone wanted God in their life, to be the King of their life. Apparently, the only way to do this was to come up to the front of the chapel, which he called "the altar." I didn't see no altar up there. But it was an Assemblies of God church, and they're big about calling things "altars" and "coming down to the front." So whatevs. Bob asked if anyone wanted to come forward. He didn't have to ask me twice.

I practically ran to the front of the room. You got me, Bob. Jesus is it.

There was one other kid who also came to the front. His name was Hung Chu, a Chinese kid from our church. In a giant room filled with white kids, it was the black kid and the Asian kid who came forward first. How very affirmative action of God.

Hung Chu was crying, and I realized I was, too. The leaders were beside themselves with joy. For us kids, camp was about fun and games and friends. But for the adults, this was why they came. Bob told us again that Jesus would not only be with us, but would change us—and all Hung Chu, I, and the rest of the kids at the front had to do is choose to follow Him.

I had no idea, really, what that meant, but I was in.

I looked at Hung Chu, and I said to him, "I can't believe I've lived this much of my life not knowing about this Jesus."

"Well," Hung Chu said, "we know now."

WALKING BACK TO THE CABIN

Chapel ended, and we had thirty minutes until curfew. That walk from the chapel back to the cabin was my own personal spiritual pilgrimage. As I took that walk back, tears flowed down my face.

There was no doubt in my mind that there was a God in this Universe, and that for some reason, He'd broken through reality to get to me. This was not like the fleeting feeling when a girl liked me. This was not like hitting a home run. This was so much bigger.

Some friends asked if I wanted to walk with them, but I hung back. I couldn't. I needed this moment to be alone. As I walked by myself, I had a deep sense, down in my bones, that my life had been changed forever, and I was trying to grapple with what that meant.

The air felt different.

The sky looked different.

The stars had a different meaning.

God was going to walk with me, now, for the rest of my life. I knew I was never going to be the same.

I was not wrong.

As you'll see, throughout the rest of my story, through the highs (and even more during the lows), from here on out, it was no longer going to be only about me.

And then I took off my Triple F.A.T. Goose down jacket.

For some reason, it just didn't seem as important anymore.

CHAPTER 8

I'M SUPPOSED TO DO WHAT?

*To love at all is to be vulnerable. Love anything
and your heart will be wrung and possibly broken.
If you want to make sure of keeping it intact you must
give it to no one, not even an animal.*
—C. S. Lewis, *The Four Loves*

*Somewhere far along this road
He lost his soul to a woman so heartless.*
—Kanye West, "Heartless"

The summer before my tenth grade year in high school, I went from being just a theater kid to ALSO being a church kid. Suddenly, I was experiencing these other kids who went to church and took God seriously not as weirdos, but as friends.

On the first day of tenth grade, I got on the bus to go back to Rancho High School. I was a bit nervous, because this was the first time I'd be learning while Christian. Would it be different? I didn't *feel* different. I started to walk to the back of the bus, because that's where the cool kids sat. Sitting near the front of the bus, with the uncool kids, was my friend John Bridges from theater class. As I got to the back of the bus, one of my classmates greeted me with a clasped handshake.

"Tyler, my dude," he said. "What the f*ck is up!"

I nodded my head and sat down. And then I pulled the hood of my black sweatshirt over my face and began to cry. I realized that was the first time I had heard a person cuss all summer long.

The speaker at camp was right. I was changing. The values of the community and people I was hanging around were shifting me from the inside. If something as basic and important as my language—how I talked and what words I used—was shifting, then maybe that meant other things were changing, too.

And now I had a new problem. I didn't know how exactly to be me anymore.

HEAVY D AND DU BOIS

Okay, let's stop for a second. Think back over your entire journey through school. How many black people in US history did you learn about? I live in Nashville now, and I asked a handful of my white friends to make a list of all the black people they learned about in school. I'm not saying "spent an entire day learning about." I'm just asking for names of black people who made contributions to the US whose names you heard and remember from school.

From all the folks I asked, I only got seven names, with most people only being able to name five. These are the names that made it on everyone's "Yeah, I know black history" list. This was the scholastic equivalent of "Yeah, I have a black friend." The names were:

- Harriet Tubman
- Frederick Douglass
- Martin Luther King Jr.
- Rosa Parks

- Malcolm X
- Booker T. Washington (maybe)
- Langston Hughes (only people who paid attention in English)

So let me get this straight. You go through thirteen years of US public education and come away only knowing the names of five to seven black people? Does that make sense to you? In the entire history of the United States, only five to seven black people did anything historically important?

At any rate, one of the most famous and important black people in American history is a man named W. E. B. Du Bois (pronounced dew-BOYS). Du Bois was the first black man to receive a doctorate from Harvard University and founded the National Association for the Advancement of Colored People (NAACP). He worked tirelessly to accomplish two things:

1. Get anti-lynching legislation passed so it would be illegal to lynch black people (he even appealed to the United Nations for help).[1]
2. Present evidence, through significant contributions of black people in both science and the arts, that black people were not inferior.

In his landmark book *The Souls of Black Folk*, Du Bois first coined the term "double consciousness" to describe the duality of being both black and American. These two aspects of personhood didn't need to be so fractured and contradictory, but because of the racial realities of the US, he was simply trying to prove that you could be black AND American. Damn. That hits hard. Du Bois writes:

One ever feels his two-ness,—an American, a Negro; two souls, two thoughts, two unreconciled strivings; two warring ideals in one dark body, whose dogged strength alone keeps it from being torn asunder. The history of the American Negro is the history of this strife—this longing to attain self-conscious manhood, to merge his double self into a better and truer self. In this merging he wishes neither of the older selves to be lost. He does not wish to Africanize America, for

America has too much to teach the world and Africa. He wouldn't bleach his Negro blood in a flood of white Americanism, for he knows that Negro blood has a message for the world. He simply wishes to make it possible for a man to be both a Negro and an American without being cursed and spit upon by his fellows, without having the doors of opportunity closed roughly in his face.[2]

This is, Du Bois says, what it means to be black in America. Let's take a moment to talk about the idea of double consciousness.

I think a lot of people have to come to terms with their own version of double consciousness. For example, I think about all the women who work in male-dominated fields. I'm reminded of all the things my mother had to go through. I know for a fact she had double consciousness—she was always aware of her female-ness.

The point I'm trying to make is that I think a lot of people have an experience of wondering how their whole person—everything that makes them them—fits into society. Because sometimes, there's something that makes you "you" that other people around you either don't understand, or don't take the time to understand, or are sometimes openly hostile to. And that feels like rejection. Which hurts.

This moment on the bus helped me realize that in addition to my double consciousness, I had even more layers going on. I had third and fourth consciousnesses going on now. I had to figure out how this new aspect of my life—this religious devotion—fit into my existing life as a theater kid. And a high school sophomore. And a black man.

Like a baby giraffe learning to walk, let's just say it wasn't pretty. There was a lot of awkwardness and a lot of falling down.

LEGALISM, MORMONS, CIGARETTES, AND A WHOLE NEW MIX TAPE

A lot of people think that religion is about "keeping the rules." After all, religions have rules. Don't do this. Make sure and do this.

But like with any rules or regulations, if you lose sight of the "why," you can get in trouble. Why shouldn't you drive fast when it's raining outside? Because you might crash and hurt yourself and others. The rules are there because the goal is safety.

I gotta be honest: early on, my focus shifted almost exclusively to the rules, instead of the reason BEHIND the rules. I thought to myself, "If I follow all the rules, then I am a good person (I'm okay!)." I would find out later that this is something called "legalism" and it's all bad, both for you and everyone who has to deal with you.

This led to me focusing on EXTERNAL stuff, instead of considering what kind of person I was becoming. Here were some examples of that struggle. I already warned you, this isn't pretty. The baby giraffe is going to fall down a lot—sometimes into a pile of elephant dung.

Mormon Kids

All of a sudden, the Mormon kids I went to high school with weren't just Mormon kids. Before, I couldn't have cared less about what they believed. But now, I had some pretty strong religious convictions. Suddenly, the Mormons weren't just the nice people in the big white church down the street with the cute girls and the free pizza. They were an opposing faith system that I thought twisted stuff about Jesus. I thought they were wrong about God. And there was a little bit of "You're kind of the enemy." And if I'm honest, I started to think that perhaps the way to show God that I was loyal to Him was to treat these people like enemies. Or at least argue with them. (I would learn later about what Jesus would say regarding how to treat your enemies and—SURPRISE!—it was not what I thought He'd say. But that's for later.) Truth? I didn't know how to have a Mormon friend anymore. I told you this wasn't cute!

No Cussing

There are certain words you don't say if you're Christian. You don't cuss. This rule wasn't that difficult for me. I already knew that you don't cuss in front of your parents or grandparents. You don't cuss in front of your teacher. Or at church. For me with cussing, I could turn it off. Like a light switch.

No Drinking or Smoking or Drugs

This was not a big deal to me, either. I didn't do that stuff anyway. It was like asking me to give up chewing tobacco or reruns of *M.A.S.H.* Not a challenge. But the next two were.

No Secular Music

Here's the truth. Up until this summer, I didn't even know what the word "secular" meant. But I was about to. *Secular* was a negative term, said in the same way one might say "scabies." It was the opposite of sacred or religious. And it was all bad.

The argument went like this: God deserves the most important place in your life. Your primary allegiance must be to God. And secular music has lyrics that are often filled with illicit and godless ideas, so you have to get rid of that influence on your mind to show God that He's the most important thing to you.

Now, I was far too immature in my faith to challenge this. And I'd like to point out that no one has ever said something like, "Hey, Christian kids. In English class, only read poems by Christian poets. Secular poems contain a worldview that is illicit and godless and it's not good for you to read them. So, in your poetry anthology, tear out all the Robert Frost and John Keats and Emily Dickinson."

But when it came to music, I was supposed to prove my allegiance to God by throwing away all my LL Cool J and New Edition and Bon Jovi and NWA.

(Okay, I could maybe see the argument for NWA.)

BUT NEW EDITION!!!

Ronnie? Bobby? Ricky? And Mike?

But I really wanted to obey God. And to be fair, there is that moment in the book of Exodus when God meets face-to-face with Moses on Mount Sinai and tells him to get rid of all his Tony! Toni! Toné! cassette tapes. "It feels good," God said. So into the trash they went.

Anyway, for the next three years, as an act of religious devotion, all I listened to were musicals and contemporary Christian music. Yes, that's a genre. This was difficult.

But not nearly as difficult as the final item on the list.

NO SEX

The Christian sexual ethic is fairly straightforward: "Either in marriage or not at all." It's not tough to understand intellectually, but, boy, is it tough to follow. It's tough to even want to follow. And for a dude like me, this was going to be a real challenge.

I felt like I could help myself by not putting myself in situations where I'd get into trouble. So I stopped going into situations where I'd be alone in empty houses with girls.

But even more than that, I had a new thing to deal with that I'd never had to deal with before.

Guilt.

Before, I'd mess around with girls and say, "That was fun." And I wouldn't think about it for two seconds. But now, I was conflicted. The things I wanted to do, I didn't want to do.

There was this one moment, midway through first semester, where I was in the back dressing room during a theater performance. The entire cast was on stage except for me and this girl LaTanya. One thing led to another, and we ended up making out as the play commenced. I nearly missed my cue.

Before, I wouldn't have thought one thing about that. But now I had guilt. I couldn't just go around randomly making out with girls backstage! That's not how you treated other people. The next day, wracked with guilt, I sheepishly approached LaTanya.

"That was fun, yesterday, huh?" she said coyly.

"Uh, yeah, about that…" I stammered.

"Yeah?" she said. "You down for round two?"

"I can't," I said.

"You can't?" LaTanya asked incredulously.

Listen. I'm fully aware that what I said next had to have sounded nuts.

"Yeah," I said. "I can't because God told me that I was wrong for doing that, and I need to stop."

Insane, huh? I know. I was there. I might as well have told her that Darth Vader had told me to stop making out with her.

So that was the end of LaTanya thinking I was normal. And I felt that Du Bois tension between the different parts of myself. I needed to figure out male-female relationships, and quick.

MY VERY FIRST CHRISTIAN GIRLFRIEND

By now, I was spending multiple nights a week at church, and I finally accepted Pastor Scott's invitation to come to the youth group. I loved it all. During this time, I met a number of good friends—a kid named Rey, who got me started singing in church; Cathleen, a white girl who loved New Kids on the Block and made everyone feel like a million bucks; Dave, a MacGyver who could fix anything with duct tape.

And then there was Kelley. She had moved a few years earlier to Vegas from St. Louis, and like former *Dancing with the Stars* contestant Nelly, she was from the Lou (St. Louis) and was proud. Her dad was a radiologist, which I thought meant he worked in radio, but it turns out that's a medical term. She was cute and red-haired, but the real reason I was drawn to Kelley is because I could tell that she was more culturally savvy than the other kids. She knew some Sir Mix-a-Lot lyrics. She got the struggle. And soon we started attempting to date while Christian. Kelley would change my life.

The main reason this was such a big deal to me was because our relationship afforded me the chance to learn how to have a nonsexual relationship with a girl. This was me working out my double consciousness. And this was not just some girl that I wanted to help me fulfill some physical needs. This was about a whole host of things, including identity. And early on, we had committed to each other—made solemn vows to each other—that we were not going to cross that line.

Both Kelley and I felt that keeping that promise to not have sex was like a tether directly back to God. As long as you didn't cross that sex line, you were still tied to God. And if you messed it up, then there might have been forgiveness from God, but like a chemical reaction, there was no going back. You can't unmix vinegar and baking soda. That's a done deal. So unlike Marvin Gaye, we were absolutely NOT going to get it on.

That was our promise.

Or so I thought.

THE ICE CREAM STORY

Well, I think it's time. I'm ready to tell you this story. It's May of my sophomore year and at this point, Kelley and I have been dating for about six months, which in teenage years is roughly nineteen years. But even though this is a silly *Saved by the Bell* romance, it was also a lot more to me.

Remember, I was a newborn baby giraffe, learning to walk, learning how to steer clear from the tall grass that always hides predators.

One Friday night, Kelley was having a sleepover at her friend's house with a handful of other girls. This girl's parents were (inexplicably) out of town, so there were some boys who wanted to come over. Now, I want to remind you, dear reader, that I still was black, and still had a black mama, so there's no way in Fresno that I was going to be allowed to stay out until midnight at some girl's house. My mama wasn't about that. So I couldn't go.

But Greg went. Greg was a dude I knew from the neighborhood. He occasionally came to youth group, but only to mack on girls. I didn't know Greg that well, but unbeknownst to me, he was sweet on Kelley.

So, I'm at my house and at some point, maybe around eleven p.m., Kelley called me and we started talking about whatever stupid stuff stupid teenagers talk about.

I wish I were there with you.

Me too.

I miss you so much.

I love you too.

I love you more.

90210 is the finest piece of created art in human history.

Fresh Prince is the finest piece of created art in human history.

You get the idea. And then, strangely, in the middle of this mindless, meaningless teenage banter Kelley says, "I want some ice cream."

That was kind of a weird thing to say. But whatever. I wanted some ice cream, too. Who doesn't want ice cream? Heck, I'm lactose intolerant and even I'm like, "Screw it. It's worth it." I ignored the comment and panned off into a series of random questions. Who's there? You guys having fun? What're you going to do tonight?

"I really want some ice cream."

This is the second time she'd mentioned this. This girl wanted ice cream.

"Uh. Okay. Get some ice cream," I suggested helpfully.

"Maybe I'll get some in a little bit," she said.

We continued talking. I asked her what the sleeping arrangements would be, or something incredibly mundane like that.

"I really want some ice cream," Kelley said.

Now I was just confused. Was this some sort of clue? Was my girlfriend hoping I could somehow magically escape my house—my military house with my military father—to go out to some store at midnight and pick up ice cream, and then romantically deliver it to her? Hope you have a magic carpet, Jasmine, because that is not going to fly.

"I really want some ice cream," she said again.

At this point, I didn't know what to say. Was she a hostage, and trying to give me a signal? Were we both deliriously tired?

"I'm going to go get some ice cream," Kelley said. "I'll call you back."

"Okay," I said. "That sounds good."

I sorta wanted her to go get some ice cream so we could be done talking about it. About twenty minutes later, Kelley called me back, and we continued to chat for another hour about meaningless drivel. I don't remember what we talked about, but I do remember how the call ended. I remember hanging up that night and saying, "I love you and I can't wait to see you." And Kelley said, "I love you, too."

Now, I know it's dumb for a sophomore in high school to tell someone he loves her. But this was the first time I had told a girl that. And when I said "I love you" to this girl, it felt bigger because it had to be. This wasn't just about a boy and a girl. It was about a boy and a girl and God.

On Saturday, the very next day, I called my friend Dawn to set up a time on Sunday afternoon to rehearse some choreography.

"Aight, so Sunday, I get back from church around one-fifteen, so gimme time to grab a quick bite and I'll be over around two p.m. That work?" I said, talking through the details.

Dawn got quiet.

Too quiet.

Like the moment before a black character in a scary movie gets killed quiet.

"Hey, Tyler," Dawn said hesitantly. "I need to tell you something."

"Yeah, what?" I said.

Dawn paused.

"So, you know last night, I was at the sleepover."

"Yeah," I said. Dawn knew I knew this.

"Well, I think you need to know that Greg came over, too."

"Yeah," I said. I didn't know where this was going.

"Well, when you were on the phone with Kelley last night, Greg was in the room with her," Dawn said carefully, as though she were a doctor delivering bad lab results.

"Okaaaaaay," I said.

"And..." Dawn paused again.

This girl was taking FOREVER to get me the deets.

"And every time she said, 'I want some ice cream,' Greg would put ice cream somewhere on her body and then he would lick it off her."

I was not expecting that.

"And then," Dawn continued, "when she hung up with you, to say she was going to go get ice cream, she and Greg had sex."

My head started spinning.

First of all, Greg was licking ice cream off my girlfriend? I started to think,

"Where did he put the ice cream?" but because I'm not trying to write a *Fifty Shades of Grey* novel, I'll move on.

Second of all, I was on the phone with Kelley as this was happening? That's just wrong.

Third of all, she had sex with a guy? She did the very thing that we had pinky-sworn to each other that we would never do? And she went and did it? With someone else?

Fourth, this was a brazen misuse of ice cream. This was now food betrayal. Don't you bring Ben and/or Jerry into your dirty philandering liaisons, Kelley!

But mostly, I felt this crushing sense of betrayal. I had been ON THE PHONE with her. I was her BOYFRIEND. We had—together—sworn before God that we weren't going to have sex. Not only did she break that vow, she then got back on the phone and talked to me like nothing had ever happened.

Ruthless.

Heartless.

There were, apparently, not any rules anymore. Not even when God was involved.

I sat down. My heart was sinking inside of me, with that terrible feeling that's a combination of the butterfly nerves you get before opening night, coupled with that weird ache you feel when you haven't eaten all day, mixed with that sinking feeling you get when you get caught cheating on a test. I could almost taste the iron in my mouth. Like I'd been sucker punched.

I wanted to throw up.

I thanked Dawn for being a good friend, and then told her I had to go.

I didn't know how to reconcile this. Is sex still wrong? Did I have to forgive Kelley? I thought I was going to spend the rest of my life with her, so now what? That's what it meant to have a Christian girlfriend, right? I was lost.

HEARTBREAK WARFARE

Later that night, I went over to Kelley's house. I had all these things to say, like a loaded gun in my mind, and I was just waiting. I had dinner with her family. I made polite conversation. But the whole time, my mind was swimming.

Finally, we were alone in the living room.

"I know what happened with Greg last night," I said finally.

"I don't know what you're talking about," Kelley said.

"I know all the details, Kell," I said, and began to tell her some.

She started to cry—but I knew that she wasn't crying because she'd hurt me. She was crying because I'd found out, and she was embarrassed. Then I started crying. I was so hurt, I wasn't even angry. I was just crushed.

The next morning was church. Kelley was there with her family, which made it more awkward. There was a whole section of the church where all the youth sat, and I was sitting there. Kelley came over and sat next to me, which made it even more awkward.

The sermon was on forgiveness. Because of course it was.

And at the close of the service, as the final worship song played, I fell to my knees, head on the chair in front of me, overwhelmed with emotion. Kelley put her hand on my shoulder.

Which was a lightning bolt.

I imagine, as you hear this story, you might think I kneeled down because I was doing some hard work with God trying to get my theology of forgiveness down. Maybe you think I was figuring out how to release the hurt I felt, and the deep betrayal, and extend forgiveness to Kelley.

And all that makes sense. And if I'd been raised in the church, maybe that's what I'd be doing. But I didn't have that kind of spiritual footing. That's not where I was going. The deepest part of me was going on a whole other journey, one that would define the rest of my young adult years in cataclysmic ways.

"I'm never going to get hurt like this again," I vowed to myself.

I was going into full-scale self-protection-at-all-costs mode. Listen, I know that we were just kids making kid mistakes. And Kelley has grown up to be a fantastic person. But back then, this hurt. And I learned that the world is harsh. The world is painful. The world is full of people who will betray you and stab you in the back, and if you leave yourself unprotected, if you let your guard down, you'll get cut. Yeah, God is good, but people are thieves and vandals. So put the walls up. The self-reliant gangsta in me was coming out.

Looking back at it, this might seem over-the-top melodramatic. This could have been handled in one episode of *90210*. But this moment messed with me in ways that it never could have mere months earlier. Now, God was involved. This was a cosmic thing. It meant that even with God in my life, I could still get really, really hurt. And because of my particular weaknesses and vulnerabilities, I was particularly susceptible to this kind of betrayal. Over the years to come, that betrayal would define all my romantic relationships with all women. I would not be hurt first. Because in that moment that Sunday morning in church, I made a steely resolve.

Never again.

I'd never be duped like this. I would never hurt this way again. I didn't care if the girl was Christian or not a Christian, because it clearly didn't matter. Girls were not to be trusted. I stood up, quietly reached over, and took Kelley's hand. I squeezed it. I looked at her, my eyes still filled with tears. Her face softened.

"I love you," she mouthed to me.

I laughed inside. It was working. She had bought it. She thought I was going on a spiritual journey of forgiveness to salvage our relationship.

"I'm gonna destroy you like you destroyed me," I thought to myself.

Spark.

Then flame.

Then fire.

Inferno soon.

Destruction inevitable.

CHAPTER 9

I'M GONNA LEARN HOW TO FLY
(PART 1)

For the next several months, Kelley and I were slow dancing in a burning room, and I was the one setting all the fires. Everything you think I might have done to hurt her, I probably did. Someone once said revenge is taking the hurt that's been done to you and paying it back with interest. I paid Kelley back double. This wasn't psychological warfare—it was a scorched-earth policy. And everyone lost. I'm not proud about it. At all.

Kelley wasn't the only one suffering from my cruelty—I was suffering, too, consumed first by jealousy, bitterness, and hate, and then later by guilt and then self-loathing and then cynicism. This was not a good time for me.

But these next two chapters aren't about that.

They are about how I escaped that whirlpool of vengeance—quite by accident. They are about a magnificent year-long distraction that allowed me to refocus all my energy, and at the very least table my pain. I didn't deal with my dysfunction. But I shelved it. But don't worry—it's gonna come roaring back at full force. If you don't deal with your stuff, your stuff will deal with you.

And it all started with a flyer.

THE NEW SCHOOL

In 1992, someone in the Clark County School District who had watched way too many episodes of *Glee* got it in their head that there should be a high school dedicated to the performing arts. The district would open a new magnet school. Thus, right before my senior year of high school, the Las Vegas Academy for Performing Arts (and International Studies) opened.

I know. That last part confuses me, too. Why did they tack that on? Did they think, "Oh, you know who loves drama and band kids? People who like to study international things. They'll be great together!" Why did the district just tack on international studies to a school dedicated to the arts? I don't know.

This high school was quite different from other, normal high schools. Most schools have departments based on academic subjects. English. Math. Science. Sports and physical education. You know, regular stuff. But this school would have six different departments, each one entirely dedicated to a visual or performing art.

- Orchestra department. Motto: Cello? Is it me you're looking for?
- Dance department. Motto: Our number system begins with 5-6-7-8.
- Choral department. Motto: Breathe from your diaphragm.
- Theater department. Motto: Eat. Sleep. Rehearse. Repeat.
- Theater tech department. Motto: Techies do it in the dark.
- International Studies. Motto: Somebody has to study math and history in this school.

This new performing arts high school had to recruit students to do an intra-district transfer to attend. Which means the Las Vegas Academy for Performing Arts (and Russian Diplomacy) would be headhunting the top musical and theater talent from every single one of the other thirty-plus high schools in the district.

How would they do it?

They did it through the cunning use of flyers.

The district direct-mailed flyers to the homes of students. I don't know if they did a blanket mailing to every student or just sent them to those currently enrolled in music or drama, but I know that my mom got a flyer. And I know that she dragged me to an open house, where teachers and administrators from the Las Vegas Academy for Performing Arts (and Espionage) tried to recruit students.

I remember thinking the idea of the charter school was cool, but I didn't want to go. I was about to be a senior, and I was Rancho Mob for Life (represent!). I wasn't about to leave my school and all my theater people.

Also, I had a few very big reasons to be loyal to the director of Rancho's theater department, Mrs. Joy Demain. Right before the end of junior year, Mrs. Demain's husband was serving as the musical director for a local professional theater group. Mrs. Demain pushed me to audition for this theater company. This was a monumental moment for me. Here was an adult encouraging me. She was saying, "I think you're talented." She was calling out a gift. And so I auditioned and was cast in *Ain't Misbehavin'*, my first professional show, as an outgoing junior. Because of this, I got a chance to work with adults. With a director. And not only that, but I had a chance to work with adult black actors and performers. That alone was more significant than you can imagine.

The point is, after opening up those doors for me and pushing me to audition, I was in *debt* to Mrs. Demain. I owed this woman.

MY MOM MOMMING IN THE MOST MOM WAY POSSIBLE. AGAIN.

On the drive home, my mom was more quiet than usual.

"What did you think of that?" she finally asked me.

"Well, I mean, it's okay," I said, casually, "but I really want to finish up my senior year at Rancho with my people."

My mother paused.

"Well, that's cool and all, but you're going to audition," she said. "And when you get in, you'll be going to that school for your senior year."

My mother was not persuading me. She was not coalition-building. She was acting on some sort of maternal instinct that because of who I was, this was the place I needed to be. And so that was that.

The biggest problem now was that some of my closest friends in life were in theater, and if I was going to make this move, then they for sure were going to need to be with me. Captain America doesn't just leave behind Aquaman and Obi-wan, you know?

(I just triggered at least four subgroups of nerd fans! Five hundred points to Gryffindor!)

If I couldn't fight with my mama, I was going to do everything in my power to make sure that I wasn't going to this new high school all alone. So I went back to Rancho and began talking up the Las Vegas Academy for Performing Arts (and Geopolitical Statecraft) as though it were the greatest school in the history of education. I made it sound like Hogwarts, only for creative people. My first targets, obvs, were my closest friends—Elysha Patino, Tim Calvalho, and John Bridges. I auditioned, and was accepted, and as my senior year in high school approached with the velocity of a freight train, I and the people who mattered most to me were changing high schools. I gutted Rancho High School's theater department. I took errbody.

(If you're reading this, Mrs. Demain, I really am sorry. You were a red-haired angel, a wildly talented performer, and your care and mentoring made an indelible impact on my life. And I will forever be thankful for it.)

My friends and I were no longer Rancho Rams, repping the green and white.

We were now the...

Uhh.

Actually, we didn't have sports teams, so we didn't really have a school mascot. This was the only high school I knew of that didn't field a soccer or football or baseball team. When he found out, my dad was SUPER excited.

So no more green and white. My new ride-or-die school colors were silver and teal, and I'm not sure but I think our informal school mascot might have been the Jazz Hands.

The Las Vegas Academy for Performing Arts (and Foreign Intrigue) Jazz Hands.

ONE ARTS SCHOOL TO RULE THEM ALL!

As I walked onto campus for the first day of my senior year, I realized this was something new. I was joining seventy-six other seniors and 735 total other students in the inaugural class of this brand-new charter school dedicated to the arts. Musical theater was no longer something I did because Kai had given me a double CD of *Miss Saigon*. It was no longer a school scheduling accident. This was now, somehow, my life.

I want to pause and acknowledge how weird this high school situation was. This was a school filled with teenagers who were told that playing make-believe was not only okay but was literally the only way forward. These students were told that creating things—dance, art, music, the written word—is not just okay, but what life is about. And then that message was reinforced in school classes and by adult mentors.

This high school was filled with students who walked around with lunch boxes filled with stage makeup. Guys and girls who were excited to put on tights. These were students who didn't just listen to music but studied it and dissected it until it was a part of who they were. These were teens who were more comfortable pretending to be orphans scrubbing floors with Annie than being a kid in their own home. A school where "first trumpet" was a much bigger deal than the quarterback on any football team. This was a high school where a legitimate part of the academic day might include a drama teacher encouraging you to pretend that you are an inanimate object.

Okay, class. For today's warmup, everyone is an orange. Be an orange. Inhabit the space. Emote! I need more juice from you, Becky!

There were gay kids.

And Jewish kids.

And Mormon kids.

Fact: This is where I met my first black Mormon kid. Who knew they had those?

You had dancers, thin and graceful, who at lunch would go to 7-Eleven, drag on a cigarette or two to abate their hunger, and then down a red Slurpee.

And there was at least one super Jesus-y black kid: me.

This was beautiful. But let's all pause and admit that it's also just weird.

And who was the person responsible for all this? Arguably the most powerful person in the high school? That was Ms. Pattie Emmett. Or, as she came to be known, Pretty Pattie, the queen. She was in charge of the entire theater department. And her power was absolute.

Ms. Emmett decided that our school's first production would be the musical *Fame*, based on the 1980 movie that chronicles the lives of students at a performing arts high school in New York. That's right.

A performing arts school.

Doing a musical.

About a performing arts school.

To quote my boy Chandler from *Friends*, "Could it *be* any more perfect?" Not since "Motownphilly" had a work of art been so meta.

But the queen wasn't just sovereign over her realm, the Kingdom of Theater. Oh no. The queen had influence over the entire land.

The orchestra department? Learn the music for *Fame*.

The choral department? Learn the music for *Fame*.

The theater tech department? Build sets and lighting designs for *Fame*.

The dance department? Work on choreography for *Fame*.

The international studies department? Prevent foreign governments from interfering with this performance of *Fame*.

All 735 of the students enrolled in the school seemed to be involved in some way or another in the production of this musical. It was an all-hands-on-deck matter. There was just one problem.

I couldn't participate.

I already had a gig.

HOW TO AVOID THE QUEEN'S GUILLOTINE

On the day that auditions for *Fame* were announced to the school, Ms. Emmett handed out scripts to the students in her drama classes.

"It goes without saying that I expect all of you to be at auditions," Ms. Emmett said, saying it anyway.

I sank into my seat. This was going to be a problem. If you recall, all my nights and weekends were currently taken up with performances and rehearsals of *Ain't Misbehavin'*. There was literally no way I could participate. I wondered if perhaps I could fly under everyone's radar, but then I realized I was still a six-foot-two black man. We don't fly under radar.

As Ms. Emmett handed me a script, she paused and privately spoke to me.

"Obviously, Tyler, I want you to audition for the part of Leroy," Ms. Emmett said to me as the bell rang. "Why, the part was practically written for you."

Now for those of you who don't know *Fame*, there's a character named Leroy who is black and from the rough side of town. Leroy is a fantastically gifted dancer, but he's illiterate. I don't know why this woman thought I was an exceptional dancer. I was an okay dancer. I mean, I could pop lock, and there wasn't a step-ball-change that I couldn't master. I was pretty good, but by no means was I a fantastic dancer. I was more of a functional dancer.

But the bigger issue was this: how was I going to tell Ms. Emmett that I would not, in fact, be playing the role of Leroy? I would not be playing any role. I had to handle this very delicately.

As the classroom emptied, I approached Ms. Emmett. What happened next was diplomatic brilliance, worthy of the second part of my high school's name. I explained to her that this past summer, before I knew I was coming to this school, I had auditioned for and been cast in a professional theater production.

"When I signed the contract, I had no idea I'd be coming to this school."

Signed the contract. Whatever. Like I was playing AAA ball for the Tigers.

"If I had known…" I trailed off, shaking my head. Now, granted, if I had completed this sentence with honesty, it would have been, "If I had known, I'd still have done it." But I didn't say that. I trailed off. I let the queen fill in the blanks. And then I finished with my tour de force.

"I think I've learned my lesson…no more auditioning for outside productions."

"Yes!" The queen's eyes lit up. "That's it. That's the new rule!"

"Yes," I said, my voice dripping with contrition. "That's the new rule."

"The new rule for the ENTIRE LAND," the queen said.

Okay, she didn't say that. But that's what she was thinking.

"Perhaps there's another way I could help?" I said.

"Yes, darling, yes," the queen said. "You will be my assistant director. By my side the entire time."

"Your wish is my command," I said, with an exaggerated, humorous bow.

But that wasn't the only bullet I dodged.

The next one was a biggie.

HOLD ME CLOSER, TINY DANCER

Every day after school for the next week, I sat next to the queen in the darkened theater as the entire student body auditioned for the various roles. It was becoming pretty clear to everyone that this cast was going to rock this musical, and that we had some wildly talented people involved. I was excited about it. Ms. Emmett was excited about it.

But we had one hole.

The part of Leroy.

One of the final auditions was for the part of Leroy, which because of the nature of the role, required that the person playing him

1. Be a minority, preferably black, and
2. Be an incredible dancer.

Ms. Emmett had asked the dance department to spend a week choreographing a piece that we would later use in the production, and then have their best dancers learn it for the audition.

"It's time for the auditions for Leroy," the queen bellowed.

Ms. Lamay, who was one of three dance instructors at this school, came forward. She had been the choreographer for this piece.

"We have one person auditioning," she said.

"One??" Ms. Emmett said, dismayed. "See, Tyler," she said with a hint of disgust, "Leroy was yours for the taking." She was right about one thing. If I had auditioned for Leroy, everyone would have remembered.

A junior came forward, a light-skinned black kid with a mid-high-top fade à la 1990 Johnny Gill. He was athletic and cut, muscles rippling in his arms and legs. His name was Brian Jason Young.

He walked to the back edge of the stage—for real, it looked like the dude was gliding. Was he walking? Did he have roller skates on? Was this brother moonwalking? I didn't know. All I know is that he landed in a pose, somehow folding in on himself while simultaneously extending his lithe, athletic frame outward. What happened next was so stunning that it would be a crime against the English language to attempt to use words to describe it.

When he leaped, he looked like something out of a nature documentary, where a gazelle bounds thirty feet effortlessly. His strength and poise were like something out of an Olympic gymnastics competition. Was this dude a Gummi Bear? He was bouncing here. And there. And everywhere. I couldn't even believe what I was seeing.

What we didn't know then was that this sixteen-year-old kid—Brian Jason Young—would go on to be a professional dancer who would be in Missy Elliott videos, star in the Broadway musical *Bring in 'da Noise, Bring in 'da Funk*, share the stage with Mariah Carey, and be the choreographer for the world tours of Madonna and Britney Spears. And he was in a Super Bowl halftime show.

This was the dude I would have been auditioning against.

Let me put you in this equation. Imagine I asked you to go grab a tennis racket to play a game of tennis against my good friend Serena Williams. That would not end well.

This could have been me, auditioning against Brian Jason "I just went to his Instagram yesterday and dammit this fool still has it" Young.

Also, in that moment, I realized that Ms. Emmett and I were having two very different experiences. She was thrilled, thinking, "Oh my goodness, this talent is off the charts! I cannot wait until the audience sees this young man."

That was *not* my immediate thought. My first thoughts were a series of questions.

- How the hell did this sixteen-year-old black kid get onto this stage and do what he just did?
- Who taught this dude ballet?
- How did he even know he was good at this?
- How did he get the training and mentoring he needed to become THAT good THAT young?

I didn't understand. How did we get here? How did Brian Jason Young get so good? How did this black kid get here? And why, in the entirety of this performing arts school, were there just a handful of black kids?

WHY DOESN'T SHAQ PLAY VOLLEYBALL?

A while ago, I was having a conversation with a good friend who is from Hawaii. The state sport of Hawaii is volleyball. And my buddy dropped this thought experiment on me.

"Can you imagine if Shaquille O'Neal played volleyball?" he said.

We spent the next five hours talking about this. Can you imagine someone of that size and athletic dexterity playing middle blocker? He would go down, without question, as the greatest volleyball player in the history of the sport. A regulation volleyball net is twenty-nine feet long, and Shaq's wingspan is nearly eight feet. With his lateral quickness, it's possible he could have blocked half the net by himself. A regulation net is seven feet, eleven inches high. Fully extended, flat-footed on the ground, Shaq's reach is ten feet. Simply standing, Shaq is more than two feet over the net! His standing vertical jump was almost three feet, which means that Shaq would be FIVE FEET ABOVE THE NET if he jumped.

"My God," I whispered. "It would be like an adult playing with toddlers."

So why didn't Shaq play volleyball?

After all, he had the chance to be the very best in the entire world at that sport, so why wouldn't he do that?

I think it's pretty simple. Shaq played basketball because of a system.

In the US, we really, really value good basketball players. We value them so much, we pay them millions of dollars to do their job. And because of that, there is a robust, properly funded, and incentivized system in place where smart adults are paid to assess young people's potential talent at basketball. And in this system, Shaq received years-long training and mentoring through robust basketball programs in middle school, high school, and even college. All of those systems helped to develop his native gifts until he became an elite, top-ten all-time NBA star.

If he had grown up in Canada, maybe Shaq would have become the greatest hockey goalie in history. If he grew up in Brazil, maybe he'd have been the greatest soccer goalie. In Thailand, the greatest badminton player ever. Who knows?

The point is, the basketball recruitment system worked. It's almost perfect. If there's an amazing basketball talent in the US, we will find that person and train the ever-loving crap out of them.

There is a system in America that creates professional athletes out of young black men. The NBA does it. The NFL does it.

But what about a system that is designed to develop the potential of young people (including young black men) beyond athletics? Let's say, I don't know, in the arenas of math and science. Well, wouldn't you know, the good old USA did just that. And the results were…fascinating.

SPUTNIK

So, check it. Immediately after World War II, only about 5 percent of all high school graduates went on to college (compared to more than 20 percent today).[1] We were still a manufacturing economy and agrarian economy, in some ways.

And then something happened.

A basketball-sized satellite named *Sputnik* was launched by the USSR on October 4, 1957. As it passed over the US, a terrible, sinking feeling came across the populace of our nation: "I thought we were the most technologically advanced nation on Earth! How did this happen?"

Our government leaders discovered that the USSR was churning out nearly three times the number of science and math graduates. To go back to the Shaq example, the USSR had developed a system where they were finding every single gifted "mathlete" in their nation and training them. It was like the NBA, only for nerds.

So, in 1958, just a year after Sputnik, Congress passed the National Defense Education Act (NDEA), a $1 billion spending package to bolster high-quality teaching and learning in science and mathematics.[2] That's the equivalent of $9 billion today, or approximately the amount white women spend on pumpkin spice lattes each fall.

Here's where it gets interesting. The government developed a test to see how all high school students enrolled in all public schools were doing in the areas of math and science. For the next twenty years, every single year, every single fourth, eighth, and eleventh grade student was administered the National Assessment of Educational Progress (NAEP).[3] The goal was simple: have (more and better!) training for teachers to teach (more and better!) science and math to see which students knew (more) and did (better) on the NAEP test.

Then, once these brilliant students were identified, the US would train them in college and then hire them at NASA (or whatever). With this system in place, we'd find every single Math Shaq out there.

There was only one problem.

We didn't.

Out! Liar! (That Was a Statistical Joke. See What I Did There?)

Buckle in, because y'all about to learn something today, and it's not about to be pretty. With all of this data, some strange trends started showing up.

Over twenty years (from 1970 to 1990) we had access to the test scores for every single seventeen-year-old high school senior across the nation. Here's what the data found. Alexa, play "California Love."

PROFICIENT AT MATH	
49 Other States:	58.65 percent
California:	21.87 percent
PROFICIENT AT SCIENCE	
49 Other States:	47.93 percent
California:	10.6 percent

Tyler Merritt

Super weird, right? But remember—just being "good" at math and science wasn't the goal of this massive educational investment. We needed to find the truly gifted people—those who scored at the very top percentiles. So let's look at those scores.

SUPER MATH GENIUSES	
49 Other States:	7.7 percent
California:	0.8 percent
SUPER SCIENCE GENIUSES	
49 Other States:	9.9 percent
California:	0.75 percent

Tyler Merritt

Now that's very weird, isn't it? You've got this cosmic boatload of data, and it turns out that the students in California (roughly 10 percent of the entire number of students in the entire nation) really aren't doing well in math and science.

How do you make sense of that?

What the heck is happening in California?

The point is, most reasonable people wouldn't say, "Those California students are so stupid. What a drain on our nation."

They'd probably say, "Man, something is wrong in California. We should really figure out what it is."

That's probably what you'd say, right? Because the wasted potential of a human life is tragic. Especially someone who has all the raw materials to be great—but never discovered that gift, or never had a chance to develop that gift, or was never mentored in that gift. That's a damn shame. And to have close to 10 percent of all students in the nation not have that chance because of a broken system is a criminal misuse of human potential.

Right?

All right, look. I'm going to stop playing with y'all. If you haven't figured it out yet, in this equation, the Californians are black people. It was black students. Here are the real numbers. You ready?

PROFICIENT AT MATH	
White Students:	58.65 percent
Black Students:	21.87 percent

PROFICIENT AT SCIENCE	
White Students:	47.93 percent
Black Students:	10.6 percent

SUPER MATH GENIUSES	
White Students:	7.7 percent
Black Students:	0.8 percent

SUPER SCIENCE GENIUSES	
White Students:	9.9 percent
Black Students:	0.75 percent

Tyler Merritt

Same numbers. Just replace "Californians" with "black kids." Now to accept these numbers—which are an average of more than twenty years of data collected by the US Federal government—you have to come to one of two conclusions.

1. The educational system simply isn't working well for black students for some reason, OR
2. Black people just aren't good as an ethnicity at science and math.

Now, there are literally some people who think the second—that somehow, black minds are less sharp than white minds. This is called "racism," kids, and it's not a pretty look. So, if number two isn't viable—or is only viable for racisty people—then how do we make sense of this?

GIMME STATS, STAT

Look, I've always hated statistics. Unless they're associated with sports, they typically are related to something I don't want to find out about. Nobody ever shares good statistics. So, here are some statistics I found that might help explain some things. Buckle up. This ain't about to be fun.

- Minority students make up 40 percent of the student population in the US, but are underrepresented in gifted programs (at only 26 percent).
- When the teacher is black, the odds of a black and a white student (with the exact same test scores) being recommended for entry into a gifted program are roughly the same.
- When the teacher is white, the odds for the white student to be recommended for entry into a gifted program stay the same, and are cut in half for the black student.[4]
- 51 percent of all students in public schools in the US are non-white.[5]
- 81 percent of public school teachers in the US are white.[6]
- In 1954, more than 38,000 black teachers in the South and border states lost their jobs[7] after the *Brown v. Board of Education* ruling because white folks didn't want their students being taught by black teachers.[8]
- 27 percent of students in the US attend a school district where more than 75 percent of the students enrolled are non-white.[9]

- 26 percent of students in the US attend a school district where more than 75 percent of the students enrolled are white.[10]
- Non-white school districts receive $23 billion less EVERY YEAR than white districts despite serving nearly the exact same number of students.[11]
- A billion dollars is a crap-ton of money.
- $23 billion is 23 crap-tons of money.

Maybe—just maybe—it's partially the fault of the system.

Look, I get this is complex. There are so many socio-politico-economic issues at work here that I don't pretend to understand. But I know this: the schools in the wealthy suburb of Green Valley, which was the first master-planned community in the lovely, manicured suburbs of Las Vegas, were a lot nicer than the schools I went to. They didn't have gangs nearby on Donna Street. They had giant, nice, plush theaters. And those schools had PTAs that raised hundreds, thousands, even tens of thousands of dollars every year because they could. This allowed for those schools' budgets to do things that other schools simply couldn't do.

And that's awesome for the rich kids.

I just…

And here's the thing. Brian Jason Young didn't go to Green Valley. He didn't go to a school with a dance program. The moon and sun and Venus and Jupiter all had to align perfectly for this black kid who lived not too far away from me to have his talent discovered and developed in something that wasn't football or basketball.

And this kid wasn't just good at dance. He was otherworldly. I think back to watching Brian Jason Young perform for the first time. I remember what it did to everyone who saw that. How jaw-dropping, mind-expanding, possibility-shattering that moment was.

And Ms. Emmett is appreciating his skill, and I'm next to her, having an existential crisis, wondering how this kid got here, and why there's only one of them. How many of those kids I grew up with near Donna Street could have real skills that went undiscovered.

To this day, I wonder how many other Brian Jason Youngs there could have been.

I read once that music is math, and math is music, so I wonder if the reason the black community had all these legends of music and jazz is because they're actually math geniuses. They just never got identified. Could Miles Davis have been a brilliant NASA engineer? Were John Coltrane and Charlie Parker and Duke Ellington and Thelonious Monk all math savants? Were they math prodigies who just happened to grow up in the South (or border states) with an impoverished educational system for Negro boys?

I'm just glad they found a way for their brilliance to make it out into the world. Can you imagine if that hadn't happened?

And yet, in 2012, the United States Department of Education released a study that showed that arts and music programs are often offered to students at wealthy schools. But students in high-poverty schools have those programs cut first.

How much potential are we missing? I can't help but think of all the Math Shaqs out there, not knowing their own brilliance. But not just them, I think about all the Art Shaqs, all the Poetry Shaqs, all the Leadership Shaqs. All the Love Shacks.

Sorry. That's one too many shacks.

The point is that black brilliance is out there. And if, as a society, we are going to make an effort to find brilliance, then that brilliance can't just be one color. We need to find it all.

DOLPHINS APPLAUDING EAGLES
AND VICE VERSA

As I sat there in the theater that Friday, next to the queen, watching Brian Jason Young absolutely upend my sense of art and reality, I thought to myself, "Where else in this whole city could this guy go and be affirmed for his gifts, and for the next few years of his life be carefully trained by three different highly skilled dance teachers?"

Nowhere else.

I realized that this magnet school was a deeply important part of our formation as human beings, not just for Brian Jason Young, but for me.

After *Fame*, Ms. Emmett decided our next production would be a revue, of sorts, where students chose their favorite numbers from various musicals, and then performed them. Because I was fresh off a "professional" stint, I chose to do the song "Your Feet's Too Big" from *Ain't Misbehavin'*. As I performed it for the first time in front of my peers, it just hit different. When I finished, the theater erupted in thunderous applause.

I remember looking out and seeing my boy Brian Jason Young leaping to his feet, clapping and hollering. Look, I could never do what he could do. But maybe I had something in me that he could never do, too. Maybe eagles marvel at dolphins, and dolphins marvel at eagles.

The Las Vegas Academy was a special place, filled with people who called out talent, affirmed it, and helped young people develop it. As I walked off the stage, I remember thinking, "This is significant."

"I guess this is who I am," I thought to myself. "This is who I am. I'm a performer. This is what I was meant to do."

This experience at the Academy, though I was only a few months into it, was already doing a thing in me. The Academy was a solution to the "California" problem. This was a place where brilliance was mined, in all its multicolored beauty. Here, I wasn't a statistic. I was being taught to dream. And honestly, the Academy was what all of us there had needed from the start. And now I, as a black kid, was getting to be a part of it. And it felt good.

Because being seen for who you are…

And then being affirmed in that by a caring community…

And then trained and developed…

To bring something good into this world…

That only you can bring?

That really is one of the best feelings in the world.

And the crazy part—we were all just getting started.

CHAPTER 10

I'M GONNA LEARN HOW TO FLY
(PART 2)

Just like the earth, just like the sun
Two worlds together are better than one
—"Worlds Apart" from the musical *Big River*

Distance breeds suspicion.
Proximity breeds empathy.
—Bryan Loritts

Looking back on it, going to this new school was a bit like being an exchange student—what I was experiencing was quite the culture shock. I was feeling uncertain and confused because the ways of doing things in this new place were so different. There was a new culture in this school that was different from any other high school I'd been in. There was a new lingo, a new value system. Even the way my classmates dressed was different. Fewer gang colors and more amazing Technicolor dreamcoats.

One day, about a month into school, one of my classmates approached me in the hallway.

"Hey, Tyler," she said. "A bunch of us are going to see the Cranberries on Thursday. Do you want to come with us?"

This is where the culture shock set in. Now at this point in my life, I was still black. I didn't follow the new genre of music called alternative rock. I had absolutely no idea that there was an Irish rock group called the Cranberries. I barely knew about Bon Jovi.

So I thought this girl and her friends were going to look at actual cranberries. Like, at an Ocean Spray farm or something.

Don't judge me.

I didn't know that cranberries are only grown and harvested in five states, none of which are Nevada.

All I could think was "Man. I *thought* that girl was pretty cool and normal, but I guess I was wrong. She's obviously involved in some white people cranberry cult."

"Uhh…" I said carefully, as though I was turning down a piece of chocolate pie made by Octavia Spencer. "No thanks. I'm good."

This girl looked at me. "Are you sure? It's not even that much money."

What? You had to pay money to go stare at this fruit? Definitely a cult.

"No, I'm good," I said.

As she walked away, my mind filled with questions. Why would a group of people go look at some cranberries? Do you pick them? It's not even Thanksgiving time. Was this some sort of weird theater exercise?

But it wasn't just that. I was only one of a handful of black kids at the Las Vegas Academy. Black people are a minority in the US at 13.4 percent, and are about the same percentage in Las Vegas, but the schools I'd gone to always had a really good number of black kids. Now I was a minority in the minority.

Secondly, I was a "religious" person in a place filled with students who, for the most part, were either devout Mormons or generally indifferent to religion. So I was a religious minority.

Here I was, a Jesus-y black kid, new in my faith, wondering how in the world to navigate this new world, knowing that I had deep religious convictions, and also knowing full well that not everyone was going to share those convictions.

But as I would soon find out, my mom putting her foot down and saying "Boy, you're going to go to that school" was easily the most dramatic career-defining, personhood-defining moment of my entire life. And to understand why we have to turn, naturally, to the Mayflower Compact. Stay with me. I don't necessarily want to go through colonial American history, either, but I'm trying to make a point here, and I don't want to hear your whining.

I'LL TAKE "HISTORY OF GLOBAL HUMAN POLITICS" FOR 100, ALEX

Now, I don't have a doctorate in political theory, and I haven't studied the entire history of the world, but my parents did have a set of encyclopedias growing up, so I know something. In sixth grade history and government class, I learned there were three basic types of government.

1. Monarchy: one person tells you what to do and takes your money.
2. Oligarchy: a group of people tell you what to do and take your money.
3. Democracy: a crazy, ill-defined mass of people tell you what to do and take your money.

Now, what I think is actually more interesting is not HOW people are governed, but WHY. How did group politics even come into existence?[*] Zooming up to 30,000 feet, throughout human history there were basically two ways that a group or society was formed.

---

[*] I originally heard this concept of government formation at a lecture given by Os Guinness, the English author and social critic, back in 2019. I don't know how to cite him. But that man is brilliant.

Family/Tribe/Kinship Organic Societies

These were local and regional societies formed by members of the same genetic family banding together for resource sharing and/or protection. Some examples are the Native American people groups, the Bedouin nomads from the Middle East, African tribes, and Scottish clans. By the way, my black manness is not too excited that I just typed the word "clan," but there it is. See how much I care about you?

Empires

These are hierarchical societies where one group uses weapons and power to conquer another group, basically swallowing them up under their banner. Empires often contain several different people groups that are now stitched together under one single ruling authority. Examples include the Incans, the Roman Empire, the Yuan dynasty, and the Lakers in the eighties.

These two options were pretty much all you saw through human history for millennia. Hundreds and hundreds and thousands and thousands of years. That's it. Those are your two options. And then something completely BRAND-NEW happened.

A group of people (all from England, and all speaking English) decided they wanted to go to the New World. But as they neared the shore after sixty-six days, they realized they had a problem. This group was going to have to live together and make rules. But they weren't family. They weren't a tribe. And they weren't an empire. So, when they landed, would it be anarchy? Some sort of *Lord of the Flies* nonsense? And so they created the Mayflower Compact. Here's basically what it said:

- Everyone freely entered into the contract (consent of the governed), but the colonists would remain loyal subjects to King James. Not LeBron. Though that would've been awesome.
- It was relational and cooperative. The colonists would create and enact "laws, ordinances, acts, constitutions and offices" and abide by those laws.

- It was morally binding. The colonists would create one society and work together for the common good.

Can we just stop right here and acknowledge how professor-y I sound right now? I'm impressing myself.

Anyway, this new form of politics was called CONSTITUTIONALISM, and it was an incredible moment in human history. By 1750, more than 1.5 million people would come to the New World under these general principles. Our current US Constitution would enshrine these ideals into our founding documents. And this is where I want to introduce you to a critically important word.

PLURALISM

Pluralism is the idea that one political body can be made up of several smaller, different groups which have different core beliefs, interests, and lifestyles and that all these groups can COEXIST TOGETHER without killing one another.

The settling of colonial America is a story of pluralism, and the colonies (which eventually formed the United States) were settled in the 1600s by people who were fleeing Europe in the face of violent persecution. There were English Puritans, French Huguenots, Dutch Calvinists, German Reformed Pietists, Scottish Presbyterians, and English Quakers. Each group was very different from the other.

Often, these communities were pretty dogmatic, and people who disagreed (Anne Hutchinson, William Penn, and Roger Williams) were expelled…but those folks would just go down the road and start a new community. The early settlers of colonial America found that religious tolerance wasn't just a good principle. It was a good practice.

But this is hard work. It's a constant balancing act between overall society and individual conscience. But—as our fledgling nation showed—it can be done. Different groups can live together in tolerance.

But.

Hear me out. Maybe "tolerance" of one another is the bare minimum. Maybe there's a better way.

Maybe there's a formula that could result in an even stronger, more robust, and more fruitful society.

And maybe I discovered this formula at the Las Vegas Academy for Performing Arts. See, I told you we were going somewhere.

RECIPE FOR BETTER SOCIETY GUMBO

Ingredient 1: Proximity
Lessons from Driving Miss Daisy Danielle

By my senior year, I had one thing going for me that most people did not. No, I am not talking about my award-winning smile, which raised questions about why I was not sponsored by Colgate. No. I'm talking about the fact that I had a car. It was a 1981 Chevy Celebrity, a car that was so cool it just screamed "I'm basically your grandmother's Buick." But I didn't care. I had a car.

One day, a girl named Danielle, a super tall sophomore with long brown hair who was in the choral department, asked me if I could drive her home from school. Now, Danielle was nice and all, but she didn't really live anywhere near me. I was thinking up excuses when she said, "I'll give you ten dollars." Danielle's mom was tired of driving her around and had given her ten dollars to pay any willing participant for "gas" in exchange for driving her home. Now this doesn't sound like a lot. But I'll remind you, gas back then was $1.11 a gallon. Danielle lived maybe ten miles out of my way. My 1981 Chevy Celebrity got twenty-one miles to the gallon, which meant it was going to cost me less than a dollar to drive her home, and I could pocket the other nine dollars.

Suffice it to say, I drove Danielle home MULTIPLE times per week. Minimum wage back then was $4.25, so driving Danielle home five times a week was the equivalent of working ten hours a week. That's a part-time job! Danielle's mother was my sugar mama, and I didn't care. I would drive Miss Daisy all day for fifty bucks a week.

On our rides home, I would often play my music, which, I will remind you, was only Christian music and musicals. At the time, the options available for decent Christian music were very slim. Very slim. Even slimmer than your chances of finding a good football team in Auburn, Alabama. Yeah, I said it. Roll Tide.

But there were some gems. Well, at least at the time I had become convinced that they were bangers, including stuff from Sandi Patty, who was like the John Stockton of gospel singers—very plain, very white, but very good. One day, we stopped singing duets to *Miss Saigon* songs long enough for me to sneak in a Sandi Patty cassette.

"I don't think I've ever heard a song like that," Danielle said, after I played "Another Time, Another Place."

"What do you mean?" I asked.

"I mean…she was singing about God, right?" Danielle asked.

As we talked, I realized that anything religious was completely outside her experience. Danielle didn't have any religious background. She'd never even been to a church. Religion wasn't really something she'd ever thought about, let alone had defined thoughts or beliefs about.

Social scientists tell us that one of the fundamental divides in the US right now is between folks who see themselves as religious and those who do not. Roughly 40 percent of all millennials identify as "nones," meaning they have no religious affiliation,[1] and only 33 percent of young people attend a church service once or twice a week. So, if you're not religious, what happens if you only hang out with people who are also not religious? What happens if you actually don't know anyone who is deeply religious? Well, I bet you'd start conjuring up some ideas about what religion is like. And vice versa, for religious people who only hang out with other religious people. Which is why proximity is so important. It destroys suspicion and mistrust. And because of our car rides, Danielle's views of religion shifted.

DANIELLE'S VIEW OF RELIGIOUS PEOPLE BEFORE THE CAR RIDES:
Weird people in weird clothes who chant things and want to turn the world into something like *The Handmaid's Tale*.

DANIELLE'S VIEW OF RELIGIOUS PEOPLE AFTER THE
CAR RIDES:
Tyler. My friend.

I had dozens of car rides with people from my school. Each one helped
with proximity. One of my friends, Donovan, once told me years later that I
was one of the only Christians he was friends with in high school.

He still remembers that it was really, really strange that I, a black man,
played Sandi Patty in my car during that year, especially considering Dr. Dre's
The Chronic had *just come out*.

That's right, folks. I missed *The Chronic*—one of the most important and
culturally influential albums of my lifetime. While the rest of the world was
learning about Snoop Dogg (1-2-3-and-to-the-fo), I was in the dark.

Donovan told me that even now, when he watches the news and sees
Christian people acting crazy, and he's tempted to write off all Christians as
whack-jobs, he thinks about me, and his stance softens. Even years later.

Distance breeds suspicion. But proximity breeds empathy.

And sometimes, it sparks interest. I asked Danielle that day if she wanted
to come to the youth group with me, and she said yes. She started going to
church and she hasn't stopped. All of a sudden, I had a neat Venn diagram
overlap of Friends Who I Went to School With and Friends Who I Went to
Church With. It doesn't always work out that way. But it's cool when it does.

Ingredient 2: Honesty
Lessons from a Paperback Bible and Sami, the Jewish Princess

With Danielle, I realized, for the first time, that I could be honest about
the most important parts of myself. Because what good is proximity if you
don't share your honest self?

This is where my new high school really stood out. The Las Vegas Academy was a place where students of different backgrounds were placed in close
proximity to one another. That was cool. But what was even more cool was
the honesty. As a school dedicated to the arts, we naturally talked about deep
things.

Queen Pattie used to say, "Art, to be effective, must say or communicate something true." And truth requires deep reflection. When you're in a performing arts high school, you're being constantly exposed to all sorts of beautiful ideas about what it means to be fully human from some of the greatest artists who have ever lived.

This is not typical. It *should* be. But it's not. It seemed like every day, every student in that whole school was scouring the face of the earth and history for songs, poems, short stories, novels, plays, and art that said something real—and then we shared those things with one another.

Sometimes, trying to share stuff can be a little awkward. Here's one for you. I remember one time, at youth group, Pastor Scott had purchased a bunch of paperback Bibles written in an English translation called the New International Version that I could read and make sense of. And he told all of us, "If you have a friend who might want one of these, take it. It's yours. It's free." I'm telling you, I was the first one up to that stack of books, and I grabbed one. I knew exactly who I was going to give it to. The next day, I went up to my friend Elysha and I gave her that Bible.

"Why are you giving this to me?" Elysha asked.

"I don't know," I said. "It just seemed important."

I realized in that moment I didn't exactly know why I had given Elysha that book. It's really strange to give someone a 1,200-page book under any circumstances. Getting a book as a gift was like getting socks for Christmas.

Hey, Elysha. How would you like a vast library of books that includes some Hebrew history, poetry, and prophetic apocalyptic literature written roughly 2,000–3,000 years ago?

No wonder people hand out New Testaments. You never go full Bible. I don't know what I was thinking. I'll be honest, I think I had read maybe 10 percent of that Bible. And I probably understood maybe half of what I'd read. But the Bible was a symbol of something. An invitation, of sorts. I was trying to say:

"Elysha. This Jesus stuff has really helped and changed me. I wanted to share it with you. And I think you're really special, and I have a good bet that God thinks so, too."

Even though this was a super awkward, almost comically inept attempt at communicating, I think Elysha understood what I was trying to say. A few weeks later, she asked if she could come to church with me. Like Danielle, she hadn't had much exposure to religion. Like Danielle, Elysha also got lost in the story of Jesus and the Bible. To this day, she's also never left.

I thought back to Kai, the overzealous fan of *Miss Saigon* whose raw passion had steamrolled over my objections and ignorance and opened my eyes to a beauty I hadn't known about before. She was just sharing something she loved. She was being honest. For me, that was what I was doing when I attempted to talk about church stuff. Only instead of sharing Lea Salonga, it was about God.

But it wasn't a one-way street. The influence of honesty went both ways.

In the final semester of my senior year, one of our drama teachers, Mr. Bryson, had us do an exercise. The entire advanced drama class sat cross-legged in a circle. Mr. Bryson gave someone a ball of yarn. You could throw it to anyone in the circle, and then you had to say a truthful statement about what you'd observed about that person. The subject of that statement then had a chance to respond.

Someone threw the ball to my friend Sami. Sami was a tiny Jewish girl. Like tiny. Like Prince tiny. Imagine a really hot Kosher hobbit. She was also a senior, a fabulous actress, and she loved black people. I don't know how else to say it. I saw pictures of her room. She had a poster of Martin Luther King Jr. in there. Also, a poster of LL Cool J, with his black Kangol hat on, and his red-and-white Adidas jacket open, showing his six-pack. But LL Cool J wasn't the only brother Sami had eyes for. She had developed a dramatic crush on me. I never gave Sami the time of day romantically, but Sami didn't take no for an answer.

"Come on, Tyler," she'd say. "Why can't we go out?"

"You know why, Sami," I said. "I can only date Christian girls."

"But we see eye-to-eye on Abraham and Moses," she countered. "We can both agree that Jesus was a nice young Jewish boy."

"I say you're just a friend, Sami," I said, walking away to class. "I say you're just a friend."

"'OH, BABY YOU! YOU GOT WHAT I NEEEEE-EEEED,'" Sami sang out after me down the hall.

This marked the only time in history that two high schoolers have talked about Old Testament prophets and Biz Markie in the same convo.

At any rate, we're all sitting in this circle, and someone threw the ball of yarn to Sami and, to get the ball rolling, said jokingly, "One thing I have noticed about Sami is that she has an undying crush on Tyler. What is up with that?"

Everyone laughed. I laughed. Sami didn't. She knew that what she was going to say next wasn't really funny.

"I don't know," Sami said, looking at me. "In the Jewish culture, there's a word we use. *Beshert*. It means a 'destiny.' It's something that happens that has God's fingerprints all over it. Sometimes, it's little, like when you were just thinking about someone and then you bump into them. But other times, it's when people come into your life and you know this wasn't an accident. Like it was preordained. And when I met Tyler, I just knew, he was going to be in my life. And that I was going to be better for it."

The room grew silent. I was stunned. This was some nineties R & B K-Ci-and-JoJo-cue-the-cellos-Baby-Baby-Baby-Baby-Baby-Baby-Baby-Baby-Baby-Baby-Baby-All-My-Life-stuff, here, people. And I was not ready.

"I just super love you, Tyler."

If I hadn't been in a room full of people, I would have started sobbing right there, on the still-new carpet of Mr. Bryson's drama classroom. If you recall, the pain of the rejection from Kelley had done a real number on me, and although for the past few months I'd found a marvelous distraction and purpose in the arts, there was still a knife in my heart. It was the kind of knife that comes when you're a teenager and you're rejected. The kind of knife whose poison whispers, "You're not really loveable. No one will ever really love you. Not the real you."

And in the busyness of school and theater, I had pretended I'd healed. But I had not. I was just ignoring this wound, hoping it would close. And in that moment, Sami was saying something that spoke to the depth of that pain. She had put her finger on it.

"I just super love you, Tyler."

I had been so wrapped up in the pain of Kelley that I hadn't considered that there could be someone beyond Kelley. Someone who could look at me and see all sorts of things worth loving. And in that moment, something shifted. I realized I had installed a protective fire ring around myself and my heart, and I had decided I would burn down every person who tried to get too close. I realized I needed to work on myself. I needed to truly forgive and move on. I needed to become the best version of myself so that when I met that person, whoever she was, I would be ready.

I still remember that moment—twenty-some odd high school upperclassmen sitting cross-legged on the ground in a drama teacher's classroom with a ball of yarn while a tiny Jewish girl gave me a bit of profound wisdom that was, unexpectedly, exactly what I needed in that moment. It was a moment of deep healing.

Sami and I are still friends to this day.

Beshert.

Proximity plus honesty are gifts. And it leads to the next part of the equation.

Ingredient 3: Value
Lessons from My Senior Prom

Because the Academy was a performing arts school, not only were the students consuming and being changed by art, we were also tasked by our teachers to try our hand in trying to create art.

So we were not only ingesting art, but also producing it. Weakly, and feebly at first, for sure. Often simply imitating (or trying to). But soon, we were producing poems, novellas, songs, dramatic scenes, and then sharing them with one another. I mean, that's just unique for a high school, right?

This meant that we not only had to live and work near each other (proximity) AND find and share deep art that moved us (honesty) BUT ALSO that we had to bring our whole, honest, entire selves to bear. That's the only way that good art can be made. So we had to bring out the things that made us... us. For some students, that meant their female-ness. Or their dancer-ness. Or their gay-ness. Or their divorced-parent-ness. And art helped make sense of how all those things tied into their human-ness.

We were like the Muppets. Whatchall know about the Muppets? They were a bunch of weirdos and cast-offs with deep flaws and insecurities, but they were a family. There's Fozzie, the jokester who is an approval addict. There's the high-energy Animal, who has anger-management issues and problems with self-control. There's the talented Miss Piggy, who is narcissistic and emotionally needy. There's Gonzo, who is a self-described "weirdo." And of course, Kermit—well, he's just green. And from what I hear, it's not easy being green. And yet, they shrug and love one another and stick by one another no matter what. It's as though the only other option is to live life utterly alone and rejected, so they choose community and friendship and devotion.

Anywho, I was the black Jesus-y Muppet. That was my role. And sometimes I didn't know how to play that role. How does one courageously play who they are, even though they're terrified of rejection? I didn't know how. But the community and the culture of the Academy helped. It helped that, even in my incredible, jilted awkwardness, my other Muppet friends could look past all that, and see that I was earnestly trying to be me. And they valued me for it. And let me be honest, because so many people had gone out of their way to do this for me, it was not that hard to return the favor.

Another example: I remember that at my senior prom, one of the guys from our school, whose name was Miguel, showed up to prom with his date. And his date was another guy.

Now, back then, that wasn't really that common. *Will & Grace* wasn't a show, Ellen hadn't come out of the closet yet, gay marriage wasn't legal, and we thought Siegfried and Roy were just two good friends who really liked hanging out with tigers. At a lot of high schools in Vegas, that move would have been really controversial. But it wasn't at the Academy.

Now, at the time, it never occurred to me to wonder what Miguel's sexuality was. It didn't occur to me that he was gay. Looking back on it, I just didn't think about it. All I knew was that Miguel was a dude who for the past year had been in close proximity to me, sharing art with me honestly. And I valued him deeply.

He could have shown up with green antennae sticking out of his head and said, "Hey, guys, sorry I've been hiding this from you, but I need you to know I'm an alien from Zork." And I would have said, "Well, I guess aliens from Zork are dope." Because Miguel was just the best.

I know that for some Christians this causes real internal conflict, but Miguel's sexuality didn't cause any internal divide inside me at all. My religious convictions didn't cause me to condemn people who didn't share them. Most people didn't share my most deeply held beliefs. That was okay. I didn't expect them to. And more than that, I valued Miguel. My legitimate value and love for him as a human being trumped any issues I was supposed to have with him. I knew (vaguely) at that time that some people thought that being religious and following Jesus meant that I was supposed to let Miguel know that I "disapproved of his lifestyle" and held his choices against him by withdrawing.

But Imma be honest: in the Bible, I don't see Jesus withdrawing a whole lot from people. Almost always, Jesus was pressing in. His critics weren't mad at Him because He maintained socially accepted boundaries really well. Quite the opposite. In my youth group, I was being taught that to follow Jesus properly meant to live out an ethic of love that surpassed everything. The ethic of Jesus was a love that was so radical, so inclusive, so sacrificial that it was transformational. Jesus even modeled loving His enemies. As He was being executed and tortured to death on a Cross, Jesus prayed that their sins would not be counted against them. Love was meant to be lived out, not only loving people in "theory" but legit making sure to erase all doubt that you were for them and liked them.

That was the love I had been shown. And it was the love I was being taught to show other people. This school had been a training ground to teach me to love people who were different from me, to get close enough (proximity) to get to know the real them (honesty) so I could see their wondrous worth (value).

Living in close proximity, with such honesty, to such amazing people, made it really difficult for me NOT to love people for who they were.

Ingredient 4: A Common Goal
Lessons from the Final Recital

As my senior year wound down, there were a number of final recitals for dance, drama, band, and the choirs. These were a BIG deal, and pretty much the entire student body attended. These performances were held in the main theater, to packed houses. I remember one evening was the final dance recital, and as my friend Brian Jason Young came out on stage, we all hooted and hollered.

Just then, a black woman who was sitting in front of me turned around and said sternly, "Young man, you need to settle down. That is NOT the way you act in the arts."

I sat back in my chair. I was hurt. She didn't know that I was a performer at that school. She probably thought I was a kid who had never been to a play and thought she had to educate me on how to act in civil society so I wouldn't embarrass myself.

I was respectful to her as she left, because my mama, but I wanted to tell her off.

Lady, this wasn't just a play. These were my people.

After the show, I was a ball of emotions. Brian Jason Young came out, and I went to hug him, and before I knew it, I was sobbing. I realized, in that moment, that the year was ending. That I was a senior. That I didn't have more time. This was it for me.

I had thought, coming to this school, that we would be working together for the common goal of making art. But looking back at that moment, as we all huddled around the stage congratulating one another, I realize that what we had actually been working on was much bigger.

Our common goal wasn't to create art. Our high school hadn't just produced musicals and plays and concerts and recitals.

It had produced people.

Our school had produced good citizens: people who knew how to work together, overcome barriers, be honest, and work hard.

We were a wild group of people, diverse, from every corner of the city, with very different views and gifts and talents and opinions—and we'd not only learned to work together for the common good, but we'd learned to LOVE EACH OTHER along the way.

As I stare at the various fractured factions of the US right now, so many people angry and upset, so many people talking past each other, so little relational trust—not only at the national level, but even at the local level—I can't help but think that the way forward in our nation was something I learned at the Academy:

> Proximity (which breeds empathy) +
> Honesty (vulnerable dialogue) +
> Value (seeing each other as having inherent worth) +
> A Common Goal (seeing that we're all in this together) =

BETTER SOCIETY GUMBO

I think that'll preach.

As I stood at the front of the stage with my friends, there were so many things I didn't realize that night that I do now, looking back on it.

I didn't realize that the reason I was crying was because it was the end of this beautiful little community.

I didn't realize how much this school had reshaped my life.

I didn't realize what an impact this single year—my senior year—had had on me. I had come in, not knowing how to be me (or what that even meant). I was not secure in my identity. And now I was.

I didn't realize how many of these relationships would continue on, and how many of these people would stay in my life. I'll be honest, I don't really remember that many people from Rancho High School. But I remember nearly EVERYONE from the Las Vegas Academy.

I didn't realize that I was standing RIGHT NEXT TO a guy who'd help choreograph Super Bowl LI. I mean, if I did, I would have asked him to hook a brotha up with some tickets.

I didn't realize we were all learning how to fly.

But most of all, I didn't realize what a kick-in-the-pants was waiting for me in college.

But that's the next chapter.

CHAPTER 11

THE GOSPEL ACCORDING TO JONATHAN LARSON

No other way
No day but today
—"Another Day" from the musical *Rent*

As my senior year wound down, I began preparing for the most high-stakes audition of my life. Athletes aren't the only people actively recruited by colleges. Colleges with performing arts programs send out scouts to high schools across the nation to recruit performers. Because our school was the performing arts magnet, the auditions were held at our facility in front of scouts from the top theater and music schools across the nation.

This was straight-up nerve-racking for an eighteen-year-old. I sang the song "Bui Doi" from *Miss Saigon*, because of course I did. They must have liked my audition, because all but two of the schools indicated they were interested. The point is that, unlike my father, whose only possible chance of escaping rural Alabama was the military, I ended up with the ability to have full-ride scholarships to several different universities with legitimate theater programs. Incredible.

Also, overwhelming. Because now I had to make a decision. If you recall, my parents didn't go to college right after high school. So they didn't really have a framework for how to make this decision. Neither did I. Here I was, facing one of the biggest decisions of my life, and I didn't even know what criteria I should be using.

In the middle of this chaos, prayers would sometimes leak out of me. Not even well-formed prayers. Just "Holy crap, what am I going to do, God help!" kind of prayers. I was an overwhelmed mess. And then. It all became clear.

TWO GREAT TASTES THAT TASTE GREAT TOGETHER

One Sunday morning, I was in church and noticed something different. A traveling choral group from a Christian college in California was visiting. During the service, this group of eighteen- to twenty-two-year-olds sang a few songs. They were aight.

After they were done, someone explained that this group was called the Ambassadors from Bethany Bible College. I knew about Bethany, because that was Pastor Scott's alma mater. Then each member of the group introduced themselves and shared their majors. "I'm Kimberly," one girl said, "I'm an early childhood education major." And "I'm Josh. I'm studying business." But then the words that would change my life flowed out of one underclassman.

"I'm Joe Vonheeder. I'm a double major in music and theater."

Whaaaaaat? I sat straight up. This Bible college had a theater major? I didn't even know that was possible! And this was the same college that Pastor Scott, a man who I deeply respected, had vouched for. It's where *he* went. At that moment, a possibility opened that I didn't even know was a possibility; I could go to a Christian college AND be a theater major. All my life, I had gone to public schools, and I'd never been in an educational setting that also was faith-based. My two favorite things, rolled up into one. Like *Star Wars* and bacon.

After the service, I went up and talked to the students. They all seemed pretty aight. They handed me a brochure about the college and encouraged me to apply. I looked at that brochure, poring over it as though it had been sent to me from Heaven. Here was the answer.

Bethany Bible College. In Scotts Valley, California, which I figured was probably right near Hollywood. True, I had never visited this school. But I knew I was going there. I went home and completed the application immediately. I sent a whole package to the theater department: professional headshots, a tape of my audition. My complete résumé. Letters of recommendation from my teachers. The whole nine yards.

By the end of May, I had received my acceptance letter from Bethany. I was in. The only question now was the matter of finances.

Now, this is where y'all are going to get mad at me. I know this because I'm still kinda mad at myself. And my parents. But remember, none of us had any experience with this. When my financial aid package came, my theater scholarship was super-duper small. Like Kevin Hart small. I stared at it for a while. My parents stared at it for a while.

"Well…you can get loans," my mother, the banking officer, helpfully said.

"Dad?" I said, looking at my father for his opinion.

"Boy. Listen to your mother," he said, non-helpfully.

"I guess I'm going," I said.

And that is the story of how I turned down multiple full-ride scholarships to several top-notch universities, instead choosing to go thousands of dollars in debt in order to go to a private Christian Bible college.

I'm gonna pause here for a second to give you time to shake your head in disapproval over that ridiculously poor financial decision. Go ahead. I'll wait.

A few days before graduation, Ms. Emmett was giving a farewell speech of sorts to the student body, sharing the good news about all the scholarships that had been offered to graduating students. It was truly a big moment for her and for all of us: this brand-new performing arts high school's first-ever graduating class contained talent worthy of collegiate recruitment. She listed off the students and the elite theater and music schools who were offering them scholarships.

"And Tyler Merritt will be attending Bethany College on a theater scholarship," she said. "Bethany, which has a *fabulous* theater department."

Everyone looked at me with puzzled looks. Nobody had even heard of Bethany College, including Ms. Emmett. Look, I loved that woman, but she was just making ish up at that point.

Nevertheless, I graduated from Academy that June. I didn't know what the future held, but I knew two things. One, I was going to go to a Christian college. And two, this school had a world-class theater department. As I would soon find out, roughly 50 percent of those statements turned out to be true.

WHAT ABOUT BOB?

At the end of summer, I drove from Vegas to California. The first thing I did was set out to go find the head of the Bethany Bible College theater department.

The faculty member I had the most interaction with during my admission process was the man in charge of the entire theater department, Bob Abplanalp. Now, I know it looks like I just pressed random keys on the keyboard to spell Bob's last name, but honest to God, that's how it's spelled. I wanted to meet Bob because I was stoked to be a part of this new theater community. I made my way to the faculty offices, and found Bob's office, and knocked on the door.

When he saw me, he said, in a loud, booming, formal theater voice, "Tyler Merritt!"

"Mr. Abplanalp," I said, "I'm so glad to meet you!"

"Welcome to Bethany!" Bob said, in the same way you might say, "Welcome to Jurassic Park!"

"Oh, I'm excited to be here," I said.

"I bet you are," Bob said, laughing.

"Can I see the theater?" I asked. I wanted to see the stage, and where my new home would be for the next four years.

"Of course," Bob said, as we walked across the campus together. "Here it is. This is the W1 Building," he said. He opened the door. It's then that I started to realize what I was getting into.

This was not a professional theater.

It was not even an amateur theater.

It wasn't even an elementary school cafeteria/gym hybrid theater.

It was a lecture hall, with tiered floors. There was not raked theater seating in this room. There were desks. There weren't curtains. There was a sliding green chalkboard that had been painted black. There were can lights hanging from the ceiling.

Forget the Academy, with its two-story fly zone, 1,000 theater seats, with Intellibeam lights and digital sound projection. We were nowhere near that. This place made my first theater, at Rancho High School, look like Carnegie Hall.

"It's not much," Bob said, in the understatement of my life.

I looked around. What was I going to do?

RAKING THE DIRT

I have a friend who once bought patio furniture from Amazon. It turned out, it was patio furniture for a doll's house. He wondered why the price was so low. 'Cause it's for Barbie, homie. That's why.

If I'm honest, that's kind of how I felt about Bethany for about ten seconds as I looked around that crappy lecture hall they called a theater. I also found out that the reason Bob was the head of the theater department was because he was the only faculty member in the entire department. There wasn't anyone else. Damn.

But as I look back at it, although I did briefly think, "Bethany College did me dirty pretending they had their stuff together," I never (not even for one second) thought, "What the heck did I get myself into? I have to get out of here, drop out, and get into a real theater school."

If the Academy had done anything, it had given me a vision for what a flourishing artistic community looked like and had made me driven to create and build things from the ground floor. After all, that's what we'd done just last year. I clapped my hands together. This wasn't a time for regrets. It was time to get to work. We had a theater department to build.

Like I learned as a kid in Eutaw, Alabama: Even if your front yard is dirt, you rake that dirt.

I had been taught to make the best with what I had in front of me. So I did.

IF YOU BUILD IT, THEY WILL COME

For the next two years, my primary labor was to work to help build a functional theater program. The first problem I had was that there were not that many people on campus who had experience doing theater, or even liked theater. So I worked to build a touring theater company. I called it Acts 2, after a verse in the Bible. There was a lot of hard work that year, but it was the start of something. The real thing that would shape the next years of my life was the team of individuals who I recruited to build up the theater program. I assembled a motley crew of theater people. I built my own Avengers. We affectionately called ourselves Theater Central.

Eric F.

I showed this dude everything about theater tech that I'd learned from doing four years of high school theater. He was a fast learner, and for the next four years, Eric was in charge of lighting and sound for everything we did. To this day, he's a professional stagehand, working with lighting and sound on a show in Vegas.

Zalissa C.

To say Zalissa was "into" details would be like saying that Shakira was "into" hip-centric-dancing. It wasn't something she did. It was something she was. She was our stage manager, who served like a cross between a quartermaster and an air traffic controller.

Amy D.

Amy started hanging around a bit because her friends were into theater, but she had no background in anything theater. But I noticed immediately she was very emotionally mature. She helped us have drama…without the drama. And with that, I had my Black Widow who could talk down any Hulk.

Todd M.

This was my dude. Todd was a giant white guy, towering over everyone at six foot six, who came to Bethany to play basketball. Todd wanted to be an actor, but he wasn't really that good at first. But Todd proved that hard work wins. Every. Time. And that he did. Work, my dude, work.

So there I was, recruiting and building. Developing the talent on campus. I knew to build a successful dynasty you have to recruit talent from outside the organization. I thought about that moment when Queen Pattie had told the entire school that Bethany's theater program was "fabulous." So I started recruiting blue chippers from the Academy to come out west.

John Bridges

As you remember, John was one of my oldest friends from both the youth group AND the Academy. John was a good actor and an even better friend. John knew he wanted to go into acting, but he didn't know what direction to go to make that happen. So, let's just say I helped him along. Boom. Recruit Number One.

Danielle

Remember Danielle from the car rides? Well, she could sing. And I mean sing. Danielle could sing the stripes off a skunk. She could sing the smug arrogance right off a Boston sports fan. (Patriots fans. Ugh. Amiright?) I told her I was building an empire, and when she graduated, she came to Bethany. I was hoping her mom would continue to pay me gas money. But no. Regardless, Danielle was Recruit Number Two.

TIME FOR A *ROCKY* TRAINING MONTAGE

After a year or two, it became clear that we were all building something. And the head of the theater department, Bob, quickly realized this and did whatever he could to support us.

First, we built a proper stage. Did any of us soft-handed theater majors know how to operate a miter saw? No. But we had friends who did. Pretty soon, we had a functional, sturdy stage. We built a legitimate sound booth. We welded together lighting bars we found for free and hung them from the ceiling. Bob located a local church that was remodeling its sanctuary and was getting rid of a whole bunch of red theater seats. We scrubbed them until they shined like new. We recruited friends who knew something about electrical work, and they rewired the entire place. We knocked down walls, built up floors, and painted until our shoes were covered in different colors.

And when we were done, we renamed it the Bethany Theater. Because hell yeah, it was. And on that stage, our little theater group punched way above its weight, putting on all sorts of shows. We did famous Greek tragedies AND the story of a beautiful woman obsessed with a dark, mysterious, musical genius. And no I'm not talking about Kanye and Kim. I'm talking about highlights from *The Phantom of the Opera*. And *Antigone*. We also did *Godspell* and *Shadowlands*.

Traditional stuff. Good stuff. But none of us were ready for what was coming around the corner.

THAT A MUSICAL OF THE PEOPLE, BY THE PEOPLE, FOR THE PEOPLE SHALL NOT PERISH FROM THE EARTH

Let me try to paint a picture for you about the world of musical theater during my freshman year of college. At that time, the most dominant shows on Broadway were the Big Three—*Les Misérables*, *The Phantom of the Opera*, and *Cats*[1]—and two Stephen Sondheim musicals, *Into the Woods* and *Sunday in the Park with George*.

If you are familiar with those shows you understand that these were not

exactly super relatable stuff to your average person, especially if you were trying to widen your audience to anyone who was, say, uh, black. In addition,
tickets to these shows were often hundreds of dollars—again, pricing out your
average person. In the middle of this, one man had a vision for a different sort
of musical.

His name was Jonathan Larson.

And he'd change all of our worlds.

Surrounded by this pain and suffering of the AIDS epidemic that ravaged
the artistic community in the East Village in the eighties, Larson couldn't
help but see the similarities to the famous opera *La Bohème* by Puccini, which
follows the life of hopelessly poor artists living in Paris in 1830, fighting off
poverty and disease (in this case, tuberculosis). Larson had an idea to modern-
ize the opera, bringing all the characters into the East Village. And what came
out was a brilliant work of genius that changed the entire musical game: a rock
opera musical called *Rent*.

Rent was radically different stylistically than anything else on Broadway at
the time, a rock opera that was forged with alternative rock and grunge and a
smattering of other modern musical styles. As Larson said, he wanted to bring
"musical theater to the MTV generation."[2] *Rent* just sounded different.

It was also younger, hipper, and more diverse. It was experimental. It was
fresh. The main characters were gay, straight, and bisexual, with a gender-fluid,
cross-dressing performance artist, a Jewish guy, and four main characters living with the HIV virus. This is very different than, say, *Les Misérables*, which
features very few strippers. It also appealed to younger, more diverse audiences. As the show began to sell out, Larson and the other producers wanted
to ensure that non-elite, non-wealthy fans of the show didn't get priced out of
tickets. The theater held an open lottery, selling seats in the first two rows of
the theater for twenty dollars per seat. Dope.

This musical changed the entire Broadway musical game. Changed. The.
Game. For everyone who loved theater. Including a certain Puerto Rican kid
from New York whose parents bought him tickets to the musical for his seven-
teenth birthday. He was so struck by it that he decided that's what he wanted
to do.[3] That kid? Lin-Manuel Miranda.

It was important.

But not just to culture at large.

It was important for us.

Starting my freshman year, for those of us in Theater Central, *Rent* was more than just another Broadway show. It was an articulation of something much deeper. I'm telling you, there wasn't a day that went by in that theater when we didn't play *Rent* through the theater sound system.

We loved it because, in *Rent*, suffering was presented as part and parcel of life. As inevitable. This is not a message you hear a lot in our contemporary culture. But suffering is part of life. You can't run from it. I knew this because I listened to the voices in the African American community. Think about the famous Negro spirituals, filled with poetic lines about hardship and trouble. For my ancestors, suffering wasn't an option: sadly, it was an inevitable companion. For them, "why" wasn't a very helpful question. The better question is "How are we going to get through this suffering?"

We loved it because *Rent*'s main characters see themselves as modern Bohemians, social outcasts who refused to go along with the status quo and who were looked upon with suspicion. And as theater people at a small Christian Bible college, we identified with that a little bit. But also, the artist community portrayed in *Rent* was a group of misfit vagabonds who looked past foibles and weaknesses and flaws and still loved one another. *Rent* showed us unflinchingly that being in an authentic community demands much: honesty, the courage to be vulnerable, forgiveness, grace. This is hard. But *Rent* showed us that it simply wasn't an option to NOT forge a loving community. I mean, what else do you got?

And we loved it because there was something visceral and true about the way love is portrayed. Love, in *Rent*, was not some sappy, sentimental idea. Love was committing yourself to someone else's good, even if it actually cost you something. *Rent* taught us that love wasn't merely a sentimental word, or even primarily a romantic word. Love was much bigger than that. If you weren't willing to let love cost you, then maybe it wasn't really love in the first place.

In the end, in a way, *Rent* was a strangely perfect metaphor for what I'd come to Bethany for—a Venn diagram overlap of theater and Christian community. It was the soundtrack of our theater group. No. It was more than that. It was a lighthouse for us.

As I neared graduation, I thought about that moment when Bob first opened the W1 building, and I first saw the theater, creaking in disrepair. I thought, "What if I had just turned around and packed up and went home? What if I'd gone and enrolled in another theater program? Would I have regretted that decision?" There's no way to know. But I do know this. I can't imagine how much life I would have missed if I had.

But there were other revelations that I learned in college, too. And some of those weren't nearly as flattering, including the next one, where I learned: no matter how fast you run, your demons can run faster.

CHAPTER 12

YOU GIVE LOVE A BAD NAME

If my past is any sign of your future
You should be warned before I let you inside
—"I Don't Trust Myself (With Loving You)" by John Mayer

I looked around, the pupils of my eyes dilating frantically, trying to adjust to the darkness of the trunk where I now found myself. The faint red light of the brake lights filtered in. I could hear the sound of the pavement. Were we still on the highway?

"Now you've done it, Tyler," I said to myself, wondering how I was going to get out of this one. I was in this trunk, and the only person who knew I was in here was the person who had slammed the trunk, pounding on it, telling me to be quiet.

The car slowly came to a stop. We were at the checkpoint. I heard the muffled sounds of the guard saying something. I heard the bright alto tones of a woman, laughing. The car shifted into drive. I exhaled a bit as the car moved. We were through the checkpoint. A few minutes later, I felt the car roll to a stop. The engine turned off. I heard a door open. The trunk swung open, and the darkness of the trunk was interrupted by the yellow-green light of the phosphorescent streetlights from overhead. I blinked.

"Get out," the voice said.

I swung my legs out and steadied myself on the ground. I knew what was coming next.

"Do you know what could have happened just now?" a woman's voice said.

"No," I said.

"Big trouble."

"Good thing we didn't get caught, then," I said, blinking.

"It's kind of a thrill breaking the rules," the woman said, walking into the light. She moved toward me. Her face was close to mine.

"I like breaking the rules with you," I said, as we dissolved into peals of laughter.

And that was the first time I was forced to sneak back onto the campus of Bethany Bible College, past the guard at the front gate, in the trunk of Joanne's white 1989 Ford Tempo.

We had been off campus, at a local coffee shop. It was 9:51 p.m. when I looked down at my watch and realized what time it was. This was bad. I was a lowly freshman, which meant I had to be back on campus by ten p.m. As I did the quick mental calculations about how long it would take us to get back to campus, I almost started hyperventilating.

"Relax," Joanne said. "I am a senior. My curfew is midnight."

"How does that help me?" I asked.

"I'll just smuggle you back in the trunk of my car," Joanne said, as though that was a normal thing to say.

Although it might sound to you like I am talking about escaping across the East Germany border at Checkpoint Charlie in 1961, this was actually part of my college experience. That's right, I said "college." We were grown-ass, legal adults, but Bethany treated us like we were preteens at a summer camp. Lights out by eleven! Also, no boys in the girls' cabins! I mean dorms!

But that was Bethany. They put the "fun" in "fundamentalist." Look, I honestly don't begrudge a private, Christian college having rules and codes of conduct. Banning all alcohol prevented underage drinking and the irresponsible choices that often follow. And there were not really any drugs on campus, but we were near Santa Cruz, where I think even the squirrels smoked pot, so I'm not sure we brought up the county's sobriety much, as a group. I get those rules. But some of the rules were...draconian.

And Joanne was the kind of girl who knew how to break the rules. In the coolest, most Joanne ways possible. But none of that explains how we met.

OUR MEET CUTE

The first few days of my freshman year of college, I began making my way around the campus, learning the lay of the land and meeting people. There were only about 600 people total on campus, and I was committed to getting to know all of them. Especially the womenfolk. Why?

Because I'm reliable with the ladies!

One day before class, as I was walking toward Victory Hall, one of the dorms for women, I saw a pack of females walking toward me with the quiet ego, confidence, and swagger that can only come from seniors. I introduced myself with typical Tyler fanfare. Their names were Charlotte, Anne, Rachelle, and Joanne. I found out quickly that these were actually the coolest girls at Bethany. Smart. Funny. All of them. An all-girl squad with all-girl squad goals. Like the Spice Girls. And Joanne was Posh Spice.

And I was David Beckham.

Look I'm never ever—for the rest of my life—going to have a chance to be able to compare myself to David Beckham, so let me have this, people!

Now, there was an ongoing joke around campus that girls only went to Bethany to get their Mrs. degree. Find a nice boy who wants to be a pastor and then live happily ever after. But Joanne was different.

First, she could sing. And she was a part of the Ambassadors. I loved her voice. Second, she was super outgoing and funny with a loud, sharp wit. I watched her slice and dice less-confident men, like a chef's knife slicing through cold watermelon, as though she were a real-life character from a Jane

Austen novel. You want to step to Joanne? You had best bring your A-game. And I loved that about her.

Third, Joanne loved life. She wanted to take it all in. Her passion for life was not only contagious but life-giving.

Fourth, Joanne loved God. She had been at this way longer than I had. Coming from a public high school, it wasn't every day that I got to interact with wildly awesome girls who also had deep religious roots. At one point, she asked me a question that several years earlier would have seemed laughable. "What is God doing in your life, Ty?" she asked me. To Joanne, God wasn't a distant, far-off force, who set the world in motion and then left. He was intimately involved.

On so many levels, Joanne was a revelation. She was just a dope-ass chick who I loved being around and who I could talk to for hours. And after a few months, Joanne was forcing me to reimagine what it might be like to like someone romantically again.

FORGET YOU, BRAD PITT.
AND YOUR SEXY-ASS HAIR.

Joanne was with the Spice Girls a lot, and I wanted to find ways to crash that party. So one weekend, I developed a plan. First, I asked five of my friends to go see a movie with me (including Joanne). Then I convinced the other four to suddenly develop unchangeable plans at the last minute. I'm not saying I paid them to drop out so I could have some one-on-one time with Joanne. But I'm not saying I didn't.

Was the reason that I didn't just ask Joanne out because I was afraid she'd say no? Maybe. Maybe I was afraid I wasn't reading the situation correctly. Was there something more to this now months-long friendship with Joanne? Was it just me feeling this way? Was there some beep-beep in her car, too? Were her feelings for me hot and fresh out da kitchen? If I turned the key, would there be ignition? Why is this sounding like an R. Kelly song? Dang it, Tyler! Pull it together! I wondered if going out on an accidental date would cement things or blow them up. Either way, I was going to know by the end of the night.

Before we go any further, I want to offer some advice to all you fellas reading this. If you're ever interested romantically in a lady, *do not* take her to see a movie with Brad Pitt in it. I repeat. Do not let Brad Pitt get close to your lady. Especially not on a movie screen. That's giant Brad Pitt. The point is, even on a screen, he will affect your lady in ways you simply are not prepared for. It's not going to end well for you.

Joanne and I saw *Legends of the Fall*, a historical Western featuring Brad Pitt in a cowboy hat riding horses, his denim shirt unbuttoned one or two buttons too low. There we were, sitting in the theater, with a fourteen-foot Brad Pitt on the screen. I looked over at Joanne, thinking, "I'm the luckiest man in the world right now." Onscreen, Brad Pitt was standing outside a gate, the golden sun shining through his long blond hair, looking his Brad Pittiest, and Joanne said, out loud, almost involuntarily, "He's angelic." Damn you, Brad Pitt.

Afterward, we went to a coffee shop called Mr. Toots. Santa Cruz was way ahead of its time in the coffee shop game. We sat down in a quiet corner and just talked. For six hours. Neither one of us wanted to go anywhere. And that's when I saw the time: 9:51p.m.

"You better get used to this," Joanne said as I folded myself into the trunk.

"What do you mean?" I said.

"I have a feeling we're going to be doing this a lot," she said. She shot me a coy smile. And as she shut the trunk, I felt my heart do that thing. That thing it hadn't done since…

WHATCHA GONNA DO WITH ALL THAT JUNK INSIDE YOUR TRUNK?

After Joanne pulled past the guard tower and into her parking spot, she let me out of the trunk. The campus was quiet. The January marine layer had come in from the ocean, blanketing the quiet campus in a soft white fog, and the chill had driven everyone inside. It felt like we were the only two people on campus.

As we walked back to her dorm, I playfully took her hand.

"Come on, I want to show you something," I said, as I flirtatiously led her into the middle of the street that wound through our campus.

"What are we doing in the middle of the street?" Joanne asked, laughing.

"What? You've never just hung out in the middle of a street before?" I said.

"Tyler Merritt, what are you doing?" Joanne said.

"I just wanted you to remember this moment for the rest of your life," I said.

"What moment?" she asked quizzically.

And with that, I took her face in my hands, and we kissed for the first time.

Oh snap! Y'all weren't ready for all that romanticity. There in the darkness, on the empty street, it was just her and me. Dim moonlight streamed down. The stars peeked through the mist. John Cusack was in the background, holding a boom box over his head that was playing "In Your Eyes." Thanks, Cusack. I owe you one.

Joanne pulled back and placed her hands on my chest. She looked up and smiled at me.

"I'm in trouble," I thought to myself.

LOOKING FOR SOME HOP STUFF, BABY, THIS EASTER

Things progressed. For the next few months, our relationship escalated. Dating was a big deal in small, enclosed Christian communities like Bethany. We really didn't want to attract unwanted attention to this relationship. But every spare moment, we were together, often sneaking off campus to coffee shops or to take walks on the beach.

As second semester sped along, Easter approached, which meant the student body had a few days off classes to celebrate the holiday.

"I had an idea," Joanne said to me after rehearsal one day. "What if you came home with me for Easter?"

More time with Joanne? I was in. We got into her trusty Ford Tempo and we drove to her family's house, about an hour and a half away.

As we were driving, Joanne turned to me.

"My dad asked me if you wanted to sing on Sunday at the church for Easter services," she said.

I was a little surprised.

"What song?" I said.

"I don't think it matters," she said.

"Wait. Has your dad ever even heard me sing?" I asked.

"No, but I vouched for you," she said.

"Okay, cool," I said. I started thinking about what song I would sing on such short notice. Probably "Bui Doi" from *Miss Saigon*. Wait. No. That wouldn't work.

"Oh yeah, and one more thing," Joanne said. "My parents kind of don't know about...us."

"Yeah, okay, cool," I said.

"I haven't told them," she said. "They think you're just a friend. They get uptight about this kind of stuff."

"I get it," I said.

I knew that Joanne's parents were pretty conservative, and her dad was a pastor. There was also probably a hint of "Young lady! No dating until you're married!"

"You know," I said, "at some point, we are going to have to discuss how your parents are still not cool with you dating, and you're a senior in college."

"Oh, they're cool with me dating," Joanne said. "But my parents would not be okay with me dating a black guy."

Her words hit me like a bullet.

I was not prepared for that.

Where were we? We weren't in some diner in rural Alabama. This wasn't the South. We were on the West Coast. When I decided to move to California, I was moving to the most progressive state in the Union. As I tried to make sense of what I'd just heard, we drove into the city limits of her hometown. I looked at the sign.

Stockton, California.

JIM CROW IN CALIFORNIA

I want to pause here and talk about Stockton. But I want to be clear. This isn't just about the city of Stockton, California. Because the story of Stockton is a very American story.

Stockton is located a little more than one hour inland from the major metro areas around the San Francisco Bay. According to a report by *US News and World Report*,[1] Stockton, California, was the MOST DIVERSE large city in the entire nation in 2018. The racial breakdown of its 310,000 residents was 42 percent Latino, 24 percent Asian, 19 percent white, and 13 percent black. Dang, Stockton! You're more diverse than a college admission pamphlet.

But when it comes to money, homeownership, and city services, the diversity ends. And that's part of Stockton's history, too.

Stockton's growth as a city is fairly easy to understand. First, it's on a major river, so it was a port city hub. It's right on a deep, inland channel with flat farmland all around—ideal for building a city. The Gold Rush hit and flooded the area with people and wealth. Then the railroads developed rapidly. And then later, highways connected Stockton to the coast. Cheap land. Loads of jobs. Great agriculture. There was a boom of migration of white settlers and a boom of immigrants. But how they were treated was wildly different, based almost entirely on race.

By 1880, because of the Gold Rush, Stockton was home to massive numbers of Chinese immigrants. These immigrants were prohibited by the Chinese Exclusion Act from owning property.[2] Later, in 1900–1923, because of a boom in transportation and farming, Stockton's population tripled, and subdivisions of houses cropped up. People could buy a home with "three dollars down and three dollars a month."[3] Except that real estate agents, developers, and the city government prohibited the sale of these houses to black, Latino, or Asian families. When the Great Depression hit, Congress established the Federal Housing Administration to make sure people didn't lose their homes.[4] From 1932 to 1964, the FHA financed more than $120 billion of loans for housing.[5] Only 2 percent of this money went to non-white people. Two percent! These discriminatory federal and local laws prevented black, Asian, and

Latino people from owning property—the primary way people in the US build wealth.

Stockton is also famous for its fairgrounds[6] having been used as a temporary processing site for the Japanese internment camps that were formed when President Franklin Delano Roosevelt passed Executive Order 9066. More than 100,000 people were relocated. The property of these individuals, many of whom were legal US citizens of Japanese descent, was seized, resulting in the loss of between $2 billion and $5 billion worth of property (in 2017 dollars)[7] from these Japanese citizens and legal immigrants. Nothing like this was ever done to citizens with German heritage or people who were German immigrants, even though we were at war with Nazi Germany. Can you guess why?

Today, in Stockton, white households have a median income of about $60,700, black households have a median income of $30,400, and Latino households have a median income of $43,900.[8]

This is criminal, isn't it? Actually, it wasn't. I just want to remind everyone that all of this ish was legal.[9] Not only legal, but in many cases fully endorsed with the backing of the US federal government. You can go online and see the official county records and city redlining maps for yourself.[10] It's all there.

This is the background of Stockton, the "most diverse city in the United States."

Of course, I didn't know any of this when I pulled into Joanne's driveway. But now I was here. And for the next two days I would be in a house with a family that wouldn't accept me dating their daughter. I didn't make a big deal out of it. I was polite. And throughout the course of the time there, I didn't detect anything from her parents that made me uncomfortable. I sang at her dad's church on Easter Sunday. Everyone was very nice to me. But in the back of my mind, this was always there. I was fine as a houseguest. Just not good enough to date their daughter.

At one point during the weekend, Joanne and I drove downtown to the train station to pick up her younger brother, who was coming home for the weekend. We had some uninterrupted time to talk.

"I'm not trying to open up a can of worms, here, but your parents seem really nice," I said. "So what makes you think they're not okay with…you know, you dating a black man?"

Joanne told me about arguments she'd had about race with her parents. They thought interracial dating was bad, and she had challenged their viewpoints. I don't remember the specifics. But as I got older, I heard similar arguments from other white people about why interracial dating was bad. Someone once said to me, "If I were to marry someone black, then my kids wouldn't look like me. They wouldn't look like our line of people. They just wouldn't look like…us."

Damn.

Look, I wasn't unclear about racism. I just hadn't experienced it like this before.*

WALKING ON THE MINES I'VE LAID

As human beings, we're remarkably resilient. We find ways to survive. We adapt. We change. When we encounter something that's a threat to us, we find ways to defend ourselves against it.

I was facing a threat to my existence. I was a man divided, because one part of me was so clearly falling in love with Joanne. But there was another part of me, too. Inside me there was still that young black kid, kneeling in that worship service, utterly destroyed by the betrayal of Kelley, vowing to myself: "I'm never going to get hurt like this again."

Now you might think knowing about Joanne's parents might have

---

*   I want to be fair here. This event happened more than twenty-five years ago. Lots has happened in those twenty-five years. Even in the past five years, loads of people in this nation have taken it upon themselves to get educated about history. And more than that, the city of Stockton has changed. Since being ground zero for the subprime mortgage crisis in 2008 and being named the most miserable city in the US in 2011 by *Forbes* magazine, Stockton has really rallied. In 2016, Michael Tubbs became the first black mayor of Stockton, and the youngest, at age twenty-six. Tubbs, a Stanford grad, whose leadership grabbed the attention of both Oprah Winfrey and Barack Obama, is leading a groundswell of renewal in that city. Places change. People change. And if I were a betting man, I'd bet that Joanne's parents have radically altered their views. I just wish that could have happened back in the mid-nineties is all. Might have spared a lot of people a lot of pain.

made me start to pull back from the relationship, just as a form of self-protection.

That story makes sense. But it's not what happened. What actually happened is far worse. And far darker.

The truth is, that moment at Easter didn't change anything. Since almost the first moment I realized my deep attraction to Joanne, the voice of that hurt, self-reliant gangsta began chirping at me. It called out, "What's your long-term play, here, Tyler? Joanne's a senior. You're a freshman. What do you think is going to happen? You're going to live happily ever after?"

The moment I had the slightest inkling that I had the chance to feel something for Joanne, I began to self-sabotage. I began to diversify my romantic investments, making sure I was secretly cultivating a relationship with another girl or two on the side. I realize how bad this sounds. But this is where I was. This is who I was. I knew that the embers of my past hurt were still there, waiting to be fanned into a raging bonfire by whoever had the audacity to try to get close to me. Joanne happened to be the first. She wouldn't be the last. But you always remember your first.

The closer I got to Joanne, the more I made sure I had multiple relational escape routes.

I am not proud of this. That unresolved hurt from back in high school with Kelley had clicked something in me that made me cruel, and it was coming back up. This wasn't fun for me. It wasn't a game. This was solely about making sure that I wouldn't be hurt again. The more ruthless I acted, the more invincible I felt. This went on for months.

Eventually, Joanne found out about the other girls. I discovered this when I found the remnants of a stuffed animal I had given her for Valentine's Day. It was torn to shreds, as though it had been tossed into a wood chipper. Completely eviscerated. Stuffing was everywhere, limbs scattered across the lawn. It was like a Muppet crime scene.

"You lied to me," Joanne screamed through the phone. "You cheating, lying motherf***er." She went on for several minutes. I sighed and sat down. "I am so glad you gave me a reason," Joanne said. "It had to end somehow, and I am SO glad you gave me a reason."

Now at that moment, I said all the right words. I'd been caught red-handed, after all. I knew I deserved what was coming to me. I made the apologies. I told Joanne how much remorse I felt for what I had done to hurt her. I told her how bad I felt for all the ways I'd done wrong by her.

And at that moment, I should have felt sorry. I should have felt disgusted with myself for the pain I'd caused.

But if I am being honest with you, I did not.

My only thought was "Better you than me."

"Look, I'm really sorry this had to go down," the self-protective voice of my past said to me. "One of you was going to get hurt. Someone was going to be screwed over, and it was not going to be us."

And with that, I hung up the phone.

"Better you than me."

The line went dead. And so did my relationship with Joanne.

Like I said, if you don't deal with your past, your past will deal with you. And in the blaze, you'll leave behind a lot of collateral damage. Here I was, my past was right in front of me, staring right at me, and I still wasn't ready to deal with it.

Far from it.

CHAPTER 13

AUGUST, BROKEN FRAME, AND EVERYTHING AFTER

Under the mid-August sun, I drove my 1981 Chevy Celebrity through the redwoods of the Santa Cruz mountains to start my sophomore year. I now had one year of faith-based collegiate education under my belt. What a year it had been. To quote the late-twentieth-century English poets Chumbawamba, "I got knocked down, but I got up again."

The semester was starting in a few days, and students were filing back onto campus. I had to go over to the Stowell Center, a two-story building whose top floor housed the campus's business offices. The lower level was a student center, with desks for studying and the familiar collegiate sound of hushed conversations. After dropping off a package, I was about to walk back outside when I heard a sound floating down to me from upstairs.

It was the sound of acoustic guitars. But what was it doing coming from the upstairs business offices? I walked up the stairs, and there, in the middle of the waiting room between the business offices, were two guys sitting on light pink-and-blue couches, strumming their guitars, clearly working on something.

Before we go any further, I need you to understand something. This moment is one of THE defining *Sliding Doors* moments of my entire life. It would turn out to be one of the moments why I'm sitting where I am. The remaining chapters of this book stem from this moment. I didn't know it, but that singular random moment of guitar playing altered the trajectory of my entire life.

I looked at the guys on the couch. One guy's name was Keith and the other guy's name won't be written in this book. My friends and I, to this very day, refer to him as "He Who Shall Not Be Mentioned." In fact, every once in a while, I'll call this dude Voldemort. He didn't actually do anything on a Voldemort level, but I'm a bit petty when it comes to this, and his name is not gonna be in this book. More on that later. But for now, back to these dudes on the pink-and-blue couches.

Guy Number 1: Keith

Keith was wearing a black Metallica t-shirt and had black hair that came down past his shoulders. To this day, I have no idea why Keith was at Bethany. I think it was because his parents were pastors. Keith was a classical guitar major, but his passion was heavy metal. Specifically, Metallica, whom he considered the greatest musical act in human history. Keith also cussed like a sailor, which made for some awkward times at our small Christian college. At one point, Keith and I were rehearsing to play some worship music for our campus chapel, and I don't remember what the circumstances were, but Keith got upset and he cussed. A Bethany staff member gently reminded him to please not curse in the chapel, and Keith said, "God hears me everywhere. Does it f*cking matter where I cuss?" Tough to argue with that one, theologically. Well played, you dark, twisted contrarian.

Guy Number 2: Voldemort

If Keith was Metallica, then He Who Shall Not Be Mentioned was Van Halen. He had long, dirty blond hair and a Peavey 5150 amp, plus this dude was a born showman, all passion, and was an excellent guitar player—just like Eddie. He even played a twelve-string acoustic guitar. I had no idea those even existed.

So these two Extreme More-than-Words-looking dudes are just sitting there strumming their guitars on the couch. I sat down. Why not? I had never seen an impromptu jam session. I felt like I was watching National Geographic, and I was getting to see white people in their native white people habitat.

"Are you guys going to start a band or something?" I asked.

"No," Keith said, looking at me as though I just suggested that we brush our teeth and go drink orange juice.

"We're just working on this song," Voldemort said, "but we don't have any lyrics, just the melody."

"Well, I sing," I offered. "How about I try to write some lyrics for you guys?"

Keith laughed. "We'd be like Hootie and the Blowfish, then, huh?"

Those were words I didn't know. I did not know what a Hootie was. Nor why one might be hanging out underwater with a blowfish. Keith saw the confusion cloud my face.

"It's a super popular band with a black lead singer," he said.

"Oh," I said, thinking it must be the inverse of Vanilla Ice. I had categories for this.

I sat and listened for a bit more, trying to memorize the chord progressions. I had been around music a lot, so that part wasn't hard. Once I got it, I stood up and said goodbye. The first thing I realized was that if I was going to write rock song lyrics, I should probably listen to some more rock songs. I promptly left campus to drive to the nearest store to buy that new CD they were talking about. I was going to get me some Hootie, and ideally also some Blowfish. And that is how I ended up with the CD *Cracked Rear View*, which is the nineteenth-best-selling album in music history.

It was at this time that my views on music were once again dramatically challenged. When I walked into the dorms of this Christian Bible college as a freshman, I quickly realized I was pretty much the only person on campus who didn't listen to all the music out there.

"Wait," I asked a senior named Scott who had an Ice Cube poster on his wall. "You listen to non-Christian music?"

"Of course," he said. "Why wouldn't I?"

"I thought…I mean…" I stammered. "I was told it was what Christians did."

"Well, you got some bad information, brother," he said.

And that was that. Later that first year, I was introduced to the Counting Crows and their debut album *August and Everything After*. The cassette actually got stuck in my piece-of-crap car radio, so for the entire summer, that was all I played. I loved the complex and mystical lyrics, and they are still one of my favorite bands.

But this night I went back to my dorm room with Hootie and the Blowfish running through my stereo, a whole summer's worth of Counting Crows in my head, and tried to write some lyrics. I'd been used to writing rhymes and bars for hip-hop and I found the process wasn't too different. And with that, I wrote these first lines:

The road is narrow
But we all walk the same one
Trying to fit in
We all come undone

Hey! That didn't suck! The next day, I went back to the Stowell Center. Keith and Other Dude were there. They looked up at me, surprised that I had come back.

"I wrote some lyrics," I said. "I can sing it for you, if you want."

Now, they didn't know I could sing. But I sat down, and let me tell you, I was legitimately nervous. What if this sucked? What if they hated it? So, Voldemort counted us in, one, two, three, and I sang what I'd written. When we were finished, Keith was excited. Because I want to keep the book at least sorta family-friendly, I'll clean up his verbiage by replacing his cuss words with the word "puppy."

"Holy puppies. That was puppy awesome. We just wrote a puppy song! Puppy!"

As we sat there in the empty hallway between the business offices, on the wall there was a framed picture of the campus back in 1919, when Bethany was first founded. It had a cheap plastic slip-on frame, and as we sat there, the bottom of the frame fell off.

"Oh, puppy!" Keith said, concerned we were going to have to pay for the damages. "Did we do that? Did we break that puppy picture?"

"No," I said. "It's a sign! We're going to be a famous band called Falling Frame!"

We all laughed. But it was electric, too. I went back to my dorm, inspired, and finished the lyrics to a song.

Picture so tight in its place
But it's only by grace
On the wall
Standing tall
And I don't touch it at all
What will you do
What will you say
When the frames fall

And that is how I wrote my first song, which we titled "Frames Fall." And where my band started. And also how a whole new storyline of my life began.

THAT THING YOU DO

As Keith and He Who Shall Not Be Mentioned rehearsed, we kept practicing writing songs, most of which were a mess. But it was a lot of fun, and I felt like we were getting better. Then I heard some pretty interesting news.

Apparently, because of budget shortfalls, Bethany wasn't going to be able to afford to continue the Ambassadors that year. So instead, they came up with a plan to send out little singing groups—duos, trios, whatever—to sing in churches instead. These smaller groups would be the new "ambassadors" for the college. The school announced it would be holding auditions, and winners would not only tour, but get a small scholarship.

Naturally, as three guys who just met a few weeks ago, I figured we should audition.

"I signed us up to audition," I told them.

"What the puppy were you thinking?" Keith said.

"What?" I said. "What do we have to lose."

"We're not even a real puppy band," Keith said.

"Well," He Who Shall Not Be Mentioned said, "we'd need a bass player or a drummer."

I was such a rock-and-roll novice that I didn't even know why that was important. But these other two dudes were musicians, so they started recruiting. This is where it gets sorta interesting.

First, there was Mike. He was a cocky, loud extrovert who made a ton of Chris Farley jokes. He was the kind of dude who brought a massive stereo system to college, put the speakers in the windows, and blared the Beastie Boys out the window into the quad on spring days. He was nonstop energy. You could say that he can't, he won't, and he don't stop. He would become our first drummer.

Second, we got Josh Combs, who was one of the most musical people I've ever met and one of the kindest.

So, to recap, we now had a band featuring:

KEITH: foul-mouthed Metallica guitar player
VOLDEMORT: Van Halen performer lead guitar player
MIKE: Chris-Farley-Beastie-Boys-loving drummer
JOSH: super nice, quiet hymn-playing musical savant
TYLER: black theater major who knew *Miss Saigon* but nothing about
    rock music sans Bon Jovi from fifth grade

The night before the audition, the five of us sat in the hallway in our dorm, trying to figure out what our band name would be. We were all over the place, but eventually we came down to three finalists. Please note, I'm not making this up, and these were the actual name choices we came up with.

- Phlegm Salad
- Stained (this was before Staind)
- Falling Frame

We went back and forth, arguing furiously until after midnight. Finally, a dude on the hall opened the door to his room and stepped out, blinking into the light.

"Look," he said, with a fair amount of irritation. "The frame fell off the wall. It broke. Just go with that. Broken Frame. Just write it down, and for the love of God, go to bed."

Broken Frame. We all looked at each other. "We can always change it later, if we don't like it," someone said. The next day was the audition, and there were several groups auditioning. Almost all of them were singing groups with names like Points of Joy who sang pleasant, Christian songs. Finally, it was our turn to go. Our newly formed quintet took the stage, and I went to the mic.

"We're Broken Frame," I said, feigning confidence.

"Dammit," I thought to myself. "Maybe we shoulda gone with Phlegm Salad." No time for that now, Tyler. Voldemort counted us in, one, two, three, and we were off.

Now, are you familiar with the late nineties feel-good Tom Hanks film *That Thing You Do*? If you haven't seen it, it's a must. Put down this incredible book and go watch it. Welcome back. Remember the scene where the band plays in front of a crowd for the first time at a talent show, and the crowd goes absolutely nuts? People cheering, standing up, clapping along. The band members look at one another, shocked at the reaction. This is exactly what happened to us that day in the Bethany Chapel. That whole room lost its damn mind. People jumped out of their seats. I was like, "What is happening?" It wasn't even all that great. But hell, there was a live audience, and the theater kid in me kicked in. I didn't exactly know what a black rock-and-roll front man looked like, but I acted like I did.

When the song was over, the crowd exploded in a standing ovation. A few days later, we found out that we were selected to tour to represent Bethany.

And that is the story of the first live performance of the band Broken Frame.

THE TOURING EDITION

Things picked up rather quickly after that. We now had a booking agent in charge of getting us gigs. And let's just say wherever we went, we made a killer first impression. Voldemort would whip his long hair around, like a rock star. Mike was a high-energy, funny drummer. And you didn't have to tell me twice to lean into a crowd. We blew the back wall off of places. Folks loved us. They'd start asking us to come back, only this time, they offered to pay us.

Whaaat?

Getting paid? To do this? We were in college, and having a blast. Along the way, we kept writing songs. Most of our songs utterly sucked, but one out of every twenty would stick, including what I would call Broken Frame's breakout song, which I wrote with He Who Shall Not Be Mentioned as a joke. We were driving along in Santa Cruz and saw a car with a bumper sticker magnet on it in the shape of a fish and the word *JESUS* written inside the outline of the fish. And then, a few seconds later, we saw another car with a fish outline, only the fish had legs, and written on the inside of the fish was the word *DARWIN*. Of course, this was the very height of American civic discourse about religion. So many people changed their minds about their most deeply held beliefs because of those stickers, which were incredibly compelling. At any rate, as a joke, we headed back to the dorms, and wrote this:

DON'T DIS MY FISH

All I want to do is be like Jesus
All I want to do is live like this
All I want to do is save the world
All I ask is don't dis my fish

Yes, it was ridiculous. Yes, someone should have pulled my black card. But the crowds loved it. It was a peppy anthem, and we sold a lot of t-shirts with the words "Don't Dis My Fish" on the back. And that's also when we realized that most bands make most of their money by selling merchandise.

For the next three years of my college experience, I remember only two things: what I did with Theater Central and what we did with Broken Frame. Were there classes? I'm sure there were. But I was busy piling into vans, loading gear, setting up shows, doing sound checks, and driving around all of God's green earth with four white dudes.

There's an old adage that goes, "If you want to truly know a person, go on a ten-hour road trip with them, and if at the end of that trip you don't want to throw them into oncoming traffic, then you can be lifelong friends."

That first year, we probably drove 10,000 miles up and down California, rocking out in small venues, and also some pretty big ones. Along the way, our college held a big outdoor music festival at the beach right on the Santa Cruz boardwalk. We had a giant stage, right on the Pacific Ocean, with teeming crowds cheering and excited to hear us play. It felt real.

The point is, that ragtag group became brothers. This was a whole different sort of experience than theater. Theater is always temporary. You were assigned a role, you played it for a bit—for a season—and you inhabited that role, but then it was over. What you had built was now gone. Theater is ephemeral, temporary. But a band is something else. A band is a team. It's you, and how you fit with everyone else. It's a group project, but it doesn't feel temporary. There's no end date. And you're not playing a part—you're being you. This was the first time since playing sports in junior high that I felt that kind of camaraderie, and it was electric for me. There's nothing like walking on stage with your band.

Which is why it was so tough, at the end of that first year, when Josh (our bass player) pulled me aside. Josh knew his end goal at Bethany—he wanted to be a worship pastor. And as his graduation approached, he knew he had some tough choices.

"Tyler," he said to me, "I'm going to have to quit the band at the end of the year."

I felt like I'd been shot through the heart. And he was to blame. I didn't know that people could quit a band. That would be like Dennis Rodman leaving the 1996 Bulls, only if Dennis Rodman were a short, introverted white dude who really, really liked guacamole. For all you musical theater people out there reading this, I know in that last analogy, all you read was sports sports sports sports sports ball. I'll put it like this. Imagine Ben Platt deciding to leave *Dear Evan Hansen* after only twelve performances.

Involuntarily, when Josh told me that, I started crying. This was deeply traumatic to me. I was going to miss this guy, and I didn't want things to change. I remember trying to talk him out of it. "Are you sure you want to do this?" I asked.

Josh nodded, slowly. He had to follow his calling to be a pastor. And who was I to argue with God?

And with that, our band was down to four. We found a guy to replace Josh (a dude named Rust; more on him later) and we continued onward.

Until we hit a brick wall.

HE WHO SHALL NOT BE MENTIONED DID THAT THING WE DON'T TALK ABOUT

For the next two years, Broken Frame took nearly every spare minute I had. For the next few semesters, our group was either trying to get a gig or preparing for our next gig. After graduation, Broken Frame continued. For the next two years, we all stuck around Santa Cruz, working odd jobs, but focusing our efforts on the band.

After we graduated, He Who Shall Not Be Mentioned got married to his girlfriend in her hometown of Oklahoma. It was a glorious celebration, and the entire band flew out to be there. Mike and I were even in the wedding, standing up as groomsmen. After the wedding, that summer, he and his new wife moved off campus to a house located at a Christian camp. The camp had a number of places where our band could rehearse at night.

One night, we all piled into the van and drove out to his house in the middle of the woods, which I know sounds like the opening scene to a horror movie. We pulled up to his house, but as we walked in, he was being all nervous and weird.

"Why don't you all sit down," He Who Shall Not Be Mentioned said.

We looked at one another and sat down. The previous week, he'd been out of town visiting his wife's family in Oklahoma, so someone asked: "Yo, how was your trip."

He looked at us and his eyes got really big.

"Yeah, about that," Voldemort said, gulping nervously. "While we were out there, I interviewed for a job at a church."

We sat there, stunned. This was the first we had heard of this.

"They want to hire me," he stammered, "so I'm going to take the pastor job out there."

I felt my heart sink. This was the guy who started it all, with Keith, up on the crappy pink-and-blue couches outside the business offices. An original founding member. I loved this guy. Look, I know I've been referring to him this entire time by the name of a super villain, but I loved him. As an only child, he was about as close to a brother as I'd ever had. It was painful. Deeply painful. I wondered where I'd felt this before, and was reminded that, oh yeah, this is reminiscent of when I learned about Kelley and the ice cream. "Oh," I thought to myself. "This is what betrayal feels like."

Let's just say the conversation didn't go great. I don't remember what I said that night. Whatever it was, it was probably unfair. After all, he was making a move to support his family. Things happen. Life changes. I can make sense of that now. But back then, I couldn't. I think what bugged me so much back then was the fact that he didn't even warn us. He had flown out to interview for a job out of state and didn't even tell us. I felt like being in a band together for the past six years had earned us a place in that conversation. Again, I know this sounds petty. He was simply making moves for his family. But maybe you're not hearing me—to me, we *were* family. He could have told us.

After we'd said our piece, it was time to go. And from that moment on, I cut him off entirely. Petty? Sure. I know some of you are thinking, "You didn't *really* cut this dude out of your life for that, did you?" And my answer is "I've given you twelve chapters of data outlining my weak spots, my flaws. If you couldn't see that coming, you haven't been paying attention."

The point is, we had work to do.

TYLER MERRITT'S SCHOOL OF MANAGEMENT 101

From that moment on, I was the CEO of Broken Frame. I had to remake and re-form this band, or it would fall apart. This was a perilous time, because Keith, the other original founder, had to leave the band to take care of his health and his wife. We respected that. But I felt like I was living the lyrics of Bryan Adams's song "Summer of '69," where people keep leaving the band.

Don't you put that evil on us, Bryan Adams!

Now let me be clear about this. I didn't just casually call myself the CEO of Broken Frame. Calling myself a CEO is a big deal, but I could truthfully and honestly say that because I had two things going for me:

1. Visibility. I was the front man for the band, and everyone knew it.
2. Real authority. I made the calls, or helped make the calls, that directed us.

When I think about black people who are CEOs, these are the folks I think about: P. Diddy, Tyler Perry, Oprah, Jay-Z, LeBron James. The list goes on and on and on. Actually, it doesn't. Because when you start talking about black people as actual leaders and CEOs in corporate America, you'd be surprised. (Or maybe you wouldn't.) So, here are some stats about black visibility and black authority in the US workplace in corporate America.

- Black people make up 13.4 percent of the US population.[1]
- Black people only represent 8 percent of white-collar professionals in the US.[2]
- As I write this, of the biggest 500 companies in the United States (the Fortune 500), only four (FOUR) have CEOs that are black.[3]
- Those companies are home improvement retailer Lowe's (No. 44), pharmaceuticals maker Merck (No. 69), financial services company TIAA (No. 81), and M&T Bank (No. 438).[4]
- The Fortune 500 has been around since 1955.[5]
- The first black CEO of a Fortune 500 company was Dr. Clifton R. Wharton Jr. with TIAA-CREF.[6] That was in 1987.
- Franklin Raines became the second black CEO of a Fortune 500 company, when he became CEO of Fannie Mae.[7] That was twelve years later, in 1999.
- There have only been eighteen black CEOs in the Fortune 500 since 1999, total.[8]
- Of all executive or senior leadership roles in the Fortune 500 (defined as within two reporting levels of the CEO), black professionals held just 3.3 percent (according to the US Equal Employment Opportunity Commission).[9]
- Among Fortune 100 companies in 2020, black professionals account for just 3 percent of CEOs, 1 percent of CFOs, and 3 percent of profit leaders like division presidents.[10,11]
- Among the Fortune 500 companies, there were 322 black corporate directors at 307 companies. Of those, twenty-one were chairmen and lead directors.[12]
- More than a third of Fortune 500 companies did not have any black board members whatsoever.
- New companies need funding from venture capital firms. More than 80 percent of venture capital firms don't have a single black investor (and the numbers show VC firms are overlooking companies with black founders).[13]

- New startups would need 6.7 times the number of Latino and 5.6 times more black executives in order to match the overall US working-age demographics.[14]
- For white people, the ratio of "workers and laborers" compared with senior-level management is roughly 7 to 1, according to 2018 statistics compiled by the US Equal Employment Opportunity Commission.
- For black people, that ratio is 105 to 1.[15]

There are a myriad of reasons for these statistics, and I'm not an economist, but it doesn't take a rocket scientist to think, "Uh, maybe we're missing out on some incredible leaders here." I don't know why more companies don't look out over the landscape of the US and think that.

To me, it's like Branch Rickey, the famed Brooklyn Dodgers executive in the 1940s, who looked around the sport of baseball and said, "Uh, why aren't we signing black baseball players?" And then went out and signed Jackie Robinson—one of the best second basemen in the history[16] of the game.[17] I think it's safe to say baseball has been improved by the presence of black players. And so would our nation's companies.

So, because I am NOT ONLY the author of this book BUT ALSO a handsome black CEO, I am now going to share my incredible management and leadership advice with you. Now, there's an old rule in business that when adding people to your team you should evaluate them on three factors:

- Character—does the person have integrity?
- Competence—is the person very good at what they do?
- Chemistry—does the person "fit" with you and your team?

Again, as a former black CEO, it is high time that the business world reevaluated this list. Here are THREE critically important business axioms from me, Tyler Merritt, former CEO and current black man, that you can take to the bank. Are you ready? Here we go.

Business Axiom 1

When hiring, chemistry is the only thing that matters.

That's right. Come at me, bro. Now I know what you're thinking. You're thinking, "Tyler, that's absurd. The most important thing for an employee to have is competence." You're also possibly thinking, "Will I make it to the end of this book without seeing the phrase 'vaginal steaming' again?"

Wrong on both counts, homie! Let me give you an example. Back when Josh left the group, we needed a new bass player. We came across a guy named Rust, a chubby white dude who had personality for days. Rust was probably 50 percent as good as Josh Combs at playing bass guitar. But he was a blast to be around and made life way more fun. And he worked his butt off to get better. He was good enough, with a hefty side of hustle to get better. In the end, I think competence is overrated. You spend roughly half your waking hours at work. Work with people you actually like. Which brings me to axiom 2.

Business Axiom 2

Chemistry is the only thing that matters. That's right. I repeated it so you wouldn't forget.

Now, I know that some people reading this are gifted businesspeople who already are forming objections in their head about what I just said. You're thinking to yourself, "Competence is so important!"

But again. It's about chemistry. Our band was incredibly hardworking, and we wanted to be good. For example, Mike was actually a killer acoustic guitar player and songwriter. In his off time, he worked on both of those relentlessly. So he got out from behind the drum kit and started playing lead acoustic.

After listening to Alanis Morissette's *Jagged Little Pill* album, and a whole lot of Blues Traveler, I decided to take up harmonica, because it was super cool-sounding. As a band, one of our core values was to get better. So, guess what? Rust worked his butt off to get better because that was a shared value for our group. If Rust had not shared that value, he probably wouldn't have fit in very well, and we'd be constantly fighting, which would throw off...

That's right.

CHEMISTRY.

If someone is good enough, and they're willing to work, you can train them to be a whole lot better. You can't train someone not to be a slacker. Which brings me to the third axiom in the Tyler Merritt Management Course.

Business Axiom 3

I'm serious. The only thing that matters is chemistry.

Do me a favor. Think about someone in your professional life who you really liked working with. I'm going to go out on a limb and guess they were NOT a slacker, and also that they weren't a jerky blowhard. Not hiring blazing jerkwads is one of the main ways to ensure you have good group chemistry. If your group is hardworking and humble, then really, all you need is to make sure you have chemistry and you're good, because the person you're hiring will automatically fit in.

At one point, we got a new guitar player named Dan, and his good friend Nate would just hang out during rehearsal.

One day, our drummer was running late, and Nate said, "Yo, let me sit in on drums. I think I know the song."

Nate made his way behind the drum set, and I counted us in. One, two, three. We started playing, and instantly we all just stopped and turned. We could not believe what we were hearing. Nate was an absolute BEAST. I mean, he was easily the best drummer I had ever heard. We were now 200 percent better. Everything was locking in so much tighter because of Nate's skills. When the drummer got to rehearsal, he was like, "Damn, well, I'm out of a job," so he slid over to play keys, and turns out, unbeknownst to all of us, he was a BEAST on keys.

And this worked because of chemistry—nobody in the band was a terrible, ego-driven churlish ass-clown, AND everyone had the humility to say, "That dude is better than me, I'll go over here."

Life is too short to spend tons of time around people who suck.

See? We need more black CEOs. I just CEO'd the hell out of that section.

ENTER MY MOM.
MOMMING SO HARD. AGAIN.

After I graduated, I continued to work various part-time jobs while pouring my time and passion into making Broken Frame work. At the same time, I was working at local and regional theaters, performing in various playhouses and productions.

The truth was, I was tired of singing other people's music. After a while, musical theater and drama began to seem so rigid to me. Theater required me to inhabit the body and voice of someone else, whereas being the lead singer of Broken Frame allowed me to be…well, me. I began to talk to Mike about this a lot, and we wondered, "What would we have to do if we really wanted to make it as a band?"

At some point, I called my mom to talk about this. I told her that I was growing weary of musical theater and that I felt my passion shifting strongly to Broken Frame.

"Mike and I were talking, Mom," I said. "We were talking about what it would take to really pursue music."

"And what would it take?" my mother, ever the pragmatist, asked.

"Well…" I hesitated. It's always dangerous to say your dreams out loud. "We'd most likely have to move to Nashville. That's where Christian bands always start. And…"

"Well, then go do it," my mom said.

"What? What did you say?" I stammered. I did not expect that.

"I said that you should do it," my mother said. "You're young. Talented. What do you have to lose? Go out there and do it."

As I hung up the phone, my hands were shaking. Was this really going to happen?

I began researching. We needed a place to stay, and I didn't know anyone in Tennessee. We lived in California, where the housing market was incredibly expensive and incredibly aggressive. I called various apartment complexes in Nashville to see if it was even possible to get housing. Finally, I found a place called Nashboro Village.

"How much is it per month for your three-bedroom apartments?" I asked.

"It's seven hundred fifty dollars," she said.

I immediately felt relief. I was paying roughly $900 per month where I was. If we all got part-time jobs, we could make that work. I sighed, doing the math in my head.

"Ok, so seven hundred fifty apiece comes out to…" I paused.

The woman on the other end laughed. "No, honey, that's seven fifty total."

Whaaaaaaaaaaaa??? I got scared. The only way you could get a place that cheap in California would be if it was in the ghetto, with cockroaches the size of shih tzus.

"What kind of neighborhood is it in?" I asked.

"Honey, it's right off a golf course," the woman said.

A golf course? What? I hung up the phone, and sat on my bed, running the numbers in my head. I called an emergency meeting with the band so that I could tell them what info I had found out, and also to tell them what my mom said.

"Hey, guys," I said. "This is what my mom said."

We were all grown-ass men, but hey, when your mama says something, you listen. I let it sink in. I then told them how much rent was.

"Seven fifty apiece?" Mike said. "That's pretty good."

"No," I said. "Seven fifty total." Everyone's mind was blown. And so we took a day to think and pray about it, and then we voted.

Rust couldn't go. But the rest did.

And so the group of us went out for one last rowdy dinner, toasted each other and to the time we spent together. Rust helped us load all our earthly possessions into a U-Haul truck. As I climbed into the truck, I realized I was leaving my first home-away-from-home, my college town, which had been the setting for the most formative years of my life. As we pulled away, the lyrics from "Mr. Jones" by Counting Crows came on, a song Adam Duritz wrote about his desire to make it as a musician, but how pursuing one's dream can result in crippling fear. To this day, I feel every single word of this song.

We drove toward Nashville, the bright dream doing something bigger guiding us. I was leaving all sorts of things behind. I was leaving behind so many memories, some bad, so many beautiful. But we were pressing onward, the four of us, traveling in a pack, a band, together, toward something.

And all of what had happened was now behind us, visible only through our cracked rearview mirror.

CHAPTER 14

THERE'S NO PLACE LIKE HOME

Let's play a game. I'm gonna say a few movie quotes, and I want you to tell me which movie the quote is from. Ready? Here we go.

- Mama always said life is like a box of chocolates.
- May the Force be with you.
- E.T., phone home.
- I'll be back.
- I'll have what she's having.
- Show me the money!
- Carpe diem. Seize the day, boys. Make your lives extraordinary!
- Nobody puts Baby in a corner.

How did you do? I think they are some of the most famous lines in movie history. It's amazing how one simple sentence of dialogue can have such a big impact.

A while ago, the American Film Institute made their list of the most famous lines in movie history. They said number one was "Frankly, my dear, I don't give a damn" from the classic 1939 film *Gone with the Wind*. Not my first choice. First of all, that movie is more than a teensy bit racisty, so I'm gonna have to bump it down a notch for not aging well. Second, I happen to legitimately think another line is more famous, simply because more people have seen the movie. It's the classic line from *The Wizard of Oz*:

"Toto. I've a feeling we're not in Kansas anymore."

That's my winner. And yo, let me tell you, driving into Tennessee after having lived my entire life in the West, I can IDENTIFY with this quote. This was going to be an adjustment. Driving through Memphis, we pulled the U-Haul into a gas station, and when we got out Mike, Dan, and Nate looked around, realizing they were the only white dudes around. And I was like, "Imagine that. It's like how I felt…oh…I don't know…every single day in Santa Cruz. Weird. I hope you all pull through okay."

We finally pulled into Nashville and made our way to Apartment 1482 in Nashboro Village. The four of us were now in our new home. There were three things that stuck out to me during this transition.

Culture Shock 1: Let Me See You Work Work Work Work Work

The first thing we learned from Nashville is that when you're trying to make it as an artist, you need a job that will pay you enough to pay for rent, gas, and food, while leaving you enough time to work on and hone your craft.

You 👏 have 👏 to 👏 get 👏 a 👏 j-o-b.

Mike and Dan got jobs in guest services at the famed Opryland Hotel working as wait staff and event staff. Nate got a job selling oil changes door to door (!), and because I had a little money saved up, I took some time to scope out the city. Okay, look, I didn't have a job, but let's get one thing straight: I wasn't a scrub. A scrub is a guy who can't get no love from me.

The first thing I realized was how big country music was in this city. I mean, I knew that, but I didn't KNOW it. One night, I was in a bar, checking things out, and sat next to this dude. We got to talking and he was really cool.

I left the bar and went home and happened to flip on the TV on to Country Music Television and a video came on featuring the guy I had just met at the bar. I was like, "Whaaaa??"

That man's name?

Garth Brooks.

Nah, I'm kidding. That would have been dope, though. His name was actually Joe Nichols. The point is, none of us in the band had ever even listened to country music. But this was Music City, USA, filled with some of the greatest musicians in the entire world. We had a lot to learn. Right then and there we decided we'd take a minimum of six months to study and grow as musicians before we decided to play in public. We had to hone our craft. So we had to get to work. But we also had to…well…get to work.

Culture Shock 2: How Is Everyone This Nice?

The second thing we learned about in Nashville was Southern hospitality. Now, people talk about Southern hospitality, with offers of sweet tea and cakes, but dang if they ain't never lied. People were uncommonly nice in Nashville. We found this out early on.

One day, I was at home, by myself. There I was in the apartment, just eating some pasta, when I heard a knock on my door. I opened the door to see a dimple-cheeked young woman with shoulder-length brown hair and perfect teeth smiling at me.

"I'm just so sorry to bother you," she said. "My friend and I are moving in upstairs, and we were wondering if you could please move your car so we could get the moving truck a little closer."

Now, at this point, I want to reveal a sad fact. My 1981 Chevy Celebrity was gone. So I didn't have a car. Wait. I didn't have a job. Or a car. Dammit. Maybe I was a scrub. Anyway, my car had died, which meant, by definition, it was not my car blocking them. But this woman was just *so nice* that it made one put down one's pasta bowl and go outside to try to help. She introduced herself.

"I'm Bridget," she said.

"I'm Tyler," I said.

And with that, I went back inside without having really helped at all. But I met Bridget, and she and her roommate became fast friends with the four of us downstairs. Pretty soon, we were hanging out all the time, eating dinner together, watching tense-episode-after-tense-episode of *24* (David Palmer is America's first black president and I will fight anyone who says otherwise), and having deep convos about life.

As I'd find out, Bridget's Southern hospitality actually had no limits. Like unlimited rolls from O'Charley's, it is endless. It's now a decade and a half later, and every Sunday night, I go over to Bridget's house to eat dinner with her and her fabulous husband, Scott, and their two kids, my niece and nephew, Zoe and Declan. Yes, they're two little white kids. But try and tell them that I'm not their Uncle Ty Ty. I dare you. I used to think that you chose your friends, but looking back at it, I'm not so sure. Maybe friends are given to us, by God, as a very good gift. I think about this a lot. What would have happened to my life if Bridget had never knocked on my door? I don't know. But thank God I'll never have to find out.

Culture Shock 3: People Are Nice, but It's Still the South

After a few weeks of not working and watching my bank account slowly trickle down, Mike came home and told me that a store in the mall was hiring. For the sake of this story, we'll say the store was called Denim. Denim was a clothing retailer whose focus was denim, and it really prided itself on customer service. The idea was to have knowledgeable employees around to help people figure out what they wanted and help them find pieces that looked good—like a personal shopper.

After dropping off an application, I had an interview with the store manager, who was a young black woman named Shymene. She was short. She was fiery. She was in charge. I liked her immediately. The job was selling jeans, but really it was about talking to people, and trying to help them. Especially talking to women. And I realized, "Hey, I think I have the personality to make this work."

Because I also realized that, for a woman, buying jeans is often a hellish nightmare that most often results in feelings of either hopelessness, depression, or wanting to stab someone. So I realized that I'd be making the world a better place—because fewer stabby women is better for everyone.

Shymene saw that I was going to be an asset to both her sales and customer service, so she decided to hire me. What I did not realize is that Shymene, as the manager of the store, had to battle for me. There was a regional manager at the store, a white woman named Brandie, and Brandie did not like me. I will give you two guesses why Brandie did not like me. Have you locked in your answer?

"That guy is not going to sell jeans to women," Brandie said to Shymene right after I left the store. She suggested that going a different direction—a less "urban" feel—would be a better look for Shymene's floor staff, and that might make customers more "comfortable."

That's when I realized that even though Nashville is cool, it's still in the South. I was now only four hours away from my parents' hometown of Eutaw, Alabama. This was different than Stockton. This was deep, ingrained segregation. Listen. Tennessee is where Martin Luther King Jr. was assassinated. In Nashville, I would drive down a road, and there would be a white Baptist church on one side of the road and a black Baptist church on the other. And nobody would even talk about how weird that is. I mean, if there's one place on the earth where segregation shouldn't happen, you'd think it'd be in a church, right?

There were also parts of Nashville where black people didn't live, and the only black people around were there to serve the white people. I hadn't seen that before. And there were other racial attitudes that crept in. This would be a good time to pour a glass of Tennessee whiskey to go with a nice tall glass of Tennessee history. I don't drink alcohol, but after reading this, I might need to start.

THE BACKSTORY

Tennessee seceded from the Union and joined the Confederacy after the attack on Fort Sumter in South Carolina in April of 1861. After Lincoln was assassinated, Tennessee governor Andrew "Jackass" Johnson became president. He's the one who took all the land that was going to be given to freed slaves and instead gave it all back to the plantation owners. Remember that guy?

THE WORST PRESIDENT EVER?

Johnson was a former slave owner. He vetoed all civil rights bills that would allow former slaves to vote. Congress, fed up with his stalling and blocking of all voting legislation, impeached Johnson.[1]

Congress then bypassed the president, passing the Fourteenth Amendment to the Constitution with a two-thirds majority, giving all black men the Constitutional right to vote.[2] White Tennesseans were enraged.

TENNESSEE FIGHTS BLACK

A former slave owner named Nathan Bedford Forrest organized a group to maintain white racial superiority in the government through intimidation of black voters.[3] This group was founded in Tennessee and was called the Ku Klux Klan.[4]

FORREST FIRES

Nathan Bedford Forrest was a successful former Confederate general who is most famous (or infamous) for the Massacre of Fort Pillow.[5] Forrest's Confederate forces captured Fort Pillow, and all 600 Union soldiers (roughly 300 white soldiers and 300 black soldiers) surrendered. Instead of treating the black soldiers as POWs, Forrest ordered his Confederate forces to kill and torture these black Union troops.[6] According to testimony by surviving Union soldiers, Forrest's forces subjected these black soldiers to extreme brutality. It's alleged they shot wounded soldiers, burned men alive, nailed men to barrels and ignited them, crucified them, or hacked them to death with sabers. Damn.

THE MORE YOU KNOW

Indiscriminately killing military combatants who have surrendered is universally acknowledged today as a war crime under international law.[7]

THE KKK

After the Civil War, Bedford used violence and the threat of violence to maintain white control over the newly enfranchised former slaves via the KKK. Nathan Bedford Forrest was the very first grand wizard of the KKK. The KKK, with Forrest in the lead, suppressed voting rights of blacks in the South through violence and intimidation during the elections of 1868.

WHO ARE YOUR HEROES?

In 1921, Tennessee declared every July 13 to be Nathan Bedford Forrest Day.[8] As of 2007, Tennessee had thirty-two dedicated historical markers linked to Nathan Bedford Forrest throughout the state. In 1973, a large, four-foot-tall bronze bust of Nathan Bedford Forrest was commissioned by the state legislature[9] and in 1978, it was installed in the state capitol.[10]

IMAGINE BEING BLACK IN TENNESSEE

Roughly 17 percent of the population of Tennessee is black.[11] That's more than 1.1 million black people. These black folks live in a state that formally recognizes Nathan Bedford Forrest Day. These black folks live in a state whose state capitol—as of the writing of this book—prominently features a bust of Nathan Bedford Forrest. It's 2021: 20 fucking 21.

The point is, racism was alive and well in Nashville. Luckily, Shymene was the manager and had authority over all hiring decisions. So I was hired. And for the next few years, I worked the floor and did my best to make Shymene proud. I was good at my job. Darn good. In fact, more than once women would walk into Denim and ask if I was working. If Brandie happened to be there, she'd offer to help, and they would say, "No thanks. I'll come back when Tyler is here." Let's just say Brandie wasn't happy about that. At the time, I couldn't understand what the problem was. But Shymene did. Shymene, being a black woman in business, she knew. She always knew. And she always protected me, and she became like an older sister to me.

Years later, Shymene left to take a different job, and not too long after she left, I got a phone call from Brandie that there would be a new manager and that my services at the store would not be needed. I could practically hear her smirking on the other end of the line. I was, and had been for a long time, the best and most reliable salesperson on the floor. What the hell?

I'm not saying this was all rooted in racism, but it feels kinda racisty, Brandie.

The point is: the South is still the South. And being black in the South is still hazardous to your health and/or employment at denim retail stores.

12TH AND PORTER

For the first six months we were in Nashville, all we did was wander around from live venue to live venue, listening to different musical acts. We listened to bands, solo artists, duos, and trios playing country, blues, rock, R & B— and we realized very quickly we were not nearly as good as we thought. So we would go back to our humble apartment and practice, rehearse, and experiment. We put in the hours.

During this time, I realized something about the music industry. As a theater guy, I knew about auditions. In fact, for years, nearly everything I did hinged on auditions. You have mere milliseconds to impress casting directors, to convince them that you are talented and capable. In theater, your success was directly tied to your audition. If you blow your audition, you blow your chance. It's harsh, but that's just how it worked. And I had an instinct that the live music scene in Nashville operated the same way. You had one shot to make an impression. So we had to be ready to carpe the crap out of that diem—if the opportunity came.

And then, it did.

Right off Broadway was a historic club called 12th and Porter, which quickly became one of my favorite places to hang out to listen to music. It was where Keith Urban and Sugarland had been discovered a few years earlier, and the place had a reputation for really caring about the live venue experience. While hanging back at the bar, drinking my iced tea (I didn't start drinking until seven paragraphs ago, after that Tennessee history bit), I overheard the bartender talking to someone about 12 at 12th.

"What's '12 at 12th'?" I asked.

"It's like an open mic night," the bartender said. "Twelve bands get up on stage, one after another. They each get two songs. It's pretty cool."

"How do you…" My voice trailed off for a second. I swallowed hard. "How do you sign up?" I asked.

And with that, Broken Frame booked its first live performance. Now all we had to do was kill it. Because in Nashville, when it comes to live performances, you can suck on stage exactly zero times if you want to make it. The good news was we only had to play two songs, so we chose the two songs that we'd been working on the most. They were our two best songs, and there was little chance we wouldn't stick the landing.

We also had a secret weapon. For the last six months, we had been making friends. So we invited everyone. Dan and Mike invited everyone from the Opryland Hotel. I am naturally pretty gregarious, but I turned into Don King, promoting the ever-loving daylights out of our 12 at 12th show. Of course, I invited Bridget from upstairs. And I told her to bring everyone she knew. I invited every neighbor whose face I recognized from the Nashboro Village apartments. I invited everyone I worked with. Shymene, as the manager, knew a lot of people, too, and also helped me get the word out. There's nothing like having those folks in your corner who you know always got your back.

We were trying to pack 12th and Porter out. And I knew, from my time in theater, that if you have energy in the room, it's contagious. Twelve acts signed up for the 12 at 12th, and for reasons I still don't quite understand, we were assigned the very last spot. Getting through twelve musical acts and twenty-four songs takes a little while. The event started at nine p.m., and as the hours clicked away, I got more and more nervous. Would the energy all fizzle by the time we took the stage? Would we be playing to a half-empty room, trying to pull energy from nothing? It was after midnight when group number eleven—the group right before us—took the stage. I looked around and somehow, the room seemed MORE full. At this point, everyone we'd invited was there. And they'd brought their friends. I saw ten people I knew. Then it was twenty. Then it was fifty. The venue at 12th and Porter was crammed.

Our band walked onto the stage, the emcee introduced us, and Nate counted us off on drums. And that was that. The crowd went nuts. And incredibly, because we were the final act, after we were done playing, the crowd started chanting for an encore. The emcee motioned to us to go ahead with a third song. We went back on stage. I counted us off. One, two, three. We played "Frames Fall," the very first song we ever wrote as a band. We had come a long way from the pink-and-blue couches at Bethany Bible College. The promoter at 12th and Porter said he'd never seen that before at a 12 at 12th—the crowd asking for an encore. He said he wanted to talk to us afterward about playing more on their stage.

And that was the very first time we ever played as a band in Nashville.

And we would never play to an empty room for the rest of our time as a band.

DEAL OR NO DEAL?

For the next few months, we did our best to pick our spots so that when we performed, we'd do a good job, but our home base was 12th and Porter. The management loved us. We'd play videos behind us—clips from movies, various pictures, pieces of art—the goal was to try to set the mood so that the audience didn't just hear the music, but they experienced it.

About five months later, we were playing at a venue called Building 8 in Franklin, Tennessee, and we got a heads-up that some A & R folks would be there. The term "A & R" stands for "Artists and Repertoire," and it's the division of a record company responsible for scouting talent. Like Minor League talent scouts for a baseball team, they always have their eyes open for musical acts and musicians to bring into the company.

Now, Broken Frame had something going for us: our band had a black male lead singer (me, in case you weren't paying attention). This definitely was not the norm and made us stand out. We played our set in front of the crowd, and afterward, an A & R executive approached us after the show. He was working for a Christian record label, and he pulled us aside and said that his label wanted to talk to us. They wanted to sign us.

By the end of the weekend, we were meeting as a band at the record label's corporate offices in Nashville, and at the end of our meeting, they slid a developmental contract across the table to us. We took the contract home to review it. Once we were back at our apartment, we all sat around staring at one another.

As our CEO, I knew we were all in over our head. I knew that we didn't know anything and needed some help.

I had someone Google "record deal contract lawyer Nashville." A woman's name popped up first. We all piled in the car and went to downtown Nashville to her offices. I later found out that she was one of the preeminent contract lawyers in Nashville. Our band sat down around a conference table as she looked over the contract we'd handed her.

"There is only one thing worse than not having a record contract," she said.

"What's that?" I said.

"Having a bad contract," she said. We all held our breath.

"And this is not a bad contract," she said.

We exhaled. It was not a bad contract.

"It's a terrible contract," she finished.

We left the office of the lawyer and went back to our apartment.

This wasn't a good contract. It wasn't going to make us rich.

But there was another problem, one we felt deep in our bones.

There was a good chance this record label—or any record label—wasn't going to like the kind of music we were writing. At the time (and even now) there was a very particular mold in Christian music, with certain sounds, certain themes, and even certain lyrics that were acceptable. And if you doubt me, go ahead and think about all the top-selling, chart-topping leading Christian artists with a song that addresses racism or injustice in the past ten years. There are a few. But not a lot. There's not a lot of room for that. And there was no room for Counting Crows in contemporary

Christian music back then, either. Our spiritually infused alternative rock sound was too Christian for most secular audiences, and too secular for most Christians.

We didn't want to play the financial game of trying to find out what was popular in the secular market and then replicate it with a fine Christian veneer. We didn't want to be a Christian knock-off of Hootie and the Blowfish. As we talked, we all slowly came to the same uncomfortable conclusion: it was highly likely that the music we were trying to make and what a record label would want were simply not the same.

And in that moment, we made a decision, collectively as a band, with one mind and heart. We weren't going to sign the contract as it was. After going back and forth, we signed a limited developmental contract with the record company to test the waters of our partnership. We released two songs with them, but both sides realized pretty quickly this was a partnership that wasn't going to work for all the reasons we talked about above. So, we parted ways.

There were no hard feelings; we just had to be the band we felt we needed to be and write the kinds of songs we needed to write. Let the chips fall where they may.

DON'T QUIT YOUR DAY JOB

For the next few years, we all kept working our day jobs and played gigs together as often as we could. We had a quarterly show at 12th and Porter that was a great creative outlet. And our band shifted members. Nate, God bless him, moved out of apartment 1482 and not much later quit the band.

We added two members to our band. Rob was an incredible bass player and he was almost equally good on drums. Rob would go on to play bass for many major country acts and just as of recent, my boy was the bass player for the house band for the 2020 CMAs. So yeah, he's dope. And this cat was our drummer.

Dan moved to playing bass, so we needed a lead guitar player. There was a local Christian band called Fusebox, and we snagged theirs—a hilarious, warm Latino dude named Ben. For some reason, Mike started calling him his

"Mijo" and it stuck. To this day, you'd be hard-pressed to find anyone who knows his real name. He's just known as Mijo.

We were always trying to create something as a band. We tried to write music that felt real and authentic to us. We had to write music that connected to our personal stories. And if you can grab fans in Music City, USA—if you can do something musically significant in Nashville—then you are definitely doing something right.

THIS CHANGES EVERYTHING

After a while, we felt like we finally had enough content to fill an album. And we said to one another, "Look, we don't have a record contract, but let's just make a record. Let's make the album we want to make." Because, after all, what was the overall point of creating? Money? Fame? Or was it about the journey of trying to be authentically ourselves, as a band?

I mean, not that we'd turn down money. Ain't nobody about to turn down some dolla dolla bills. Just that it wasn't about that. It had never been about that. So we found enough money to buy studio time and hire a producer and sound engineer. And in the fall of 2007, after months of hard work in the studio, we finally recorded eleven songs for Broken Frame's debut album, which we titled *This Changes Everything*. It's still available anywhere music is streamed. Plug.

We were going to have a CD release party concert. And of course, it was going to be at 12th and Porter. And of course, everyone we knew in the whole city was going to be there. My friend Shannon (remember that name) knew what a big deal this was for me and played an integral part in making sure that my parents flew out to attend the concert. I don't think she really fully knew what a big deal this was for me. Since I'd quit baseball back in eighth grade, my dad hadn't seen me do anything related to the performing arts. He hadn't come to see me in any of my musicals, or any play or concert. And even though I had now been in this band for the past twelve years, this would be my dad's first time ever seeing me play.

Right before the concert, the five of us stood together at the side of the stage. I looked at Mike and thought about that moment in California by the van where we decided to keep going with Broken Frame. Now, we were here.

The venue at 12th and Porter was packed to the back wall, and you could practically feel heat from the bodies. As we were announced, the five of us walked onto the stage.

I am telling you.

I have stood in front of crowds. I have walked on stages for musicals and plays and all manner of dramas.

But there is nothing like walking onto a stage in front of a live crowd with your band. The group, the team that you toiled with as you wrote every chord and every lyric of every song. The group, the team that you practiced with until the late hours of the night. The group, the team that became like brothers. Co-collaborators. Co-performers. Co-creators. There is just nothing like it.

As we walked off the stage, I looked out at the crowd and made eye contact with my dad. I didn't know what kind of reaction I'd get from him. I realized I was still a lot like that little boy who'd hit the game-winning home run for my dad. Did I still really need his validation as much now as I had then? "Boy," he said shaking my hand. "You did good."

A few months later, at Christmas, I went home to visit my parents in Las Vegas, and I overheard my father in his Alabama-themed man cave, talking to his friends. "Oh, you should have seen him," he said, bragging to his boys. "There were all of these people, so many people. The girls loved him. The guys loved him. He had the whole crowd in the palm of his hand." My dad's voice was brimming with pride. I knew it wasn't likely he would ever say those things directly to me. Why? I don't know, a different generation, I guess. But you know what, he was trying. And it was enough for me.

"Boy, you did good." Four words that contained a universe.

I thought about how far away from Santa Cruz we were. Like Dorothy, taken from her home by a whirling tornado and dropped in a strange new land, we had come to Nashville. The yellow brick road we'd been following was a dream of creating something, and we'd done that. But just like Dorothy, I'd discovered that "meeting the Wizard"—which seemed like the ultimate goal—wasn't really all it was cracked up to be. It wasn't the destination that was ultimately important—it was the people I'd met along the way.

I'd found a brain when we met Mijo and Rob, who made us so much smarter and better as artists.

I'd found courage when I met Shymene, my sister who taught me how to navigate a new world where the color of my skin was going to matter far more than it ever had.

I'd found a heart when I met Bridget, whose friendship and kindness were a never-waning constant in this new town. Without her, I don't know if I'd have made it.

I don't know how, in this analogy, I ended up as a six-foot-two, dreadlocked Dorothy. But here we are. But you get what I am saying. We weren't in Kansas anymore. There was no place like home. And somehow, improbably, Nashville had become our home.

I'll never forget that night. For as long as I live.

And there, in the venue at 12th and Porter, surrounded by my closest friends, my parents, and my band, performing deeply personal songs from the album we'd labored for years to create, I felt like everything in my life finally made sense.

My life was finally together.

I was finally together.

Until I wasn't.

CHAPTER 15

THE BENCH

No one, no one, no one
Can get in the way of what I feel.
For you.
—Alicia Keys, "No One"

Sometime after Broken Frame's album release, my life took a dramatic turn when a man named Harry made an unusual request of me.

Harry was a pastor at the church I attended, which we'll call Nashville Christian Church. That's not the actual name of the church, but the name doesn't matter. The story does.

Harry was an older, white-haired white dude with the heart of a saint. Harry trafficked in extreme love, the kind that made people uncomfortable. Harry was the kind of dude who kicked it with homeless people under the bridge, handing out "socks and smokes" because those were the items most requested by the homeless. Harry had an edge to him, too, telling folks in our church to "get up off your ass and help those who don't have as much as you." And no one argued with him because nobody wanted his job.

Well, it came to Harry's attention that East Nashville Magnet High School needed some help. East was an under-resourced, under-performing school in our area where about 94 percent of the student body was black, and

93 percent of the student body qualified for free lunch. Harry—because he's awesome—asked the high school how the church could help, and the head coach chimed in and asked if the church could bring a pregame dinner for the struggling football team. Harry agreed and asked if we could say a few words before dinner to spiritually encourage the kids.

So Harry cooked dinner for the whole football team and asked me to come along to say some words. Look, I'm not saying that Harry invited me because I'm black, but Harry invited me because I'm black. Good call, Harry.

FRIDAY NIGHT LIGHTS

Hanging out with the team at East reminded me of my time at Rancho. When I looked at those kids, I saw myself. I had been an athlete, so I got that world. I knew what it was like to want to win. But I was also someone who could make a current topical joke, unlike Harry, who thought Snoop Dogg was related to Charlie Brown and Woodstock. After dinner, someone started banging out a beat on the table, starting a cypher (white people translation: an informal freestyle rap competition).

I walked up. "All right, who got bars?" And the kids were like, "Whaaaa." And as we battled, I'm gonna be honest, I got emotional. I thought about how far I'd come from the playground back at Jim Bridger Junior High where I used to do this as a kid. And now, here I was. I don't know, I just connected.

After dinner, the head coach asked the team to thank the church for the food, and the grateful boys exploded in applause. Then he asked me to say a few words.

I realized I had exactly one minute to catch their attention before they tuned out.

I opened with a story about my childhood, about a time when my two friends and I formed a rap group for the eighth grade talent show. During the performance, I was the last one on the mic, because I was the best emcee. But right before my verse, I tried to hype the crowd up by dancing. This was not what we'd rehearsed. I tried to do the caterpillar, a move when you dive to the floor and move like a worm.

I don't know if I just didn't time it right, or if I was just too hype and had too much adrenaline running through my system, but I launched myself into the air and came down way too fast and basically busted my chin onto the stage floor.

The boys howled with laughter as I described seeing stars and trying to take the microphone, but unable to rap because I had just given myself a stage two concussion.

"Now bow your heads with me," I said, and confused looks went around, as heads politely bowed.

"I didn't even know we were having church right now," said an assistant coach, Brian Waite, who was a compact black man built like a wrecking ball.

And they didn't. Because I had snuck church in. I went on to talk about the danger of overconfidence, and how if you let your ego go, you'll end up in ruin. I quoted an ancient Hebrew proverb, using the New Tyler Merritt (NTM) translation:

> *Folks with big egos fall flat on their faces,*
> *but humble people will stand tall.*

We chatted about braggadocious people, and how irritating it is to deal with them. As I talked, I saw Coach Waite put down his charts and plays and look straight at me. He'd tell me later, "I've heard hundreds of pregame speeches, but I knew from the start that you weren't afraid to keep it real with these kids."

"Bro, these kids come from the real world, and deal with real issues," I said. "I have to be real with them. You feel me?"

"Bet," Coach Waite said.

After my talk, I prayed for safety, humility, and for the team not to be filled with ego. The LORD heard a brotha because they lost that game by thirty-four points. For the rest of the season, I came out with Harry to East to speak. I let them get to know the real me, as I asked the same of them. It was the highlight of my week, a lot of weeks.

The next season, Coach Waite became the head coach for East. He called me to tell me that he'd gotten the job.

"Yo, congrats," I said.

"The first thing we're going to need is for you to be a part of this team," he told me.

For Coach Waite, like all excellent coaches, football was not just about football. It was a chance to learn about life. He knew that a lot of the young men on that team didn't have an active, loving father at home, so he and the other coaches had to play that role. This was bigger than Xs and Os—it was about helping young men mature.

"I need you for that heart component, Tyler," he told me. So, every Friday, I spoke to that team—at home games and away games. I was becoming part of the team.

SMELLS LIKE TEEN SPIRIT

Driving home from that first night at East, Harry turned to me.

"You really know what you're doing with these students," he said. "You have a gift."

Which is why, eight months later, I wasn't too surprised when Harry called me. He told me that our church was losing its youth pastor and needed someone to fill in as interim for the summer. Now if you'll recall, I had just gotten fired from Denim, so a brotha needed some work.

But an interim youth pastor?

Me?

With the title "pastor" in front of my name.

What?

"This is the right move for you and for the church," my friend Shannon said.

Which brings me to Shannon, who holds such a significant place in my life.

THE KEENLY IMPROBABLE STORY
OF SHANNON

I met Shannon when she was just a kid. She was the daughter of Dr. Dan Albrecht, who taught Old Testament at Bethany and was arguably the best professor on that campus. When Broken Frame would be rehearsing in the chapel, she'd be the high school girl in the back row, just hanging out.

A few years after I graduated, while I was still living in California, I was at a local grocery store, probably buying pasta, and I came around the corner, and Shannon was there with her friend.

"Hey, Tyler, remember me!" she said. "I'm at Bethany now," she said, as I slowly pieced together that she was Dr. Albrecht's daughter.

"Oh, cool, cool," I said. And then I said something to try to be polite. "We'll have to hang out sometime," I said. And then I nodded to her roommate and turned to go.

"Yeah, totally," Shannon said.

And that probably should have been the end of the story. With any normal person, it would have been. But Shannon was not a normal person.

The next Saturday, I was in my apartment with my two roommates, Amy and Todd from Theater Central. We had been invited to go see a movie—an arthouse film. I didn't know anything about it but agreed to go. As we were getting ready, there was a knock at our door.

"Is Tyler here?" I heard a voice say. I looked around. I wasn't expecting anyone. I went into the living room, and there in the doorway was Shannon.

"Hey," she said, smiling brightly.

"Hey," I said, genuinely confused. "What are you doing here?"

"You said we should hang out sometime!" she said.

"I...did?" I said, genuinely wondering not only when I said that, but how she knew where I lived.

"Hey. Aren't you Dr. Albrecht's daughter?" Todd said.

"Yeah. So, what are you guys up to?" Shannon said, as though this wasn't super weird behavior. How did she get my address again? What was happening? Amy must have read my face.

"Oh, we would love to hang out, but we're actually heading out to a movie," Amy said.

"Awesome. I'm down. What are we seeing?" Shannon said.

We all looked at one another. What the fresh hell was going on?

"I actually don't know," I said, not lying. "Some arthouse film, I guess."

"Well, let's hope it's good," Shannon said.

"Yes, let's," said Todd, shrugging.

And with that, we left to go see the movie with Shannon in tow. That singular event changed my life. And pretty soon, it became clear that Shannon was dope. From that day forward, Shannon became part of our core group of friends and—more important—she became one of my best friends.

When we moved to Nashville, she came to visit us. After she graduated, she decided to move to Nashville. Her dad knew a few people who worked at Nashville Christian Church, and she got a job working for them. And to this day, she lives only a few houses away from me. And that's how Shannon became my ride-or-die homie. But, now, back to the story of how I—Tyler Merritt—became a (gulp) pastor.

SMELLS LIKE TEEN SPIRIT (CONTINUED)

"This is the right move for you and for the church," Shannon said. She knew the youth department could use some help. She also knew I was unemployed, and that I'd bring energy to this group of kids.

Now, it's time to talk about the general church culture at Nashville Christian Church and how that played out in the youth group. Nashville Christian Church was a church located in the heart of downtown Nashville, in a historic district and beautiful old church building. But almost everyone who attended the church did not live downtown but drove in from the surrounding suburbs. The staff was all white people. The congregation was almost all white people. But the area around the church was not. Less than one mile away, there was a poor, almost exclusively black community called Edgehill that had low-income apartments, liquor stores, and broken-down homes with boarded-up windows. Nowadays, that area is completely gentrified, and the homes go for $900,000. Yea, capitalism! But back then, Edgehill was a struggling, low-income, urban black area.

And nobody from Edgehill attended Nashville Christian Church, which was literally right down the street.

The youth building for the church was across the street. I walked in and saw twenty white (mostly) homeschooled kids hanging out on beanbag chairs. As I would find, this group was a dynamic group of kids, but they had created their own clubhouse—an environment for them and by them, complete in and of itself.

One of the kids ran up to me. His name was Nick, and I'd met him a number of years ago when Broken Frame had played at a youth camp. He was a tall, lanky, piano-playing music-head eighth grader back then, and now he was a tall, lanky, piano-playing music-head tenth grader. He ran up to me, excited as a puppy.

"Are you going to be…our youth pastor?" he asked.

"I'm here to help over the summer, buddy," I said, unable to call myself a "pastor."

"Nice!" Nick said, then paused. "Man, are things gonna change around here."

But neither of us knew the half of it.

THE TIMES, THEY ARE A-CHANGIN'

The first hint I had that things were going to be weird was my first full week of work at Nashville Christian Church. The family pastor, Lon, called me in and told me that there was a mission trip to Mexico.

"Almost all the kids are going on the trip," Lon said. "So don't take it personal when nobody shows up."

"Well, there's a whole lot of kids right down the street," I said.

"What?" Lon said.

"Down the street. By the Edgehill Apartments," I explained. "I drive by a whole mess of kids on the way in here."

"Oh," Lon, said. "Yeah, those aren't really our kids."

I thought—and still think—that was a curious thing to say.

The next day, I started recruiting. Remember where I had come from. I was in the first class of drama kids at the Academy. Bethany didn't have a theater department, or a rock band, when I got there. My name is Tyler, and I build things. I was going to build, create, grow a thing. Build a family, like I had before.

The first thing I had to do was fix the environment. Those beanbag chairs had to go, man. I brought in chairs, cleared off and repainted the stage, and installed some stage lights. I recruited as many people as I could. We got that youth room into tip-top shape in no time.

The only thing that was missing was teenagers. But I knew where to find those. I walked down the street to the basketball courts and started talking to kids. I found out from Harry that on Saturday mornings, our children's department would go out to the park near the Edgehill Apartments and do a program for the elementary-aged kids. It was summer, so we played games in the field and we brought Popsicles. So many Popsicles! But man, the kids loved it. I figured the kids *had* to have older brothers and sisters, so I went out just to meet people. I told every teen (or anyone who even looked like a teen) the same thing:

Yo. The church up the road? We have a thing on Wednesday nights at seven p.m. You should come by and check it out.

I must have said that 11,000 times.

Over the next few Wednesday nights, we held youth services, and students from the Edgehill neighborhood came by, and the other adult youth leaders and I took time to get to know them. I played some videos on the screen, gave a brief message, and we ordered pizza. It was going…okay…until I accidentally hit the jackpot.

I decided to play a game I called "Win Tyler Merritt's Money." I bet a couple kids the entirety of the cash in my pocket if they could beat me at a challenge. I called some kids up, and they competed against me in a dance-off. One kid clearly beat me, doing the Michael Jackson "Billie Jean" moonwalk dance, and I gladly reached into my pocket and gave him all nineteen dollars that was in there. The kids went nuts—you would have thought I was giving away free cars.

"I didn't know you could go to church and come home with money," the kid said. He later thanked me, saying he was gonna buy some snacks for his kid brothers on the way home. I told him, "Look, I'm glad you got money, but what we do here on Wednesday nights is worth so much more than that," I said. "I hope to see you next week."

The next week we had even more kids. And I played another rousing round of "Win Tyler Merritt's Money." This time, it was a hot summer night in the South, so we had a contest to see who could leave their foot in a five-gallon bucket of ice water the longest. I had to stop the game because I thought this kid was going to get frostbite. That determined kid took home all my money, which was twenty-seven dollars this time.

For the low, low cost of forty-six dollars, I had bought enough word-of-mouth advertising to spread through the entire teenage community at Edgehill. What. A. Deal.

But not everyone was happy. After the core kids from the youth group got back from Mexico, they experienced another sort of culture shock. Their old youth room now looked completely different, in more than one way. Now I had a new problem. Not only "how to get the kids from the community nearby to come" but also how to forge a community from kids who were very different from one another.

For example, some of the kids thought that playing games in church was inappropriate. One time, one of the girls from the original youth group won "Win Tyler Merritt's Money," and after the service, she came up to me.

"You don't have to bribe me and the kids like me to come to church," she said, handing me back the twenty-dollar bill I'd given her earlier.

"Then take this money and give it to someone who needs it," I said, looking around the room. "This isn't about you."

Like I said, this wasn't easy. The white kids didn't get the kids from Edgehill ("You cuss too much!"), and the Edgehill kids resented how rich the suburban white kids were. It is never easy to break down both socioeconomic and racial barriers. That doesn't happen overnight. But I figured if I could get these students to see all they had in common, and slowly get them to become actual friends, then the rest would take care of itself. My whole life up until this point had been a testimony of the power of proximity to break down barriers and forge real community. I knew it worked. It just needed time.

But that doesn't mean it was easy. It also wasn't easy for me, personally.

After one Wednesday night service, I discovered that someone had stolen my backpack from the sound booth, with my Bible and my iPad in it. I knew exactly which kid stole it, too. And, man, I felt betrayed. I wanted to confront this kid, grab him by his shoulders and shake him like a Polaroid picture, and yell: "What the hell, man!! After all I do for you, every week, you come in here and steal my iPad?"

But—as a pastor—I couldn't just blast this kid. The thing was, I knew exactly why this kid stole it. It was simple math. He needed to take care of his mom and siblings at any cost. In his mind, I could afford to lose an iPad. I was collateral damage. He was just trying to take care of his mama. That I can understand.

I had a new choice. Condemn and push this kid away. Or lean in, show mercy, and work for reconciliation.

I chose the latter. I went over to the kid and took him to the side. I let him know that I knew what he'd done, but that I wasn't mad about it, and I forgave him. I then opened my wallet and gave him a wad of cash that I'd collected from not only myself but from the other youth leaders.

"Every single one of these adult leaders, they willingly gave me this money to give to you," I told him. "You don't ever have to steal from us. We are your family, too. We'll take care of you."

I don't know if I did many things right that first year of doing youth ministry, but I felt like I got some of those moments right. But don't get it twisted: it wasn't a walk in the park.

Another thing that wasn't easy was navigating through the hordes of now angry white parents who didn't like how the youth group was changing. Again, none of this was easy. But nothing worth anything ever is.

Soon, the vast majority of my focus, time, and creativity was being funneled not into Broken Frame but this growing community of teenagers. I lived and breathed for Wednesday nights, and as a result, the band deeply suffered. I admit that. But something was shifting in me. For all those years that I had been using my voice, in a way, I felt that now I was finally finding it.

Summer turned to fall. The church offered me a job. After all, I was growing the program, and the numbers of teens showing up was six times what it used to be. And so, for the next several years, I labored to build a community. We all worked to bridge the natural divides within the group and learn to grow and serve and love together. Together, with a team of incredible adult volunteers, we built something really special on Wednesday nights.

Until it all came crashing down.

HOW DO I SAY "NO" TO THIS?

I know I've mentioned this before, but one of the most difficult parts of the musical *Hamilton* is watching a man with so much giftedness and promise—with so much to offer the world—crash and burn because of the cracks in the foundation of his character. Alexander Hamilton was a brilliant man whose flaws eventually caused his downfall.

When you're watching the show, you know it's coming. But that doesn't make it any easier. As you know, my "fatal flaw" was my woundedness when it came to females, my inability to trust, and my tendency to sabotage relationships. This didn't stop when I graduated from college. And maybe, like in *Hamilton*, you've been hoping I could avoid reaping what I'd sown. But that's not how things work.

After college I went from broken relationship to broken relationship to broken relationship—and each time I detonated things by cheating or being unfaithful. It was the same cycle:

1. Get close to a woman.
2. Realize my heart was at risk.
3. Take defensive measures to make sure I wouldn't be the one to get hurt.

Well, this pattern resulted in a lot of heartache and a trail of women who had been betrayed by my treasonous behavior.

Now that I was working as a pastor, those deep issues didn't just magically go away. Like Godzilla, frozen in the ice under the Arctic, they were going to surface at some point. And there'd be hell to pay.

Her name was Nina, and she was an adult volunteer who worked with the youth. She'd been a part of the church since before I took the job. She was hysterically funny, driven, and quickly became a key leader in our group. But we both quickly realized—as two grown, adult single people—that there was a lot of physical attraction between us.

We were both in our early thirties, and not married and…well…the chemistry was real. And before long, we were entangled in an on-again, off-again sexual relationship. Let me be clear here: I knew it wasn't right. It was a shortcut for me to fulfill my individual needs. Messed up, I know.

You see my mind was tellin' me no.

But my body?

My body?

My body was telling me yes.

Sometimes, people try to meet a legitimate need in an illegitimate way. I knew using Nina to fill some sort of need that I had, without any real concern for what might be happening to her, was wrong. It was akin to using a person for their body. Nina and I would get together, vow to never do that again, and then, a few months later, come right back to it. This pattern went on for a while. And we were careful to keep it a tight, tight secret.

Eventually, as time progressed, I started to realize that every time we got together, she'd want more exclusivity from me, from our relationship. It wasn't just sex with no strings attached. After multiple times of trying to end this, finally, I told her, "Nina. We simply cannot do this anymore."

And that was that.

Six months later, Nina was still processing everything. She told her friend, an older person on staff, in confidence about the turmoil she was feeling because of the ending of her "relationship" with me. She told me she had done this, and I was fine with it, saying, "It's your story to tell." And it was.

But, as often happens in these kinds of situations, that staff member told other people, who told other people, and a few days later, I was called into the senior pastor's office.

But here's the thing.

The church didn't have the foggiest idea how to deal with my lapse in judgment. They didn't have the theology to deal with this situation properly. And I know. Because I had been on staff for a while now, and I had seen some things.

A few years earlier, a prominent member of the church (who for the sake of the story we'll call John Smith) had his wife leave him in a messy divorce. But nobody asked the question, "Wait. Is this dude okay? Think about what he's going through." This dude's arms had just gotten pulled off, and nobody thought to give him first aid. Instead, they basically said, "Hey man, pull yourself up, dress yourself, and for God's sake, try not to bleed everywhere."

Months (maybe it was years?) later, John (now a single man) got romantically involved with one of his kid's elementary school teachers. Well, the woman didn't handle John's attempts to end the relationship well. One evening, she walked into a board meeting, and in front of half the staff and the entire board of the church, she confronted John and told every sordid detail about what had happened in their relationship. She then turned, walked out, and slammed the door. Caught red-handed, John did what he had to do.

He denied it.

He claimed she made all of it up, that it was revenge for him rebuffing her advances. In his version, she was Potiphar's wife and he was the virtuous Joseph. And the board and the staff believed him, summarily dismissing her claims without even bothering to do an investigation. And John kept his job. Because who isn't going to believe a pastor? Right? The point is, John knew something I did not. He knew that in some sectors of the church world, there's no coming back from sexual misconduct. Sexual sin was seen as a different sort of sin, different than greed, or abusive narcissism, or even a cocaine habit. Those sins? Those can be rehabilitated. But sexual sin was a sin so dark it meant you were rotten to the core. And because of that, no one will help you. You have to hide, and you have to lie. John knew that.

So, when I was confronted by the same church leaders, I had a model for how to handle accusations of sexual impropriety. I could have lied, like he had. I had that option. After all, I had lied to women. I had lied to protect myself. But this was a chance to tell the truth, and walk through this time with the church, like I had with many of my students from across the street.

I told the truth. After all, what's that saying? When you tell the truth, everything works out.

Yeah.

Except when it doesn't.

THE BEGINNING OF MY END

Like I said before, Nashville Christian Church didn't have the ability to think well about human sexuality, as evidenced by the way they had dealt with their worship pastor. Eventually, I was called into a room with the senior staff of the church. Lon was there. John Smith was there, too. So were a few other men.

"First of all, we only want the best for you," they said.

"And I take full responsibility for any hurt I caused in this situation," I said. "Whatever Nina said I did, I'm gonna be honest with you, I probably did. I need you to know I own that."

"This is a safe space to talk," one of them said.

"In fact," Lon said, "I'm not just the leader of your department, but I'm the family counselor here. You can tell me everything."

And I believed him—which was, looking back at it, probably one of the biggest mistakes of my entire life.

I didn't know how this would go, but I was eager to talk about what was going on with me. I talked about how I was constantly self-sabotaging my romantic relationships. I shared briefly about Kelley and Joanne and all my past failures—and wondered aloud how all that might tie into this mess with Nina. I knew I had hurt people.

When I was done, I was almost in tears. I had bared my soul, vulnerably sharing some sensitive parts of my life and heart. They looked at me.

"So," Lon said, carefully, "at any point in time did you touch any of the children."

"WHAAATT??" I said incredulously.

"Did you have sexual contact with any of the students?" Lon asked.

"What are you talking about! NO!" I said, leaping to my feet almost involuntarily.

Here's what I wanted to say: "I had a consensual sexual relationship with another consenting adult, you sicko." But shame, guilt, and deep embarrassment caused me to say nothing.

"Because to us, it sounds like you have the markings of a sexual addict," someone said.

"Someone who cannot control their sexual urges," someone else said.

I couldn't believe what I was hearing.

"I had a consensual relationship…with an adult," I said.

"We're just worried about the kids," someone said.

I shook my head. Was this a joke? Was this really happening?

The men explained that I would need to take some time off from the youth group while they got this all sorted out. They told me to come back in a few days, after they'd had time to think about things. And with that, I exited the church.

THE BENCH

I walked out of that church, staggered out down the stairs, shell-shocked. I felt about as low as a person could feel. First, I was angry. I wanted to go back in there and tell John Smith, "Hey, bro. I could have just denied all this like you did. Seems like it worked out okay for you, huh?"

Yeah, there was anger. But mostly, there was a new feeling.

Shame.

I kept thinking back to that moment when they asked me that question. I wanted to throw up.

They treated me like a sexual predator. I realized what I was feeling. It was the feeling of condemnation. It's the very thing I'd promised to never make one of my students feel. Ever. Because it feels like shit.

My sins and brokenness had been weaponized against me.

You're broken, Tyler.
You are disqualified.
You cannot help our youth.
Your brokenness is all we see now.
Your identity is now this wrong thing you've done.

A panel of grown white men had judged me and found me wanting. For the next few weeks, my job was on hold. And I didn't know what to do, so every day, I went for a long walk around the Percy Priest Lake Park. And that's when I discovered the bench.

At the end of a grassy point, overlooking the J. Percy Priest Dam, there was a simple bench along the path that was nearly always empty. I would walk to this bench, and sit down, and look out over the water. These were dark times for me. And for the next several weeks, as I walked around the dam, I had a constant companion by my side.

Shame.

It yelled at me. It yelled loud. And from the moment I woke up, until the moment I slipped into unconsciousness, it was pretty much the only voice I heard. And it was a cruel companion. It told me, with certainty, that:

I was broken.
Beyond repair.
It was hopeless.
I was unlovable.
Worthless
All I had built was a farce.
Meaningless.
A lie.

That I was now disqualified.

Done.

Even as I write this, my heart swells with pain. I can't put into words the isolation that I felt in those moments. I sat on that bench, a broken and defeated man. At so many points, I just pulled my hoodie over my face and wept. I don't know if I was praying, in those moments. Mostly, I was sobbing. Just pain falling out of me. I guess I was praying, even if I didn't have words. All I wanted was to get rid of this shame, to be free from this crushing sense that I was broken, irrevocably.

MOM. AGAIN. (OF COURSE.)

My mom has stupid-crazy mom-intuition. Even to this day, there will be times where I will be sick as a dog, and nobody else could possibly know, and my mom will call me out of nowhere. I don't know what it is. Just black mom magic, I guess. And as I sat on that bench one day, dying inside, my phone rang. It was my mother. Of course it was. I broke down and, through tears, I told her everything. I told her about Nina. I told her about our broken relationship. I told her how the church found out. I told her how I was being painted as a sexual deviant who was a threat to the youth group.

Here's what I expected, honestly, to happen. I thought my mother would pat me on the head metaphorically, and tell me, "This too shall pass, Tyler." Because here's what you need to know: black people have been through too much stuff for my mom to blow a gasket over this. But that is not what I encountered. My mom got angry. Like, red-hot angry.

"Tyler, son, you listen to me and you listen closely," my mother said, with a steel in her voice I had not heard in a long, long while.

"Forget that man, Tyler," she said, practically hissing. "Forget that man."

"People make mistakes," she continued. "This is not your first, and—hear me, son—it will not be the last. You are still my child. You are still the boy I raised. I will not sit here and let this man—this white man—this stranger—define my son. I will not let him define who you are. Do not believe those lies. Do not let this man define you. Do you hear me, son?"

I could hear her, but only barely, because I was sobbing. This was the first time in weeks that anybody had confronted that loud voice of shame and dared to shout back.

Quiet, you.
Shut up!
You are a liar.
This does not change Tyler's life.
This does not change Tyler's effectiveness.
This does not change his worth.

I sat on that bench, soaking it all in, gulping it down like a man emerging from a desert. Sometimes, you just need to hear your mama's voice reminding you of who you are.

VOICES CARRY

There were other voices of hope and life that soon entered. During this time, I continued to go over to Bridget and Scott's house every Sunday night for dinner. At this point, my adopted niece Zoe was three and nephew Declan was one. When I entered the house, Zoe would run to me and scream, "Uncle TY TY," and demand that I pick her up, and she would squeeze me with her little arms as though I was her favorite person in the world.

I can't tell you how healing this was. Because during this time, I had powerful, grown men in a church telling me I was sinful, beyond repair. And dammit if I didn't almost believe them. I might have believed them if I hadn't seen the unconditional love in those two kids' eyes. They didn't see me as a woeful failure. To them, I was beloved Uncle Ty Ty. Love heals.

There were other voices of grace, too. There was my brother and band-mate Mike. And Shannon. Shannon might have suffered the most collateral damage. The church asked her to stop volunteering in the youth group because she was close friends with me. At that point, Shannon had a choice to make, so she did the only thing a ride-or-die would do. She quit. And then she got a much better job. I cannot tell you what a gift it is to be able to share the depths of your brokenness with someone, and have that person say, "Don't worry. I'm not going anywhere." That love feels…

Well.

It feels a lot like being loved by God, I would imagine.

THE FINAL WORD

After a few weeks, the leadership of the church called me in to "talk."

"The way we see it, Tyler," they said, "you have two options. You can go through the following procedures that we've outlined here…"

I'm not sure about all the specifics they were expecting of me, but in that moment it really didn't matter.

I looked out the window of the office, across the street to the youth building. I thought about the youth group we'd built over the past few years. I thought about that kid who stole the iPad. I thought about the gay kids who had come up to me because they didn't have anyone to talk to, but I seemed safe. I thought about the messages I'd shared, about the never-stopping, never-ending, always-and-forever kind of love that Jesus showed. To everyone. Even folks who didn't deserve it. I thought about how much I'd tried to convey to these teens that their failure was never final. I wanted to be a part of that kind of church.

I didn't see much resemblance to that community in this office, surrounded by these men.

In fact, I didn't trust that any of these men even knew me, let alone had my best interest at heart.

"I'll leave," I said, interrupting them.

"You sure?" one asked.

"Yes," I said. I thanked them for the chance to serve the last few years and walked to the door.

"One more thing," someone said. "We're going to need you to stop speaking to the football team on Fridays, since we're affiliated with that. We hope you understand."

I nodded. And with that, I walked out, and stopped being a pastor.

WINTER ALWAYS COMES BEFORE SPRING

That evening, I went for a walk and, as the sun set, found my way back to the bench. This was my bench now. It was the bench where I'd been broken, and the bench where I was slowly being rebuilt. I wondered what was next. And as I sat there, the phone rang. I looked down at the number. It was Coach Waite, from East Nashville Magnet High School.

I sighed and picked up the phone. I explained to him that the church had just fired me.

"Why?" he said, shocked.

"I had an inappropriate relationship with a woman, and I was let go," I said.

"And?" he said.

"And they don't want me to go out and speak to your team at the dinners," I said.

"Yeah, cool. We don't need dinner," he said. "But we need you."

I sat there, genuinely shocked. I had told him I'd been fired, right?

"Look, I can always get different food," Coach Waite said. "What I can't get is another Tyler Merritt."

"I guess I'll see you on Friday," I said.

"Damn straight, you will," he said.

That next Friday, Coach Waite told me, "You walked with us when we weren't strong. Now let us walk with you when you aren't." In the end, I spoke every Friday night to Coach Waite's teams for ten years. I was there when the team was 2–8. And when the team was one of the best in the state. Yeah, I graduated from a high school in Vegas, but I think I'll always be an East Nashville Eagle.

But that evening, as the sun set on my time as a pastor and on that season of my life, I sat on my bench, looking out over the water. I'd lost a lot, and a lot of it was my fault, the result of my own brokenness. But I'd also gained a lot. I felt like I had grown a lot, like some sort of surgery had been done on me, and that I was healing—or at least on the way to healing. And I had quite a few things going for me. Friends. Zoe and Declan. My mom. A good coach in my corner. Some stellar best friends. And God.

A song came over my headphones. I sang it, out loud, with no one around, at the top of my lungs, tears streaming down my face.

No one.
No one.
No one.
Can get in the way of what I'm feeling for you.

Was I singing it to God? Or was He singing it over me?
Maybe a little bit of both.
Yes.
Both.

CHAPTER 16

THE TYLER MERRITT PROJECT

People fail to get along because they fear each other;
they fear each other because they don't know each
other; they don't know each other because they have not
communicated with each other.
—Martin Luther King Jr.

Our lives begin to end the day we become silent
about things that matter.
—Martin Luther King Jr.

BACK TO LIFE. BACK TO REALITY.

Immediately after getting fired from the church, I decided I simply wanted anonymity, so I took a job running the denim department at a store at a mall way out in the suburbs. It was a good half hour away from downtown Nashville. I just wanted to get away from everything and be as far away from the church as I could. I was grateful for this job, and this time. I could go, set up the displays, fold some jeans, and clock out. I just wanted a job where people were no longer my business. I guess I basically went into hiding.

It was winter in Nashville. But it was also winter inside me. I was closed up against the harsh cold. Dormant. It's a funny thing about trees and plants: sometimes, when they're dormant, they look completely dead, like sticks in the ground, as though nothing will ever grow ever again. And then, one spring, just when you've stopped looking, there's the appearance of the smallest buds. And then one day, an explosion of color. I guess the lesson is that even in winter, life still makes a way for things to grow. One of my friends from California grew up with vineyards on his property, and he told me that vintners never water the roots of grapevines, but water in the space between the roots so that the water they need is actually three or four feet away. This forces the plant to dig and burrow and grow deep roots so that it will be stronger. Tough times might seem unfair, but they can grow you in ways that would otherwise be impossible. And I didn't know it, but I was being watered three or four feet away, shaping me for what was next.

Now, while I was working at the church, a man in the congregation named Gary had called me. Gary worked at a company called LifeWay, which is the publishing and distribution arm of the Southern Baptist Convention, the largest Protestant denomination in the US. They produce books and curricula for churches. Gary called me up and told me he was working on a project and wrote something with me in mind as a narrator.

So, before all the stuff at the church went down, I went in to do some voice-over work for a video, which was designed to tell kids the story of the Bible. They gave me a script, I learned the lines, I came in, and they filmed me. It was a cool gig. I didn't think much of it, and in fact, didn't even see the final cut.

Well, a little while later, I got a call from Gary. Apparently, this little project had blown up. What I didn't know is that LifeWay markets all their products to churches affiliated with the Southern Baptist Convention, which includes more than 47,000 churches—and this new product quickly became a giant hit. Now, I'm not saying that all of the churches in the Southern Baptist

Convention used this curriculum, but let's just say there were an awful lot of little white kids across the nation who suddenly had a new big, black Sunday school teacher. The project picked up steam, and LifeWay called me in to be the host for more episodes. We did a complete season one. Then season two. Then season three.

Pretty soon, my beautiful black face was being shown to literally hundreds of thousands of kids across the nation. I was the voice—the narrator—of the Bible for them. My friends started tagging pictures of them watching me in their churches—from Shreveport to Sacramento to Scranton. At one point, I got a text from a friend of mine who was teaching English in Korea and said, "I just saw a clip of the Gospel Project for Kids translated into Korean." KOREAN!

CARTOONS WITH JESUS

I think I still dramatically underestimated the reach and impact of what this curriculum meant to people. But I was about to find out. Remember, I was still working in retail, running the denim section at JCPenney, just trying to blend into the background. Around this time, there was a fair deal of national discussion about health care. Who deserves it? Who should pay for it? Et cetera. And so, I found a cartoon of Jesus, standing over someone on a stretcher, and made my own caption that said, "Yes, I'd love to heal you, but can I see your medical insurance card first."

Honestly, I didn't even think it was that controversial. I lived in the city that's the buckle for the Bible Belt, where Jesus is the model for our common humanity. So isn't it fair game to use Jesus to point out that "barriers of bureaucracy" and "concerns about profit" aren't really good reasons to deny hurting (or poor) people the medical care they need? I thought so. People clicked "like" and posted the 😄 emoji, and I didn't think twice about it.

And there's a reason I didn't think twice about it, because that night, my ride-or-die Shannon had secured us tickets to Dave Matthews and Tim Reynolds, who were playing at the Ascend outdoor amphitheater. It was an epic, sold-out concert, and I was marveling at the sheer skill of Dave Matthews's guitar playing and drunken dance moves when my cell phone vibrated in my pocket. It was a text from Gary.

"I don't ever want to see you posting a cartoon with Jesus on social media ever again. Can you assure me that this won't happen again?"

I felt blindsided. I quickly typed back, "Yes," and then stood there, a little upset that Gary had ruined my Dave Matthews Band high. Also, to be clear, when I say "Dave Matthews Band high" I do not mean I was using recreational marijuana—just that I was really, really enjoying the music and live show. Don't get me wrong. There were a lot of people smoking weed around me. And I'm sure there were many people at the concert who had "contact highs." Wait a second. Maybe I was high. Anyway.

The next day, I called Gary, and we chatted about it. He explained how I represented a "brand" at LifeWay, and that I had to be very, very careful with what I posted. Again, it was like I was back at Nashville Christian Church. The mantle was back on my shoulders. And from that moment on, I was incredibly conscious about everything I posted on social media. I made sure my political affiliation box on my profiles were left blank. I thought about everything I posted, like I had my Obama Translator right with me. One time, my ride-or-die Shannon scored us tickets to the concert of the year at the State Farm Arena in Atlanta—Jay-Z. Did I mention that Shannon is really, really good at finding amazing tickets? Sure, we paid through the nose for them, but some things are worth it. And this was worth it.

So, we drove four hours to Atlanta to the sold-out show to watch (arguably) the best rapper of my lifetime put on the show of a lifetime. Black excellence. Opulence. Decadence. Tuxes next to the president. And I was present.

At the concert, I had Shannon snap a picture of me throwing up the ROC pyramid symbol in front of the stage, with Jay-Z looming on the giant screens behind us. In my excitement, I was about to post it on the 'gram, but then my Obama Translator kicked in. I thought, "Wait a second. Can I post this? Perhaps people will think I'm throwing up gang signs. What if they think I support the Illuminati? Or that I don't worship Jehovah because I'm in a concert with a man who calls himself J-Hova. Plus, Jay-Z does say some bad words in his songs…"

Let me make this clear to you. Here I was, a six-foot-two black man, raised on hip-hop, watching my favorite rapper of all time. And in the back of mind, I cannot share this specific black experience with the rest of my world. My mind started racing. I had become incredibly self-conscious. So I didn't post that pic of me at the best rap concert I had—or have ever—been to.

As we drove home, I realized I was now in a new situation. It's true, I no longer worked for a church, but because the Gospel Project had blown up, I had to monitor my public profile in a way that I never had to before. I began to get angry. I had been chastised over a Jesus cartoon that made the incredibly controversial point that Jesus wanted to heal people. All of this was training me—unknowingly—to be the kind of person who never posted anything that could possibly offend anyone. I was like a neutered Pit Bull (the dog, not the rapper) on a chain in the pleasant white man's yard. I was a nice, smiling, non-controversial black man. Tame. Meek. Safe.

I hated it.

THE FIRST AMENDMENT FOR BLACK PEOPLE

Now, at this point in the story, I know that some of you are about to explode. You're putting yourself in my shoes and thinking, "Oh hell naw! Do not be muzzled, my man! If you want to post something, Tyler, you go ahead and post something. As long as it's true, then who cares!"

First Amendment rights of free speech, and all that.

And if you're white, that makes sense. But the rules don't always apply in the same way to white people as they do for black people. And for a long while, for black folk it felt like there really was not such a thing as a First Amendment for us. Hear me out.

Let's go back to my family in Eutaw, Alabama. Remember, my father was a sharecropper in Alabama, whose annual income depended entirely on the sale price at the time of harvest. Both my father and my grandfather would tell stories of being cheated out of fair prices on their harvested corn by local merchants who gave higher, fair prices to white farmers. Why? Because the white men who owned the mill knew that the black farmers had no recourse.

And why did they have no recourse? Well, first there was no legal protection in Eutaw, Alabama, for black folks. What are you going to do? Sue? Bring your case to the white judge who was appointed by the white mayor, who were both friends with the white owner of the white mill? And let's be honest, they were both probably drinking white milk. But seriously, though, black people in the South had been sufficiently taught by the terror of murderous lynchings what happens to black people who fail to hold their tongues.

From 1915 to 1940 throughout the South, lynch mobs targeted African Americans who protested being treated as second-class citizens. If a group of farmers tried to organize to demand, for example, fair weights and measures to be used to weigh their crops so that they were not cheated, whites responded with swift, deadly, and terrifying violence.

One example. In 1935, when my grandfather was a young man, there was a man named Joe "Spinner" Johnson, who was a sharecropper in Perry County, Alabama, which is about forty miles to the east of Eutaw. Johnson, tired of the unfair labor practices, unfair wages, and unjust working conditions started the Alabama Sharecroppers Union.[1] The idea was there was safety and power in numbers. There was not.

Now I wish what I am about to tell you wasn't true, that there weren't eyewitness historical accounts of this event. But there were. One day, Johnson was called in from the field by his white landlord, where he was delivered into the hands of a white gang. The gang tied Mr. Johnson "hog-fashion with a board behind his neck and his hands and feet tied in front of him" and beat him mercilessly.[2] They took him to the jail in Selma, Alabama, where other inmates heard him being beaten and screaming. Mr. Johnson's mutilated body was found several days later in a field near the town of Greensboro—which is about twenty minutes away from Eutaw.

Let's just say the n*gg*rs got the message.

Loud and clear.

The point is NOT that I was undergoing anything even approaching what Mr. Johnson went through. The point is that as a black American, you learn very quickly that the rules do not always apply to you. Not really. If you are a black man, you must learn restraint. Or you will pay the price. Black people cannot be like Karens in a Walmart. That's how you get the police called on you. And that's how you end up dead.

So I had to be careful with my speech.

But like those grapevine roots being watered three to four feet from their base, this time was also growing something—in this case, a larger, broader, far more diverse demographic of people who were following me. But that came with some challenges.

OBERGEFELL V. HODGES
AND TYLER V. FACEBOOK

In 2015, the Supreme Court of the United States decided one of the more important cases (at least in its cultural impact) in recent memory. The court ruled 5–4 that the right to marry was a constitutionally protected right for same-sex couples. The court saw the right to marry as a fundamental individual liberty (under the Fifth Amendment's Due Process Clause, which prevents the government from depriving any citizen of a fundamental right, and the Fourteenth Amendment's Equal Protection Clause, which requires laws to be evenly applied to all citizens for fairness).

Now, this bothered some people a LOT. Including a lot of Christians, for whom same-sex weddings seemed to rewrite the traditional definition of marriage.

This wasn't really a confusing moment for me like it was for a lot of other Christians, mainly because since high school (and especially since my time at the Las Vegas Academy) I have not only had gay friends but have had very close gay friends.

My brother John Bridges has been a part of my whole life story. We used to ride together on the bus to junior high. John was in theater with me at Rancho High School. I recruited him to come with me to the Las Vegas Academy. I brought him over to California with me to go to Bethany. When I was building Theater Central, there were a few non-negotiables, and John being a part of it was one of them. And one day during our senior year, while we were roommates there at Bethany Bible College, John sat on the edge of his bed, and I sat across from him, and he told me that he was gay.

"I've known you ever since we were in elementary school," I said to him. "My mother invites you to our house for Christmas every single year. You are family. You're not like a brother to me. You are a brother to me. This changes nothing."

But as John told me, I also felt sadness. I knew it wasn't going to be easy for him, because sometimes people are horrible to you. I didn't want that for John. He is an amazing person and deserves all the love in the world. And I remember thinking, "Man. I really hope that people aren't cruel to you and that you find people who love you for who you are."

John's not married, but if he were ever to get married, I would be there in a second.

The point is, on the night that the *Obergefell v. Hodges* decision was announced, I wanted to write a post on social media saying something like:

To my brothers and sisters who are gay: I see you! I love you! I am here for you!

But then I started thinking about it. If you thought my posting a cartoon anti-HMO Jesus got a lot of pushback, I can only imagine what writing something that seemed like it was supporting gay people might do in Tennessee. But I obviously had some convictions. As a black man, you might be able to understand why I think equal protection of all citizens under the law is a good thing. You know, because of history. Let me say that louder for the folks in the back: equal protection of all citizens under the law is a good thing. You know, because of history.

Now I had a problem to solve: how could I show support for my close friends who were gay...without getting chewed out about it?

As I walked around the Percy Priest Dam, the idea hit me like the beat at the end of the eighth measure of the intro to "No Diggity." If I posted something every single day on Facebook, celebrating someone I loved and respected, and I just happened to fold a slew of gay folks into the mix, then nobody could be mad about that, right? I mean, I'd just be loving everyone? No diggity. No doubt. So, as the New Year came, I started a project. Every day on the socials, I would choose a person to celebrate and show love to. Every day, I'd write a post explaining what they meant to me and why they were significant. I tagged it #thisiscrazylove2016. Things were looking up. It was summer of 2016. Pokémon GO had united the world. The Olympics were coming to Rio. Everything seemed like it was going well. But I would like to remind you, I was still a black man.

ALTON STERLING

On July 5, 2016, just after midnight, two Baton Rouge Police Department officers named Blane Salamoni and Howie Lake responded to a call[3] that a man in a red shirt who was selling CDs was threatening people with a handgun outside a Triple S Food Mart. Based on bodycam and cell phone video footage, Salamoni and Lake immediately saw Alton Sterling sitting outside the store where he routinely sold CDs and DVDS, wearing a red shirt. They told Sterling to put his hands on a nearby car.[4]

"What I did?" Sterling asked, as the officers grabbed him and pushed him toward a nearby silver car.[5]

"Don't fucking move or I'll shoot your fucking ass, bitch," Salamoni yelled, drawing his weapon. "Don't you fucking move or I'm going to shoot you in your fucking head," he said, while putting his gun to Sterling's head.[6]

The officers instructed Sterling to put his hands on the nearby car, while telling him not to move.

"All right, all right," Sterling said. He complained that the officers were hurting his arm. He continued asking what he did wrong. The officers then used a stun gun on him, ordering Sterling to get on the ground. The two officers pinned Sterling to the ground. While he was (seemingly) immobile, one of the officers yelled, "He's got a gun!"[7]

Officer Salamoni aimed his gun at Sterling's chest. Seconds later, the officer[8] opened fire, firing into his chest six times. Seconds later, Alton Sterling was dead.[9]

I awoke to the news story and could not believe what I saw.

I want to be clear about this: my dad was active military for most of my formative years, so I understand weapons and violence. I understand that in our world, there are agents of the state who carry deadly weapons and who sometimes use deadly force. But in the military, every soldier is carefully trained and instructed on the clear rules of engagement.

If you are a soldier in a foreign country, during peacetime or times of conflict, you simply cannot fire upon civilians without provocation. You can fire if there is an attack, or a clear and present threat of an attack. If this is true in wartime with soldiers on foreign soil, then how much more true should it be for agents of the state policing US citizens?

I watched the lumbering Sterling, flat on his back, after being stunned, his arms pinned by officers kneeling on him.

And then bam, shot six times.

I couldn't understand how this was a justified use of force. I was staring at the footage of the situation, right in front of me. How did this fit the legal definition of proper use of force? To top it off, Alton Sterling was about my age, and his skin tone was about my same skin tone. The whole incident was terrifying to me.

Shell-shocked, scared, and grieving, I posted my reaction, saying how much this incident of police violence had shaken me.

I had been shocked by what I had seen on the news.

But I was about to be even more shocked by what I saw on my social media feed.

A MISCARRIAGE OF JUSTICE

Unfortunately, I have had quite a few women in my life who have experienced the incredibly painful and heart-wrenching tragedy of miscarriage. Being a man, I often don't have the proper words, and sometimes all I can say is "I am so, so sorry."

But do you know what I would absolutely not say? Under any circumstances? I would not say any of the following sentences.

- Well, were you taking good care of yourself while you were pregnant?
- I don't know if you know this, but it's actually pretty uncommon, statistically.
- Did you smoke, at all, while you were pregnant?
- It's actually not even really that developed—just a bunch of cells, really.
- At least you weren't further along.
- Be grateful for what you have.
- It's tragic, but what about all the lives lost every year to abortion?

Go ahead and read those. Can you imagine saying those to a friend who just told you that she had suffered a miscarriage? No. Some of them are outrageous because they imply that she did something wrong to cause the miscarriage. Some imply that that situation isn't really that bad(!). And some shift the topic to a non sequitur in a way that is so emotionally cold that it's tough to imagine saying something worse. Right? Even the most socially obtuse person would not say those things. Because they range from callous to outright cruel.

So, imagine my surprise when the comments on my social media were exactly that. I posted:

Broken-hearted about the death of Alton Sterling. Really has me shook. Much love to you tonight.

From there, the uncompassionate comments rolled in. I could not believe what I was reading, from people who were acquaintances and friends.

Did you know he had a police record?
He shouldn't have been outside the store that late.
Statistically, a black person is far more likely to be killed by another black person than by a cop.
Are you saying the police don't have a right to defend themselves?

He was probably high on drugs.

Shouldn't have had a gun on him, if he didn't want to get shot.

And the one that hurt the most:

Homeless grifter. Armed. Criminal record. Is it really that sad?

That last comment came in as I was watching the press conference with his family, who tried desperately to make a plea to the public that Alton Sterling was not who the media were portraying him to be. During the conference, Sterling's baby-faced fifteen-year-old son put his arm around his mother, and as she spoke about a man just trying to provide money for his family, he broke down sobbing. This giant boy, just a boy, remembering his father, realizing that he was gone, covered his face as he sobbed, then collapsed in sorrow into the arms of family members.

I couldn't stop sobbing. I saw myself in that boy. I saw myself in his father. I saw myself.

Go ahead. Find it. Put down this book, go to YouTube, and search for "Family Members Speak Out on Death of Alton Sterling." Watch the clip. Then tell me if you would type this.

Homeless grifter. Armed. Criminal record. Is it really that sad?

I realized then that something was deeply, deeply wrong. The comments that were the most callous were—respectfully—all from white people. It was painfully clear that the folks writing these comments did not realize that black Americans experience these news events as group psychological trauma. Because of our present and our past, we experience news events like this collectively. And these white people were treating this as a news story—as something to be dealt with as facts. The relational blindness was shocking.

It would be like a wife saying to her husband, "You don't even love me!" and the husband pulling out an Excel spreadsheet:

That is false. I changed the air in your tires here. And did our taxes on time here. Not to mention, look how much I spent on dinner last Valentine's Day.

It was astonishing. And it showed a horrible, horrible lack of empathy. It was a deep, deep blindness. I knew I had to do something, because this was bad. And it was about to get worse.

A LAMENT

Two days later, on July seventh, as I was gathering my thoughts to make a video trying to express the grief I felt not only over Alton Sterling, but over the responses I'd received from some of my white friends, the news broke.

In a suburb of Minneapolis, police officers Jeronimo Yanez and Joseph Kauser pulled over a white 1997 Oldsmobile 88 for a traffic stop. The car was being driven by Philando Castile, who was driving home from dinner with his girlfriend, Diamond Reynolds, and her four-year-old daughter, who was in a car seat in the back seat.

The officer asked for Castile's license and registration. Castile produced it, and then said, calmly, "Sir, I have to tell you that I do have a firearm on me." Here's how the next sixteen seconds went, according to the official police reports, testimonies, and dash cams as reported by CNN:

Castile told Yanez: "Sir, I have to tell you that I do have a firearm on me." Before Castile completed the sentence, Yanez interrupted and replied, "Okay" and placed his right hand on the holster of his gun. Yanez said "Okay, don't reach for it, then." Castile responded: "I'm…I'm…[inaudible] reaching…," before being again interrupted by Yanez, who said "Don't pull it out." Castile responded, "I'm not pulling it out," and Reynolds said, "He's not pulling it out." Yanez screamed: "Don't pull it out," and pulled his gun with his right hand. Yanez fired seven shots in the direction of Castile in rapid succession. The seventh shot was fired at 9:06:02 p.m. Kauser did not touch or remove his gun. Reynolds yelled, "You just killed my boyfriend!" Castile moaned and said, "I wasn't reaching for it." These were his last words. Reynolds said "He wasn't reaching for it." Before she completed her sentence, Yanez screamed "Don't pull it out!" Reynolds responded. "He wasn't." Yanez yelled, "Don't move! F***!"[10]

Five of the seven shots fired by Yanez at point-blank range hit Castile.[11] Two of those pierced his heart.

All of it was caught again, on video. Castile, slumped over the wheel, his shirt bloodied, dying in front of us, his final words to his murderer.

"I wasn't reaching for it."[12]

I remember being hesitant to click on this video to watch it. After the video was over, I immediately regretted that I'd seen it. I'm not built to watch men get killed in front of me. This wasn't TV. This wasn't a movie. This was another man who looked like me, losing his life. And this time, in front of a four-year-old child. I'm just not built for that.

Trauma. New trauma. On top of trauma. I could not take this anymore. Well-meaning white friends called and texted, trying to ease the anxiety it was clear I was carrying.

Don't worry, Tyler.
That would never happen to you.
You're one of the good ones.

So was Philando.

Hours later, I listened to Minnesota's governor Mark Dayton give his comments:

Would this have happened if those passengers, the driver and the passengers, were white? I don't think it would have. So I'm forced to confront, and I think all of us in Minnesota are forced to confront, that this kind of racism exists.[13]

Then I cried. I cried for Alton. I cried for Philando. I cried for myself. I cried for us.

IN MEMORIAM

Although the deaths of Alton Sterling and Philando Castile brought a sharp national spotlight to the issue of racialized police violence, it did not reveal a new problem. The issue had always been happening. The only difference was that now, because of the ubiquity of cell phones, it was being captured.

The following is a list of unarmed black people killed by police since I first heard the news of Alton Sterling, that Tuesday, July fifth, back in 2016. The names in bold garnered national headlines. I'm asking that you don't skim through this list, but as an act of respect, that you actually read their names. They deserve that.

Alton Sterling
July 5, 2016
Baton Rouge, Louisiana

Philando Castile
July 6, 2016
Falcon Heights, Minnesota

Joseph Curtis Mann
July 11, 2016
Sacramento, California

Korryn Gaines
August 1, 2016
Randallstown, Maryland

Terrence LeDell Sterling
September 11, 2016
Washington, DC

Terence Crutcher
September 16, 2016
Tulsa, Oklahoma

Alfred Olango
September 27, 2016
El Cajon, California

Deborah Danner
October 18, 2016
The Bronx, New York City, New York

Chad Robertson
February 15, 2017
Chicago, Illinois

Jordan Edwards
April 29, 2017
Balch Springs, Texas

Charleena Chavon Lyles
June 18, 2017
Seattle, Washington

Unborn child of Charleena Chavon Lyles (14–15 weeks)
June 18, 2017
Seattle, Washington

Aaron Bailey
June 29, 2017
Indianapolis, Indiana

Stephon Alonzo Clark
March 18, 2018
Sacramento, California

Saheed Vassell
April 4, 2018
Brooklyn, New York City, New York

Antwon Rose Jr.
June 19, 2018
East Pittsburgh, Pennsylvania

Botham Shem Jean
September 6, 2018
Dallas, Texas

Chinedu Okobi
October 3, 2018
Millbrae, California

Charles "Chop" Roundtree Jr.
October 17, 2018
San Antonio, Texas

Emantic "EJ" Fitzgerald Bradford Jr.
November 22, 2018
Hoover, Alabama

Sterling Lapree Higgins
March 25, 2019
Union City, Tennessee

Ronald Greene
May 10, 2019
Monroe, Louisiana

Elijah McClain
August 30, 2019
Aurora, Colorado

Atatiana Koquice Jefferson
October 12, 2019
Fort Worth, Texas

John Elliott Neville
December 4, 2019
Winston-Salem, North Carolina

William Howard Green
January 27, 2020
Temple Hills, Maryland

Manuel "Mannie" Elijah Ellis
March 3, 2020
Tacoma, Washington

Breonna Taylor
March 13, 2020
Louisville, Kentucky

Daniel T. Prude
March 30, 2020
Rochester, New York

Michael Brent Charles Ramos
April 24, 2020
Austin, Texas

Dreasjon "Sean" Reed
May 6, 2020
Indianapolis, Indiana

George Perry Floyd Jr.
May 25, 2020
Minneapolis, Minnesota

Tony McDade
May 27, 2020
Tallahassee, Florida

David McAtee
June 1, 2020
Louisville, Kentucky

Carlos Carson
June 6, 2020
Tulsa, Oklahoma

Rayshard Brooks
June 12, 2020
Atlanta, Georgia

Dijon Durand Kizzee
August 31, 2020
Los Angeles, California

Jonathan Dwayne Price
October 3, 2020
Wolfe City, Texas

Marcellis Stinnette
October 20, 2020
Waukegan, Illinois

Sincere Pierce
November 13, 2020
Cocoa, Florida

Angelo "AJ" Crooms
November 13, 2020
Cocoa, Florida

Casey Christopher Goodson Jr.
December 4, 2020
Columbus, Ohio

Andre Maurice Hill
December 22, 2020
Columbus, Ohio

Angelo Quinto
December 23, 2020
Antioch, California

Vincent "Vinny" M. Belmonte
January 5, 2021
Cleveland, Ohio

Patrick Lynn Warren Sr.
January 10, 2021
Killeen, Texas

Marvin David Scott III
March 14, 2021
McKinney, Texas

Daunte Demetrius Wright
April 11, 2021
Brooklyn Center, Minnesota

THE BIRTH OF A NOTION

As these events of police killings of unarmed black people began to build, I felt hopelessness come crashing down, like a great wave over me. I felt like I was drowning. I was at risk—and my personhood was desperate to survive. I felt that primordial "fight or flight" instinct kick up, but there was nowhere to run. So I was going to have to fight back the only way I knew how.

My name is Tyler, and I build things.

But what? What could I build this time? I thought about a quote that I first heard from Dr. Bryan Loritts, which I think he might have adapted from a quote from Dr. Eric Mason. It went like this:

Distance breeds suspicion.
But proximity breeds empathy.

I had a hunch deep in my bones that proximity was key. And throughout my life, although I hadn't realized it, I was accidentally developing and building a life of proximity, where I was living near and around so many different sorts of people. Some people might call that "luck." I'd call it Providence. I often think, "What if my dad had stayed stationed in Alaska for twenty years?" I think your life experiences really do shape how you view the world. And my whole life had been one giant exercise in proximity.

It was time to build the Tyler Merritt Project.

THE SAFE PLACE

There were forty people invited from around the city. All of them were carefully screened. The invitations were hand-delivered, which explained the purpose of the event, and some key conditions. None of the invitees would know the location of the meeting until the day of. No one. There would be no cameras. No microphones. No media. No press. Just a large room, and forty or so people from all over Nashville. Black men. White men. Black women. White women. Some young, some older. Some were wealthy. Some were not as wealthy. Some gay. Some straight.

The goal: this group of disparate strangers would sit down and talk about what was going on in the nation and our city regarding race. We would have an honest, and painful if needed, dialogue. It would start as a room full of strangers. By the end, maybe something would have changed.

I called it "The Safe Place," and it was the first test of my theory that I could use my unique life experiences and I could leverage proximity to do something significant to make the world a better place. I rented out the clubhouse of my apartment complex because there was plenty of room. At three p.m., I emailed and texted out the address and location to all the participants, and they filled the room by seven p.m.

As each guest came, they were given a paddle. One side was black and said "Yes," and the other side was white and said "No." We sat in a large circle facing one another, and the ground rules were laid out:

1. What was about to happen in this room would stay in this room.
2. Everyone in this room is worthy of respect from one another. Everyone. So, raise your paddle if you want to talk.
3. No one was allowed to say "they." As in "You know how they are"

or "You know what they say." Stereotypes and exaggerations were out. Stick to "I" or "me."

And then, for the next two and a half hours, I moderated the discussion. Nobody could have anticipated what happened in that room. In that evening, this group could not point nor dodge behind the cowardice of anonymity on social media—they had to deal with the people in front of them. It was forced proximity. And it was working.

And it resulted in some powerful moments.

One black woman said that she had been trained since her earliest memories to never trust white people, under any circumstances. "You must always be on your guard," her mother used to tell her at night, when she was tucking her in. "They will steal from you. They will take from you. They will lie about you to the authorities. Never trust a white person, ever."

"Why would someone teach their child that?" a white woman asked, genuinely baffled.

"Hundreds of years of lived experience," the woman replied.

Another woman, a white woman, spoke up.

"My family definitely owned slaves," she said. "I still have the receipts at home."

"Why the fuck do you still have receipts for slaves at your house?" a black person asked.

"I...don't know," she stammered. "Family history?"

Gregg, a guy I knew from church circles, was there, too. At one point, he broke down, almost in tears. "My office, it's just stacked with white people," he said, shaking his head. "Everyone who leads it is white, everyone who directs it is white. And looking at it, I can see how it got built that way, and it's this racially segregated reality."

Throughout the next two hours, we delved into some pretty volatile topics. Does privilege exist? What is racism? Does systematic racism exist? What is the way forward? Can America ever heal from slavery and Jim Crow, or are we doomed to keep repeating this?

Here's what I saw: the conversation was more personal, more honest, and more empathetic by a hundred times than anything I have ever seen online. There was more dialogue, and way less grandstanding and monologues. Far more active listening. And it was a hell of an emotional ride, a deeply bonding experience, and every single person said it had changed them in one way or another. Proximity for the win.

One moment in particular hit me.

A middle-aged man with a military background raised his paddle and got right to it. He explained how he hated it when people talk about white privilege. He shared his story of being born in a very poor, rural area in Tennessee. His family was ravaged by alcohol abuse and poverty and the schools he attended were terrible.

"I didn't have any privilege!" he said, with deep pain and emotion. "Tell me what privilege I had."

The room went silent. A black man spoke up.

"I gotta say, brother, I don't know how you're standing here," the black man said. "I can't believe you came out of that. I got mad respect for you."

The group slowly nodded.

"That must have been a nightmare," he said, and the larger group began to affirm this man and his journey.

"When you talked about being afraid of your daddy, I just need you to know, that I felt you," the black man said, clutching at his chest. They looked at each other, tears welling up.

"I just need you to know that I didn't come from a place where everything was lined up for me," the white man said. "I didn't."

"I know that, brother. We know that," the black man across from him said. "Nothing was lined up for you. You weren't given nothing. Nothing."

He paused.

"But nothing was stacked against you *just because of the color of your skin*," he said gently. "Poverty is color-blind. But racism is about one thing only." He pointed to the skin on his arm. "Racism is about hierarchy based on skin color."

"No one has ever explained privilege like that to me before," he said. "I get it now, brother. I get it."

Right there in front of me I watched a black man speak to a white man, and the white man got it. How do I know? Because he said so.

After the meeting, the two men exchanged numbers. They hugged. Respect and friendship began to flow. Again, proximity for the win.

Because proximity breeds empathy. And with empathy, humanity has a fighting chance.

MARTIN OR MALCOLM

Because of my personal history, and because of black American history, I am a black man who has two black impulses inside me that sometimes want to duke it out. These are two voices from history, speaking to me from the pages of the past, with powerful, intelligent, compelling rhetoric. Two leaders, presenting different visions and reactions within. Sometimes these paths seem to converge. Sometimes they seem to split, in the widest possible gulf. They're the voice of Malcolm X and the voice of Martin Luther King Jr. Here's how they sound, in my head. First, Martin with his soothing "we gonna be all right" tone.

MARTIN VOICE: We can build a coalition. This nation is not without hope. Buried in its founding documents—buried deep, perhaps—is a seed of freedom. A promissory note, as I called it in my famous speech—a check of freedom that will someday be cashed. By appealing to universal ethics, we can build a coalition of justice to stand against the evils of racism. Because the arc of the universe bends toward justice—not because it is inevitable but because God is just and will bring it about in us. Resist giving in to fear and hatred. If we use violence, we lose both politically and morally. In the end, we can forge brotherhood. We can do this.

Now, Malcolm. "Nah, son."

MALCOLM VOICE: My brother. You are far too optimistic. The situation for the black man in this country is not just "going to get better" on its own. Racism is woven into the very fabric of this nation. The white people have all the money and power, and they will not just give it up quietly. You want to build a coalition of wider support? From who? We are not wanted.

Our dignity will never be recognized. No, black people have got to organize, we have got to rise up and protect ourselves against violence and exploitation "by any means necessary." And if it comes down to it—we will protect ourselves.

As I sat in the empty clubhouse of my apartment building, after the Safe Place event, I realized that both voices were never going to go away. I would lean on the awareness of Malcolm, but take the posture and follow the voice of Martin.

I was going to build allies. I was going to lean into proximity. I had seen it work.

And for the first time since I was fired from the church, I realized that I could use my life to make a positive impact. The stress on the vines of my life, after years of strain, had caused my roots to burrow deep. At long last, the vine of my life was beginning to produce clusters of fruit. Finally. I could see it. I could use my acting background. I could use my background living in so many different places. I could use my voice. And my experiences living in proximity to so many different types of people would be my superpower.

BEFORE YOU CALL THE COPS

I set up the lights and stepped into the bright, white light. I checked the audio levels. The camera was focused tightly on my face and neck. I took off my shirt. I am still not quite sure why I did that. But I knew that I had to appear vulnerable. I knew the tone I was going for. I was going to speak in a voice barely above a whisper. The tone would be pleading. Almost desperate.

You see, for the past few months, I had undertaken a social experiment. Armed with the experience from the Safe Place, I set out to create content that would aid in creating proximity. I made videos, using my voice, my face, my acting, my humor, and my mind to disarm (white!) viewers so that they would let me, a giant, six-foot-two, dreadlocked (black!) man share with them.

And now this video that I was about to shoot would be the next experiment of the Tyler Merritt Project.

Would it fly? I didn't know. But I was going to try.

One night, at almost midnight, I had an idea for a video. And yes, the idea came like a flash of lightning. And I knew I had to create this video right then and there. And the script came to me, flowing out of me like water. But even though it felt like the script came to me all at one moment, as I wrote it down, I realized that wasn't true. I realized I had been working on this script for my entire life. Here it is:

BEFORE YOU CALL THE COPS

Before you call the cops
I just want you to know
The first thing I did this morning was yell at my alarm clock.
My parents were raised in the South.
I have to Roll Tide or they'll disown me.
They raised me in Las Vegas.
That city still has my heart.
I hate spiders.
I'm a vegetarian.
I'm not proud about it.
I've done goat yoga.
I'm really not proud about that.
I can tell you every single word off the NWA Straight Outta
     Compton *album.*
I can also sing you every word from Oklahoma!
Bananas are disgusting.
I am a Christian.
I spend almost every Sunday morning teaching kids in Sunday school.
I am often asked if I am a Muslim.
I'm okay with that.
I'm pretty much convinced that if you met my mother…
You'd automatically become a better person.
My father is a veteran.
He taught me how to say "Yes sir" and "Yes ma'am" to everyone that I meet.

I don't hate our president.
I pray for him.
I love basketball.
And also hockey.
This is my brother James.
This is my brother Mike.
This is my brother John.
And this is my brother Rob.
I've never been to jail.
I've never owned a gun.
I hate that anyone at all might possibly be afraid of me.
I'd go around the world and back again if I knew that single act
Might make your day better.
I'm a proud man.
I'm a proud black man.
Does any of this really matter?
No.
I just wanted you to get to know me better.
Before you call the cops.[14]

Every word in this video was intentional.

I uploaded the video to my social media accounts. I didn't know what was going to happen, but I liked what I'd tried to do. I had tried to use a medium that's largely impersonal to be deeply vulnerable. Why?

To achieve proximity, of course.

20 MILLION IS A LOT OF ZEROES

Within a few hours, the video began blowing up. A few months earlier, I had a video that reached 10,000 views. I wasn't about numbers, but it meant that people were talking.

It quickly became clear that's not how "Before You Call the Cops" was acting. Pretty soon, the video was at 400,000 views. Then it was a million.

A million.

A million! If you counted to a million, taking one second per number, it would take you 11.5 days. One million is every single word in the entire Harry Potter series. A million inches is more than 15.78 miles. A million miles is forty times around the globe, plus an additional 4,000 miles. A million miles is also roughly 1,000 times how far Vanessa Carlton would walk just to see you tonight.

Because she misses you.

And she needs you.

Pretty soon, the video was at 2 million views. People were messaging me, sending me emails. I got messages from around the world. One person wrote me from China (China!) asking me "What is a 'Roll Tide'?" I blocked that fool, because if you don't love 'Bama, then I don't want you in my life. Proximity has limits.

I'm kidding. But I say this because comments and questions started pouring in. POURING in. Good-hearted, honest people, asking me to help them make sense of the world. And in that, I got a glimpse that this was actually working. I got message after message and email after email. People saying "thank you" and "this really matters" and simply "I love you" or "we're so, so different and yet the same" or "bananas suck."

The "bananas suck" people? Those are my people. People like bananas in ways I simply don't understand.

A teenager from rural Arkansas wrote me, saying that he was deeply moved by the video. Rural Arkansas! I realized that I really could bring people together in a way that an argument never could. I started to realize that the Tyler Merritt Project was accomplishing what I hoped it would: increase proximity in a way that led to empathy.

And that's when things began to get out of control, for a few reasons:

Reason 1: I was ill-prepared.

I was not ready for the flood of attention the video would send my way. I did not make my social media accounts private, and soon I was overwhelmed with requests. I had made a video about proximity and suddenly had hundreds of thousands of people trying to get in close proximity.

I made it my goal to respond to every DM, every text, every message, to read every comment, and respond back to every email, educating everyone. That is just impossible, even if you devote every waking hour to it.

Reason 2: My personality.

I am not uniquely suited to simply brush off criticism. In the height of my Broken Frame days, the entire show could go great, but if I missed a note, or missed a lyric, my perfectionist brain would go crazy with self-criticism. If ninety-nine things went right, I would focus only on the one thing that went wrong. And if ninety-nine people came up and said "I loved it" and one person was critical, my focus would not be proportionate. That one criticism would get 99 percent of my attention. Some of you know exactly what I mean, how this works, how this feels. A spare wasn't enough: it was a strike, or nothing.

Reason 3: The Trolls.

Trolls are people who are trying to deliberately post the most insidious, vile, or provocative things in order to draw attention to themselves. Their first tactic is to comment on everything and anything except the actual content of the video. Their second tactic is to just think about what Satan would post, and then try to be 10 percent more evil. I had to deal with racial slurs. People telling me to shut up, and then threatening violence if I did not comply. One person was shockingly specific about how they would silence me, saying they would both staple AND superglue my lips together "in my sleep." Now, I'm a deep sleeper, but I think I might wake up during that. One person made a sexually suggestive comment about my mother. Another threatened to find where my family lived. But perhaps the worst was when someone said that my video was worse than the song "MMMBop" from Hanson. How dare you. How dare you, sir!

Reason 4: The Pressure.

Once you have a video go viral, people are expecting you to release more content. Now, if you're making funny cat videos, or basketball trick shot videos, that's not that difficult. But if you're trying to make compelling social commentary to confront prejudice and challenge perspectives, well, it's not that easy to just crank out another video. But all that was on my shoulders. And I felt it.

In the middle of all this, I had a political action committee reaching out to me (because I had said I prayed for the president) wondering if I would speak on their behalf and make commercials advocating for President Trump. I guess they were having a hard time finding black folks to endorse him. But I also had black folks who were angry with me. "How dare you try to humanize yourself to be accepted," they yelled. I could hear the Malcolm X in their voice. I recognized it. They weren't wrong. "It's not our job to make them see we are human!" Their criticism was easily the hardest part of this entire situation for me emotionally. It hurt. Feeling like you were letting down the very people you represent. That one got me. That one hurt.

It all came in so fast. I started thinking and strategizing about how to get out and break away. I could see clearly that even after only a few weeks, this had become a burden that was too large and too heavy for me. I had started the Tyler Merritt Project to help people, but it was getting to be too much. I had some soul-searching to do. I decided that I was going to take a break—a sabbatical of sorts—from all social media. I just didn't know when or how.

But I knew that if I wasn't careful, this could crush me.

And then, it did.

CHAPTER 17

NEVER GONNA BE PRESIDENT NOW,

AKA MY HUSBAND FOUND YOUR PICTURES

Now I'm right here, and I'm right now
And I'm hoping, knowing somehow
That my shadows days are over
My shadow days are over now
—"Shadow Days" by John Mayer

Imagine Netflix had a show called *Surprise! Look What You Did!* This show would contain footage (somehow obtained) of the ten worst things you had ever done in your entire life. Just stitched together footage of you, at your absolute worst.

Now imagine the show premieres for the people in your life that you spend the most time with—your co-workers, neighbors, friends, and family.

No, really. I need you to stop for a second, for the sake of this experiment. What is one thing? One of the worst things that you've done that you wouldn't want ANYONE to know about.

Got it? Now, imagine that moment—and nine others like it—displayed for all to see. What would you feel? In that moment? And then, what would you do?

I think the only reasonable answer would be to literally move away, change your address and cell phone number, quit your job, and hope that you never saw any of those people ever again.

The word for that feeling is shame. My girl Brené Brown defines shame as "the intensely painful feeling or experience of believing that we are flawed and therefore unworthy of love and belonging—something we've experienced, done, or failed to do makes us unworthy of connection."[1]

I'm not trying to be cruel here or drag up past trauma, but when you thought about that one moment—the reason that's so difficult is because of the pain and shame it brings up. I haven't met a person who doesn't hide things from their past, fearing that if someone were to actually find out about that moment, that it would confirm what they always feared: if someone saw your worst moments, they would turn and walk away in disgust, disappointment, and disapproval.

That's what I believed for a long time.

For this penultimate chapter, I'm going to share one of my "Netflix" moments. Not because it's fun. God, it's not. I would rather not go back to this moment and dredge all these painful memories up. And honestly, even as I write this, I'm still debating if the end really justifies the means.

But in sharing one of my darkest, bleakest moments, it's my earnest hope that we can experience something that's pretty rare these days: a formative moment from true vulnerability.

I WAS CHILLIN'
CHILLIN' MINDIN' MY BUSINESS

I remember, it was October and I was eating Caesar salad. Extra croutons. And I was watching the Dodgers and Astros take it to game seven. My phone lit up and I saw the DM pop up.

"Hey Tyler!"

I looked at the name. Who was this? The name on the message said Baby Girl. I only vaguely remembered her.

"I saw your video."

What was her name? T…something? Tiana? Was that it? I didn't remember much about her. Had she dated someone I worked with at some point?

"I think it's so cool, what you're doing. Really trying to make an impact."

I was also pretty sure she'd come to a Broken Frame show or two. Yes. She was friends with…who, again? We continued to chat. I thanked her for her compliment. This was months and months before I made "Before You Call the Cops." I had just posted some encouraging videos. I was glad people were responding. I said something polite. The convo ended. I went to bed. Two weeks later, it was late, and I was sitting in my house, watching reruns of something when my phone lit up.

"Hey Tyler, you up?"

It was that girl, T…something. What did she call herself? Baby Girl?

"Just needed some handsome in my life right now."

Well, hello! I mean, I mighta been watching some reruns, but this was new. Then I thought about it for a second. Wasn't she…married? I hit her back.

"You need some handsome? Ain't you got some handsome at home?"

Turns out she got separated from her husband a while ago, and they were no longer together. We got to chatting. It was a long thread. She opened up. I listened. I know what it's like to be single and in your thirties, and not really have planned for it to be that way. We chatted. We got flirty. She sent me some photos she took from my social media accounts that she'd stitched together. She complimented me and asked me if I have any more pictures of myself.

I don't want to delve into the lascivious details, but the conversation turned into a bit more than flirty, which then shifted to provocative, which then transitioned into steamy, which then jumped the shark into dirty. Pictures were sent. And if you're wondering what kind of pictures, let me save you the trouble of guessing: yes, those kinds of pictures. It was a guy who was alone late at night, connecting privately with a seemingly lonely woman. I know, I know. It wasn't right.

SIDENOTE: Now I know not everyone reading this is single, but us grown single folks know that if you're messaging someone after one in the morning, it's safe to say—ain't nothing holy happening at one in the morning. Not to make light of this, but some of y'all who have been married since you got up outta high school need to understand that ish gets real real fast out here in these single streets.

I went to bed, thinking that was the end of it. Rarely in my life have I been that wrong.

FAST-FORWARD NINE MONTHS

I picked up my phone. There it was. A message from that girl. What was her damn name? She called herself Baby Girl. I read the message again.

"My husband found your pictures."

What. The. Actual. Fuck.

My mind spun. Time stopped. Had it been a minute? Six minutes? Thirty seconds? As the blue and red lights flashed behind me, my mind raced through four thoughts which all flooded my head, one after another.

Thought 1

What do you mean "my husband"? She had told me, in no uncertain terms, in plain language she was NO LONGER WITH HIM. Had they gotten back together? Had she been lying? Did this man know that I didn't know that she was still married?

Thought 2

What pictures? What kinds of pictures had I sent her? I didn't exactly remember. Had she…saved them? Did her husband have them? Would they…get out?

Thought 3

Oh, man. Mike and I had talked about this. I once said to Mike, "If you ever mess around with another man's wife, and that man says he's coming over here to fight you, I'll open the door and step outside, bro. You're on your own." And he nodded. We agreed: you don't mess with another man's wife. This was bad. Bad. Bad. Bad.

Thought 4

How was this happening? I was no longer working at a church. I thought that my private dating (or whatever you call it) was now back to being PRIVATE because my employer certainly did not care. This was like getting fined by the NFL, only I had been retired for three years. The church had written me off, and so had most people from the church. It was just me. Me and my private life, dating and all. It was PRIVATE. But now, this? I worried about all the people who still saw a "flawless" man on their TV screen in Sunday school every week. Would they find out about this? How would they find out? What about my friends? What if they find out? I'll never be able to show my face again.

I had dinner plans to meet some friends at Slim and Husky's. If you don't know, Slim and Husky's is a Nashville original hip-hop black culture concept pizza restaurant, started by three best-friend black entrepreneurs. I love me some Slim and Husky's.

But not tonight. The friends who I was meeting didn't know what happened. Let's just say I might have been physically there, but I was not present at that dinner. The whole night, I kept thinking, "Who knows about this?"

But even worse, I had this sinking feeling deep in the pit of me. Look, I've been trying to tell you that if you don't truly deal with your demons, they will deal with you. Yeah, it's true. I hadn't known that Baby Girl was still married. But if I'm being honest with you—I was so deeply selfish at that point—*it wouldn't have mattered.*

THE FALLOUT, BOY

I was secretly glad I was out of my house at the pizza place, because if I had been home alone, I think I might have gone crazy. I got back in my car and took out my phone. I messaged Baby Girl. I'd been thinking about this. This wasn't a conversation.

"I need to know that the pictures are no longer on your phone.

"I need to know that you've deleted them and no one else has them."

I waited. She hit me back, assuring me, "yes, yes." I breathed. I didn't know what was next, but I knew who I needed to call.

James.

James Monroe Iglehart.

The story of how James and I met is one of the more important moments of my life. We met at an audition right after I graduated college. It was a weird audition. The director had twelve of us in this large, open room, with a single piano. It was me, this other black dude who I had never seen before, and ten white dudes. I looked down the row and made eye contact with the other black dude. He looked down the row. And that's when I knew.

I knew.

That moment was like a unicorn looking around the world and finally finding another unicorn. What was this black man, so skilled, so talented, doing in this room with me? Whatever his journey was, I knew that it had to have been similar to mine. He had to have been cut from the same cloth that I'd been cut from.

Look, it's difficult enough to find another human being on the planet who knows who Billy Porter is, or why the name Norm Lewis is historically important. Or why the musical *Ragtime* really matters, how it ties to *Rent*, and how it leads directly to *Hamilton*. It's tough enough to find someone who gets all that.

Let alone another black man.

After the audition, we walked straight to each other.

Yo, I'm James.

I'm Tyler.

We start chatting. It was the early 2000s, and I worked at Blockbuster Video.

So did he.

We both sang at our local church.

And we were two straight black dudes who were into musicals.

Are we the same person?

Did we just become best friends?

"Here's my number," I said.

We clasped hands, and as we did, I knew this was the beginning of something. A brotherhood. Something positive, dynamic, bonding, and life-changing.

I was an only child, for sure. But I felt like in James, I'd found my brother.

James would go on to be kind of a big deal—winning a Tony Award for his scene-stealing performance as the Genie in the Broadway production of Disney's *Aladdin* and playing the role of Lafayette/Jefferson in the Broadway company of *Hamilton*. That's my bro right there.

And if you don't know, now you know.

I knew I needed to call James. He and I had both seen a measure of fame in our lives, and now, here I was, in the middle of an inundation from a video that was going viral with more than 20 million views—and this hits? This scandal. What if 20 million people find out about this? What if 20 million people…

I called James. I told him everything, and he listened with the calm patience that I recognized. His tone was not patronizing, just searingly realistic. He was affirming, but honest, encouraging, and kind. Sure, he cracked a few jokes, but if you have never kicked it with two black dudes in crisis, we do what we need to do to handle the moment. I knew I had work to do, but I also knew that I had at least one brother in my corner who would stick by my side. It turns out the ancient Hebrew proverb is right: there is a friend that sticks closer than a brother. And what a gift that is. I would need him.

THE RECKONING

Baby Girl's husband began stalking me on the internet. Everyone called him Big Skip, and he began writing profanity-laced posts under a picture of me, and then would tag my name calling me a "homewrecker" and a "adulterer." He was so angry. He wrote my friends Shannon and Shymene and told them what I had done. He threatened to expose me as a fraud to the entire world. It was a nightmare I could not stop.

As I was leaving church one Sunday, my phone vibrated. It was Baby Girl calling. What in the actual? I could not believe her gall.

"What," I said, answering the call as coldly as I could.

"I-I-I," she stammered.

"Why are you calling me?" I said, again, with more ice than Elsa.

"My husband's...he...he is gone," she said. "So, I can be with you now."

"What??" I almost exploded through the phone. "I said I never wanted to talk to you ever again. What in the world would make you think that I want to be with you?"

"Will you be with me, now?" she said, her voice shaking.

"No," I said. "Let me say this as clearly as I can. I don't want to be with you. You ruined my life."

Another voice clicked on. It was Big Skip. But now, he was Big Angry Skip.

"Oh, you think she ruined your life?" he screamed through the phone. "You ruined my life, motherf****r."

Suddenly this whole phone call made a lot more sense. This was some sort of test the two of them had worked out. And I was in the middle of it. Just where I absolutely did not want to be.

"Real talk? You're just the man I have been trying to talk to," I said.

"Oh yeah?" he said. "What do you have to say to me?"

"I think you misunderstood some basic facts, man," I said. "There is not a situation in the world where I would have done this to you if I had known you two were still married."

"Talk is cheap, I want to see you face-to-face," Big Skip said.

"Sure," I said. "When?"

"Now," he said.

"Okay," I said. "Tell me where, Skip, and I will meet you."

I hung up the phone and walked to my car in the church parking lot. My friend Will knew something was up by the look on my face.

"Wait," he said. "You're about to meet this guy? He's going to shoot you, bro."

I hadn't thought of that.

But I can talk my way out of a paper bag, and I had a hunch this man did not know that I did not know Baby Girl was still married. In no way did I try to purposely mess up his life. I figured if I could look this guy in the face, I could clear my name.

A KMART IN THE MIDDLE OF NOWHERE

Will agreed to follow me to the meeting spot, and then, about a mile away, we switched cars, and I drove his blue Honda Accord to the outdoor strip mall where we were meeting.

"This way," Will explained, "if things go sideways, he doesn't know your car."

Will parked on the other side of the parking lot and was watching from a distance. The entrance to the store was all the way at one end of the long, rectangular building. I stood alone, all the way at the other end. I anticipated an animated conversation, so I wanted someplace rather private, but not so private that no one would hear my screams or find my body.

I heard Skip's vehicle before I saw it, as the older-model red-and-white GMC truck barreled into the parking lot. I inhaled.

"The last breath before the plunge," I said to myself, quoting Gandalf, which was not exactly the blackest thing I have ever done, but whatever.

Now, I wish I were making this next part up. But it really happened.

"Oh, hey, Pastor Tyler," I heard a voice say. I turned to look. It was Kirsten, one of the girls from my old youth group. She was standing there, leg cocked, ribbons in her blond hair. What are the chances? My eyes bugged out.

"Hey, Kirsten, good to see you," I said quickly. I needed this white girl to get out of here. I heard a door slam. I looked up and getting out of the truck was a giant of a man, easily 350 pounds, barrel-chested, with a Big Dog oversize shirt and shorts.

"Is that the motherfucker!" I heard him yell, as he stared at me and walked toward me.

"Right now is not a good time, Kirsten," I said, trying to get her to move away quickly.

"Is THIS the nigga that is fucking around with my wife," Big Skip bellowed, from about four rows away, as he hit shopping carts out of his way.

Kristen looked at me. Then she looked at the man. Then she looked
back at me. I could tell she was trying her hardest to use her teenage white
girl brain to piece together a coherent story about why her old youth pastor
was the subject of a vulgarity-laden tirade in the middle of a Kmart parking
lot.

"You the nigga?" Skip yelled. "Is that you? You the homewrecker!"

"Uh oh," I thought. The script that I had been writing in my mind was
going to need some adjustments. Starting with the white girl from my old
youth group, who, when I mentally ran through the thousands of ways this
could go down, was never part of any scenario.

"You need to go," I said to Kirsten, almost hissing.

"Okay, well, gosh, see you later, Pastor Tyler," she said, scuttling away,
hopefully to her therapist.

As I looked at Skip, it took me about two seconds to think, "I probably
should have thought this through a bit more." I saw Baby Girl, wrapped in
a blanket, slowly emerging from the GMC truck. Her eyes were red from
crying.

As Skip got close, I could tell he had been crying, too. Maybe now it was
tears of rage, but tears nonetheless. As he stood in front of me, it occurred to
me that this was not a fictitious character. This was not some guy blasting me
on social media. This was a man who my actions had hurt.

No.

Check it.

Let me take more responsibility.

This was a man I had hurt.

A black man.

As we made eye contact for the first time, I thought about the first
time that James Monroe Iglehart and I had made eye contact. I knew back
then that he and I were the same. Of the same cloth. And as I looked at Skip,
I felt that same feeling. I had known that animal rage and psychic pain Skip
was feeling. I knew it. Like Skip, I too had felt betrayal, deep, profound

betrayal, and wounds that cut deeper than flesh. Like Skip, I had felt something snap inside me that was so painful, I thought I might die.

I could see all that in Skip's eyes, too. We black men are proud, and we are toughened into coarse leather by the cruelty of a world hostile to our existence. But black men can be broken, too. Just like any other man. I realized in that moment that something had to shift. I had come to that Kmart shopping center in the middle of nowhere because I wanted my own nightmare to be over. I wanted the weight of this situation off my back, so I could be free. But this selfishness was exactly my problem, this self-centeredness, this belief that the world revolves around me. I should have never been involved with Baby Girl in the first place. But the same thing that had made me heartless, ruthless, and inconsiderate of women had never changed.

Couldn't I see?

I was the villain here. I was now playing the role of the guy who licked ice cream off some other guy's girlfriend. No. Wife. I was the one, standing by, not caring while another man was crushed. I was the one inflicting the pain.

Whatever anguish I had been going through—worried about bad publicity online and all that—this man's anguish was a hundred times worse. This was his wife. And I had caused him that pain.

Me.

Whatever happened next, I knew I had to get the weight off this man. I saw him as I remembered myself, like a wounded animal, wondering why the one I trusted had left him for dead.

And just like that first time meeting James, I was seeing another black man, and although I did not know this man's story or how he had gotten there, I knew that our stories were very similar. I spoke in quiet tones, because I wanted to take a humble, soft-spoken, and contrite position. I had no defense.

ME:

> Skip. I am sorry. I am sorry that you have to be standing here. I am sorry that you're in so much pain. But you need to know. I didn't know. I didn't know you guys were still married. I didn't know. I didn't.

HIM:

> You telling me you didn't know? She DM'd you. There's pictures
> of us all on her page. You telling me you didn't know?

ME:

> I didn't know, man.

HIM:

> No! You are out here trying to be with my wife.

ME:

> No. That isn't true. I don't want to steal your wife. I didn't know
> you two were still married.

HIM:

> Is what he is saying true?

I looked at Baby Girl. She looked to the ground, and wrapped her head
in the blanket, like a shawl.

ME:

> Tell this man that what I am saying is true.

I looked at her, and then I looked at Skip. I was in the middle of this thing
that I should have never been in the middle of. The thought hit me, "What
if he doesn't have a mother like mine? To pull him back from the brink. To
restore him? What will he do then?"

ME:

> I am so sorry that I have done this to you.

HIM:

> I got laid off, three weeks ago. I have kids to take care of.

His words stabbed me. He was cataloguing for me all the black trauma.
And here I was, adding to it.

ME:

    God, I'm sorry.

HIM:

    And you're a pastor! You are the reason I will never go to church.
    Why I will never be a Christian. You hypocrite.

His words stung. They went deep. In his pain, he was trying to dismantle me with his words, to inflict pain back. It was working. And I realized that I deserved it. I deserved every word.

ME:

    Listen to me, Skip. I don't love your wife. I am not a threat. I am
    not trying to ruin your life.

HIM:

    So do you think she loves you?

ME:

    No, man. She doesn't love me. She barely knows me.

Skip started to calm down. I could tell that the story she had been feeding him, partially to save face and partially to save their relationship, wasn't factual. It was obvious she loved him and that he loved her. Relationships are complicated, and I didn't know all their history and what they had been through to get to this place, but here we were. Skip was working it all out real-time. I wasn't a threat. I was backing away. Hopefully, with that space, he and Baby Girl could work on their relationship. He started to back away, and then the question came into his mind, like a fiery dart.

HIM:

    Did she message you first, or you message her? Did she ask to see
    photos of you?

ME:

    Look, man. You don't really want to know.

And with that, Skip took a step forward, and with his whole person and whole body, he hit me. It was like slow motion. He hit me hard, in the face, full force, kind of an open-hand slap that connected across my entire face.

It hurt, but I thought I deserved that.

Tears welled in my heart, as I stared at this man I had wounded so badly. It was like this man was slapping all my years of dysfunction. All the people I'd hurt with my selfish behavior. All the wounds I'd caused. All the tears I'd caused. All the heartbreak.

"I deserved that," I said, leaving my face to the side where the force of the blow had taken it.

I locked eyes with Skip. Like James, we were united, the same, two black men, so different, yet the same.

"I'm sorry," I said softly, again. "I am so sorry."

And I meant it. From my core. I was tired. So tired of being that person. I don't know what was wrong with me, what broken toxicity kept leaking out, but I was tired of it. I needed to change. That old part of me needed to die.

I cannot be this person anymore. I cannot be this guy.

In that moment, Skip and I looked at each other. And he saw something in me that he recognized. Because broken recognizes broken. There was some commotion from the people nearby who had just watched one big black man verbally assault and then hit another big black man. I'd like to remind you we're still in the South, and white people still think black people are trespassing, so it was a good bet that some well-to-do white woman was just about to pick up her cell phone and call the police.

Skip saw the situation clearly, too, and moved into escape mode. "Come on," he said to Baby Girl. "We need to get out of here before some white people call the cops." And with that, they got into his battered GMC truck and sped away.

And like that, they were gone. Will pulled up a few seconds later, and at the same time a white woman came over, talking into her cell phone.

"Yes, he assaulted him. Yes. I saw it. My name is Karen, K-A-R—"

"Dude, you okay?" Will asked me.

"No," I said.

A few minutes later, the police pulled up.

"I saw it, officer, I saw the whole thing," the woman said. "This man was assaulted!"

The cop pulled me to the side. I had no idea what to do in this situation, but I knew that I really just wanted to go home.

"Just so you know, we have his car stopped just down the street," the officer said. "All you have to do is say the word, and we'll take him in. We have more than enough witnesses saying he assaulted you and that you did not retaliate."

"Naw," I said. "He didn't do anything."

I got up and walked to my car, gingerly touching my face.

"He didn't do anything," I said again, tears running down my face. I finished the sentence in my mind. "At least not anything I didn't deserve."

The officer radioed to his partner. Skip was released. And that was the end of it. Except not really.

THANKSGIVING AND MY FORCED SABBATICAL

From that moment on, I went completely dark on social media. I was disconnected for months—knowing that I had some real issues internally I had to address.

My mom flew to Eutaw for Thanksgiving, and I drove to see her. I told my mom the whole thing. All the sordid details. All of them. Yes, even that detail. Yep. Awkward. She spoke to me like James had spoken to me, without a hint of surprise or condemnation.

"Well," she said. "This isn't your first mistake and it won't be your last." I had heard this before from her.

Okay, to be honest, there were a few times my mother rolled her eyes and said, "Really, son? Really?" But overall, very supportive.

Being able to admit that to my mother, face-to-face, was big, because there's a difference between "I'm worthless" and "I have some work to do." A month passed, and that Christmas, I was back in Las Vegas with my parents. Two days after Christmas, I got a text from a friend.

Skip was posting inflammatory stuff again. He had more questions, and this was his way of trying to get in touch with me.

I still had his number, so I just called him. Maybe it was the time that had passed. Maybe it was the fact that we'd met face-to-face. Maybe it was his heart softening. But this time when we talked on the phone, when he asked me questions and I answered, he accepted them.

He just wanted to make sure that I was really out of the picture. I assured him again that I only hoped the best for him as a man. As a black man.

There was silence on the other end of the phone for a beat. It sank in.

"All right, bro," he said. "All right."

And with that, Big Skip hung up. I haven't heard from him since.

THE SECOND SURGERY
ALWAYS HURTS THE WORST

For the second time in my life, I had been leveled, and reduced to ash. But this moment was different from the painful experience at church. This failure wasn't institutional—it was personal. It was caused not by others, but because of my own issues. It was a battle with my own demons that I'd been unwilling to face. There were four elements to this time in my life. Four things that helped me heal.

One: Music

Someone once told me that true change always begins in our mind, and that people who live great lives are people who habitually think great thoughts.[2] So I created a playlist on Spotify that contained nothing except gospel music. I wanted music forged in the black church, in the experience of suffering and lament, that came from a people who knew they needed a real and tangible hope. Saccharine theology wasn't going to work. I listened to that playlist every day. I understood why my mom and dad raised me on this music. They knew something I didn't know. They knew one day I would need this. And I did. I needed the lyrics of those songs like I needed air.

Listening to this music reshaped my own narrative, and the music and theology of my people helped form me, just like it has since our days in the cotton and rice fields. Listen, I know that sounds dramatic—but it was the truth.

Two: Serving

In 1946, an Austrian psychiatrist named Viktor Frankl who survived the horrors of Auschwitz wrote, "In some ways suffering ceases to be suffering at the moment it finds a meaning, such as the meaning of a sacrifice."[3]

If that's true in the most extreme situations humanity can face, then it's probably true everywhere. And I found it to be true.

Life is miserable, when you're floating around, feeling as though you don't have a purpose.

Shannon and I had now found a church we had fallen in love with, called Cross Point Church. One day, while we were walking past the children's department, the director looked at me and her eyes got really big.

"Oh my gosh, it's you!" she said.

She recognized me from the Gospel Project, and she asked me to help her with their upcoming Easter service. I wasn't even sure that I wanted to be a part of a church again, so I asked for some time to think about it. What pushed me over the edge was the thought that I could help with something that Zoe and Declan might one day go to. So finally, I agreed.

I basically started serving like a theater stage director. I started teaching the stage hosts and weekly teachers stage presence and delivery, worked on the scripts, trained the folks running the media in the back, and in general, made sure things ran well. I don't think I'll ever work for a church again—but if I were to, these are the kind of people I'd want to serve with.

Every Sunday when I walk through the doors of the church, at the far end, they have the church's official motto stenciled, high on the wall, for all to see.

Everyone's welcome.

Nobody is perfect

Anything is possible.

A church full of broken people. Working to heal. These are my people.

Three: The Bench (Again)

During this time, I took a lot of walks around Percy Priest reservoir. Each time, I would stop at my bench. And I would sit. And I would think. And I would pray. And sometimes, when the days were really dark, I would call someone. The two people I called the most were my mom and James.

My mom would remind me that suffering wasn't wasted if it grew you, and that often the greatest lessons in life can't be taught—they have to be experienced. There's also just something about talking to your mom. Truthfully, writing this book has forced me to see just how pivotal my mother has been in my life. I know not everybody has this. But what I do know is that my mom would love to meet you. And if you did meet my mom, I know you'd automatically become a better person.

Next, James. First of all, James is just plain funny. He has the innate ability to just make me laugh. Sometimes, in a world that feels bitter and cold, moments of joy can save your life. Sometimes, he'd make me laugh so hard, people passing by probably wondered if I was insane. But it was more than just laughs. There were a number of moments when I questioned if I'd ever come out of this storm, and James would thunder back with his signature line of encouragement:

"You better remember who you are. You are TYLER MUTHAF*CK*N' MERRITT!"

Now, I know that might sound a little vulgar, but go ahead. Try it. Take your first name. Then take your last name. Then insert a little MUTHAF*CK*N' right smack dab in the middle of it. Got it? Okay, NOW, imagine a big black man yelling all that at you. Feels good, doesn't it? Yeah it does.

Sometimes, he'd just leave me a voice mail with that line. It was James saying, "Look, I know today is a hard day, and that you feel down, and you're fighting shame and feelings of worthlessness.

"But I need to remind you—you're not defined by this mistake, or this failure. You never could be. The deepest part of you is NOT your mistakes or your failures. When God looks at you, He sees so much deeper than your mistakes to your actual identity, your true worth and value. And those of us who love you can see that part, too. So get a better perspective and live that truth out."

There was something about James's voice—something about being seen by another black man as a whole person, and being told that you have worth. His voice was validation and hope and love—spoken in a world that sometimes felt cruel. It was the voice of friendship, is what it was. And it was life to me.

Four: No Social Media

For two years, I was not on social media. If you searched for my name, Google would autofill it to "Is Tyler Merritt dead?" Thanks, Google. But do you know how good this was for me? It was not a punishment. I started noticing how distracted people were by their phones. They were always buzzing, grabbing people's attention, demanding to be looked at. I saw how it affected human interaction, like it was a wall preventing human connection.

Nah. It was good being free. I had real dinners, real conversations. My outrage level was WAY down. I could think long, deep thoughts without interruption. Sure, there were times when people would say, "Hey did you see that thing?" and I would have to say, "No, I did not." But then they'd explain it to me. It was not like a punishing monastic vow I had to struggle through. It was more like my chrysalis.

COMING OUT OF THE DARK

During this time, I felt a bit like an athlete who had just suffered a catastrophic injury. When that happens, you know that you're going to be sidelined for a while. But you're not just sitting around: your life turns into rehab. Rehab isn't fun. It's always painful, which is a sharp reminder that you're hurt. It's a daily reminder that you're not in the game. The point of rehab is to get back in the game. I felt like I was never going to be well enough to play. And I wasn't even sure I even wanted to play.

For two years, I didn't say or write or produce anything. My mind didn't dream up ideas. I had nothing to say.

One day, as I was taking my daily walk, I realized that I had begun to see some of the same people. I had the thought, "I bet those people would be surprised if they knew what I was listening to."

I thought it would be a cool thing to document. So I just filmed myself out for a walk, heading to my bench. The video starts out in black-and-white, because this first part of the video is in a world of music. A world where color doesn't matter. It's about sound. You see me, putting on my headphones and pulling up the hood to my sweatshirt. For the next few minutes, the viewer is going to hear what I hear, including my interior monologue.

"Let's get this walk in," my voice says. "Now what to listen to?"

I start walking, with the streets of Nashville in the background. And the viewer is treated to my playlist and my running interior commentary:

"Izzo" by Jay-Z.
Naw. Thank you, J.
"All I Really Want" by Alanis Morissette.
Ooo! Still one of the top five albums of all time. Come at me.
"Wanted Dead or Alive" by Bon Jovi.
Bon Jovi and them were gangstas. You can't tell me nothin'. They was
    gangstas.
"Boyz-n-the-Hood" by Eazy-E.
Yeah, we were gangsta once. Back in…junior high.
"Waving Through a Window" from the musical *Dear Evan Hansen*.
I am not too old to play Evan Hansen. I could do it. Okay, maybe his
    grandpa.

"Single Ladies" by Beyoncé.

Ha!

"Don't Take the Money" by Bleachers.

Man, I wish I wrote this song.

"Made a Way" by Travis Greene.

Lord, you're so good to me. And God I really don't deserve…

"All Falls Down" by Kanye West.

I don't mess with Kanye no more. Who am I kidding, man? Haha!

"Love Story" by Taylor Swift.

Can these folks tell that I'm listening to Taylor Swift?

"Round Here" by Counting Crows.

This record changed my life. For real.

"So Will I (100 Billion X)" by Hillsong UNITED.

It always comes back to you.

In the video, as I come around a corner, the lyrics spill out from the final song by Hillsong UNITED.

On a hill you created, abandoned in darkness to die.

Then, in the video, I stop walking. My face changes, from surprise to recognition to abject fear. I blink. I swallow hard. My lip trembles in terror. I reach up and quickly remove my hoodie and my headphones. The music disappears, and the video changes back to color. A world in which color matters. A world in which we're the same. Until we're not.

"What's your name, boy?" a voice says. It's clear I'm being stopped by someone, though they are out of frame. I do not move. My face is painted with fear.

"I said, what's your name?" the voice says with a menacing tone.

"It's Ty—"

And the video goes to a black screen. And these words appear.

For all those who never made it home.

I made that video in April of 2020, still carrying the stories of Alton and Philando and the rest with me. I titled it "The Playlist." I thought, "Man, that is powerful." But I had made this one just for me. I wasn't going to release it. I was still too fearful to let something out into the world. I wasn't ready. But sometimes, life doesn't care if you're ready.

MEMORIAL DAY WEEKEND 2020

Over Memorial Day weekend 2020, toward the beginning of the COVID-19 pandemic, three things happened in quick succession. Three tragically important videos flooded the internet.

Video 1: Amy Cooper, a white woman in Central Park, threatened to call the cops on a black man who was bird-watching because he dared to tell her to put her dog on a leash.

In the video, Cooper calls 911 and then using false histrionics, claims the man is threatening her.[4] A white woman, lying, making a threat, and weaponizing the police against a black man. This is how black people used to get lynched.

Video 2: Right on the heels of that video, another horrific moment caught on tape, one we already covered in chapter 7: the lynching of Ahmaud Arbery.

Video 3: And then, a third video surfaced, showing Minneapolis police officer Derek Chauvin kneeling on the neck of George Floyd for 7 minutes and 46 seconds.[5] With a smug look on his face, ignoring the pleas from bystanders, Chauvin kneeled on Floyd's neck until he died. The world watched as an officer of the peace killed a man.

An unarmed man.

An unarmed black man.

Again. Trauma. That could have been me.

Suddenly (and tragically), the "Playlist" video I'd made mere days earlier seemed even more relevant.

And with that, I posted the "Playlist" video. None of my social media accounts were even open, really. I was not even sure how anyone would find the video. I had the thought that perhaps I would share the link with a few friends. Not a major step, but it was a step. A baby step back.

The next morning at seven a.m. my phone rang. It was my mother.

"Someone from Jimmy Kimmel's show is trying to reach you," she told me. "Get a pen and paper and write this number down."

Get a pen and paper? Mom, I haven't had a pen and paper since I was in high school. It turns out that late night talk show host Jimmy Kimmel had seen my "Before You Call the Cops" video, and in the wake of a shocked nation, wanted permission to play it on his show. I had seen Kimmel handle other important and sensitive topics, most notably the issue of national health care. In a powerful monologue back in 2017, Kimmel shared about how his newborn son had been born with a rare heart defect[6] requiring open heart surgery just hours after his birth.[7] Kimmel, talking through his own tears, shared about how deeply personal this was for him and how not everyone has the same access to the level of medical care that he did. I remember thinking that had to be one of the most exceptional moments in the history of late-night television.

I called the number my mother had given me back and gave Jimmy Kimmel and his crew full permission to use the video.

And that Friday night, I watched his segment about George Floyd. Kimmel began talking about the weeklong tensions that had erupted in violence in Minneapolis and began talking about the tragedy of George Floyd. It was so moving that I got lost in it, and about three-quarters of the way through, it hit me that I was also a part of this segment. Jimmy ended saying:

> We need to work on this problem we have. This blatant double standard. Because when you stand in front of the flag, you put your hand on your heart and you pledge allegiance with liberty and justice for all. We don't have that "for all." I mean, I have it. A lot of you have it. But it's not "for all." So, my wife showed me a video last night. It's a couple of years old but it really is relevant, I think.

And before I show it to you, I want to say that it's a shame that it even had to be made. But it's very powerful and I think it's worth seeing, especially right now.[8]

And then he played my "Before You Call the Cops" video. I was humbled to be a part of this moment. After the show aired, I thought to myself, "Well, we are in this fight now. If I've never had the title 'activist' before, I do now."

Soon, I began getting alerts on my phone—"Before You Call the Cops" was going viral. Again. Another 30 million views. How many videos go viral twice?

But that wasn't all. Just two days earlier, I had sent a link to "The Playlist" video to a few of my close friends just to get their feedback. The texts and emails began to flow in.

"Post this everywhere. Right now," my friend Joy texted me.

"The world needs to see this, brother," James texted.

Jimmy Kimmel messaged me, telling me to reopen my Twitter account to the public and get back on social media in full force. "What you're doing is important," he said.

Get back in the game?

I felt fear rising up inside of me. But I also felt something else. As I sat on my back porch, music from my headphones poured out. It was the song "Thank You" by Anthony Brown. The lyrics from this gospel song arrested me.

You did not create me to worry
You did not create me to fear.

I had just spent two years in the wilderness. Two years doing the hard, inner work of confronting my past and my weaknesses. And just because I had failed, in small and big ways, so many times, and just because I was a massive, messed-up wreck of a human being did not mean that I couldn't say something true. That did not disqualify me from trying to do something significant. It did not prevent me from trying to use my life to help.

I was beginning to feel—and I mean really feel—that maybe my shadow days were over.

And with that, I decided.

Oh, sure, I was never gonna be president now.

But I had work to do. We had work to do.

We have work to do.

So, let's go change the world, shall we?

CHAPTER 18

IF SHE ONLY KNEW
(PART 2)

Every single day, I try to exercise.

I set out this morning on the typical five-mile route that I take around Nashville. I go down my street, through my neighborhood, and then out to the J. Percy Priest Dam, where I can look out over the lake and the water. There's a bench along that route that is my bench.

I even call it that.

I approached the intersection on my way to the trails and quieter side streets that lead to the dam and the lake. As I approached the crosswalk, I thought back to something that had happened a little while ago. How I was about to walk across an intersection and there was a woman sitting there, in a blue-and-white older-model Ford truck. As I was about to cross, I knew—and man, I just *knew*—that I was going to startle her. So I took off my sunglasses and pulled down the hood of my Alabama sweatshirt and took off my headphones and tried to think my best black Mister Rogers thoughts, so she wouldn't be frightened by me.

But that didn't work. As I passed in front of her blue-and-white older-model Ford truck, she saw me.

"Oh, my GAAAWWWD," she said, terrified. She grabbed her purse from the passenger seat and then frantically rolled up her window. I heard the *click* of her automatic door locks activating.

And then she stared straight ahead at the stoplight. She wouldn't look at me. She tried to pretend I didn't exist.

It hurts when someone pretends you don't exist.

It hurts even more when someone secretly wishes you didn't exist and they let that secret thought leak out, and you see it.

Because I've been black all my life, and that happens so much, you think maybe by now I'd be used to it. But I'm not. It still hurts.

As I walked, I saw my bench around the bend.

When I see it, I say to myself, "That's my bench."

As I sat and stared out at the water, sipping on my Smartwater and drinking in the crisp fall air, I thought about that lady in the blue-and-white older-model Ford truck. Why had she been so scared?

I think it's because she didn't see me. I mean, she saw me. But all she saw was a six-foot-two black man in a hoodie.

If she had known everything I had to go through in my entire life to get here to this moment—all the failures and heartbreaks and triumphs and tragedies that have made me who I am in this moment in this instant—if she had, oh, I don't know, read this whole damn book—then maybe she'd know my heart, and she'd know all the love I have tried to give to this world, and then she might have leaped out of the cab of her car and ran to me, saying, "Is that Tyler Merritt? Oh, you brilliant, beautiful, black king!" And we would have hugged, like old friends.

Did I mention I'm the best hugger in the entire greater Nashville metro area? That is quantifiable.

But she didn't. So I worked to make myself small for her. To do whatever it took to make sure she wasn't frightened.

Because that's what real kings do. They serve. In love.

I wish that's the way it went down. But it didn't.

A young couple jogged by me. They smiled at me just now. I smiled back. That made me feel good, because it's not always like that. Sometimes, when

I'm out on my walks, people get nervous when they see a six-foot-two black man with dreadlocks coming, and they cross the street, even though I try my very best to smile brightly to everyone I see. They probably don't think I notice. But I notice every time.

Because I've been black all my life, and that happens so much, you think maybe by now I'd be used to it. But I'm not. It still hurts.

Why did that couple that was jogging smile at me, when this lady in the blue-and-white older-model Ford truck got so scared? I don't know. I was only a few feet away from her, but the separation was immense. Worlds apart.

If she would just get close enough to really talk and really see me, I bet we'd realize we have so much in common. So much.

Like you and me.

Look at us. Hey! Look at us. Who woulda thought? Not me! But here we are, eighteen chapters later. You just spent a crap-ton of time with me, from elementary school to now. Heck, look how much you know about me. If you're ever on *Jeopardy!* (RIP Alex Trebek) and the category is Tyler Merritt, you will score some major points.

- This fruit is hated by Tyler Merritt, who thinks it is utterly disgusting.
- You don't have to enumerate black ravens to know how influential this nineties alternative rock band was in Merritt's life.
- This Broadway musical was Tyler's first, a can't "miss" production.
- This dairy product is something Tyler thinks you should never lick off another person's girlfriend.

You would clean house in that category. You know about my past. You know about some of my deepest religious experiences. You've heard about some of my most profound failures. And you know how much of my story is due to the fact that I experience this life as a black man in America.

A very sexy black man. Arguably as sexy as Denzel. Arguably.

But a black man, nonetheless.

In a real way, because you and I took the time to connect, now you know me. I wish I could have had that kind of conversation with that lady in the blue-and-white older-model Ford truck. I wish I could do this with everyone, honestly. I wish we could go out and get a cup of coffee together. I wish we could sit down together.

I'm not sure what we'd talk about. Just to get the ball rolling, maybe I'd share about me a little bit. Probably start at the very beginning. That's a very good place to start. I'd share about how so many roads in my own life go right back to my father, and somehow, trying to understand him has helped me understand myself.

I'd share about my mother's life, how she grew up in the South, and how that turned her into a woman who was driven to escape from the prison of poor circumstances. She was running hard for a long time. She ran hard up a corporate ladder. Always running, my mom. But she eventually slowed down enough to have me. And now I feel like when she's talking to me, she slows all the way down. My mama is a queen. When you get to meet her, you'll see.

I'd share about the things that have hurt me. Those sorts of things are often difficult to talk about. But we've both got them in our lives, don't we? I've put my heart out to people I thought would be safe, and they hurt me. I bet you do, too. That's hard.

Maybe that's as far as we'd get. But maybe not. Maybe we'd keep talking. Maybe we'd keep talking about the wounds that life has given us. Those can be difficult to talk about. But I find that the toughest things to talk about are the things that I've done to hurt other people. Damn. I feel a lot of shame about those. I want to hide those things, and disappear, behind my coffee. Shame is powerful, huh? Yeah, I know shame too well. It's been an unwelcome companion for too long in my story. I'm afraid if I told you those things, you wouldn't like me much anymore. And that you'd stand up and leave, maybe because my bad things remind you of your own bad things.

But I'd hope that you'd stay. Because shame is not where the story ends.

Because there is another story—a story that's older than me by a good measure. A story that was told in the fields by my people a long time ago and a story that was told many ages before that. It's a story that I heard for the first time at a summer camp in Las Vegas wearing a Triple F.A.T. Goose jacket.

It's a story I first heard that says despite the bad things we've done, that we can be cleansed and forgiven by a Love that's more wild and rushing than the fiercest river. It's a story that I used to think was too good to be true, that there was a God who sees all, but doesn't reject me, or look at me with disgust, even though I wouldn't even blame Him if He did, because the truth is, I deserve it. I know what I've done. I deserve it a thousand times over.

But this Love is bigger than even a thousand times over. It doesn't just stay far away but comes close.

Close.

Closer than my very breath.

I remember walking back to my cabin at that summer camp that night in Las Vegas, feeling like I had just heard a story that would change me for the rest of my life.

And it did.

And I would sit across from you, emotional about how far I had come, choking back tears.

And if you shared your stories with me, I'd show you where and how our stories are the same. I'd laugh with you, because it's good to share joy.

And when it got time for you to tell the hard parts.

The sad parts.

The broken parts.

The parts where you didn't know if you could even go on because the pain was so deep.

Well, I know I would cry with you, because I've known pain, too. And you'd find a friend in my tears.

And when you had to tell the hard parts of your story. The times when you fell down. Or lost yourself. Or lost your way. Or did a bad thing. You'd look up and you wouldn't see any judgment in my eyes.

Because I've known the darkness, too. I know what it's like to be lost. You'd see that in my face.

And I would tell you, "Thank you for telling me that," and I would mean it. To the core of my heart. Because now that you told me that, I know that we're the same.

But we are also so very different from each other.

Yeah, that's what I want. I want more time, sitting across from people. People like you.

And at the end of that time I would hope…

That if the time came…

And life got tough for you…

(And it will get tough.)

That you would know you'd found a friend. A person who would always be a soft place to land, when life crashes down.

And I would hope that if things got tough for me…

Maybe really tough…

Maybe because of the color of my skin…

Maybe because some people don't see me as a real person because of my melanin…

It's my hope that you'd stand.

And that you would say.

In a loud and clear voice.

Stop.

I know that man.

He's a mix of the good and the bad, for sure.

But I know him.

And he's my brother.

I hope that you'd stand with me.

You better believe that I would stand for you.

That's what I hope for, that somehow by sitting across from each other, we'd end up side by side.

And that somehow by sitting across from each other, we'd end up standing up for each other.

All because you decided to join me for a conversation.

Yeah. I'd love to share that moment. Over coffee.

And oh. By the way.

I take my coffee black…

ACKNOWLEDGMENTS

God, you really do see us. Thank you that you see us and still choose to love us.

Mom and Dad, in so many ways this book is simply a tribute to all that you have poured into my life. I've only ever just wanted to make you proud.

Shannon Albrecht, you've walked through most of these stories and you are still here. Thank you.

Thank you, Las Vegas, you raised me well.

Eutaw, Alabama…So much for nobody knowing anything about you. You deserve for the world to know your story.

Gigi and Bella, we are working on building a better world for you.

Sandra Seaton, thank you for showing me the stage.

Joy Demain, thank you for showing me how to own the stage.

Pattie Emmett, thank you for showing me that I could use the stage to change the world.

Mr. Morris, I see the same skies through brown eyes that you see through blue.

The Las Vegas Academy, in one little year you changed the entirety of my life.

Bob Abplanalp, you let a group of nobodies take over a whole department. We've never been the same since. Is there such a thing as a Theater Dad?

The Broken Frame family: Mike, Keith, Tyson, Josh, Adam, Charlie, Don, Dave, Nate, Blue, Rob, Ant, Mijo, Andrew, Ron. There are only a few in the world who know what it's like to walk on stage and take on the world with your band. It's a bond you never outlive. Thank you for being a part of some of the best memories of my life.

Theater Central, you all know who you are. In so many ways you were so crucial in teaching me how to build things and learning how to dream.

The Bay Area theater community, please take this as my official apology for not telling your stories in this book. I could write a whole other book just on how the years I spent with you shaped so much of who I am.

Mike Holser, you are legitimately the closest thing I have to an actual brother. I'm just glad that if I had to lose you, it was to the incredible Erin.

James Iglehart, we've come a long way from the Denny's parking lot. Sharks and Seahorses, my brother. Love you, too, Dawn!

Rob Cureton, you are my brother for life. You are a creative genius. The world is yours.

Dan, Reba, Ally, Justin, and Jordan, please know that everything I do, you all are a part of it!

Ben Rodriguez, you will always be our little Mijo.

Antjuan Johnson, you are such a huge part of all of these musical stories, but like a good song, editing sucks! You are in all of this.

John Bridges, we've come a long way since Beverly Village, my brother.

Todd Metzker, just pour some Coke up in it.

Bridgey, Scott, Zoe, and Declan, I'll see you Sunday. For the rest of my life.

Sara Horton, you continue to help me make it through. I only hope I can do the same for you someday.

Nick Miller and Mosaic Youth, this gray hair is all y'all's fault. You all aged a brotha in the best way possible. I will always love you all.

Shymene, big sis. Yo, you were everything I needed at the perfect time in my life.

Lisa Portale, you've been a steady rock. We all so badly need a Lisa in our lives.

Brian Waite, all you ever have to do is call, my brother, and you know I got you.

Donnie, Kindred, Aaron, and Wes, who would have guessed that folding jeans would teach us so many lessons.

Jim, Mel, Tish, Jordan, Savannah, sometimes family just calls out to you. Here's to answering the call. We miss you, Mel.

Cathleen, I love you, and Elysha, get back to writing.

Sami Klein, I wrote a damn book and of course you are in it. That is all. Love you, Sami.

Kelly McDonnell, you are a poet and I'm so glad that you finally know it.

Maddie, let's cure JM. www.curejm.org

Sophie, thank you for continuing to help the world to breathe.

Posh Spice, thank you for letting me write about you.

Dave Tieche, I never want to write anything again without you by my side. Two heads are always better than one, especially when the two heads can both quote New Edition accurately. I'm glad I found you before the rest of the world catches on. Look at what we done did.

Erin Niumata, you scare me, my friend. I never want to not be on your team. You're the best.

Josh Shipp and my folks at Folio, all of this is your fault and I couldn't be more thankful.

Beth Adams, it started with sweet and sour vegetarian chicken and ended with Adam Duritz. I can't wait 'til the next one.

India Hunter, having you (specifically) be a part of this book is exactly what I needed. Thank you, India. Yes, I sang that in my head.

Daisy Hutton and my Hachette family, thank you for believing me when I told you that I wanted to change the world. You didn't ask questions, you just wanted to know how you could help. Superheroes you are, all of you!

To my Houghton Talent family, I'm honored to be taking over the world with you.

Cookie at the McCray Agency, we all get better because of how much you believe in us.

Talent Plus, thank you for seeing that "it" factor before anyone else did.

Nakia Tomlinson, Jason Arel, Tim Rabdau, Jessica Gebhardt, and Comcast, I can't thank you enough for allowing me to be me.

Joy and Michelle, the best part of making a viral video is the two of you coming into my life. Not really sure how I existed without you two before now.

Jimmy and Molly, thank you for being so wonderfully gracious when you simply didn't have to be. My promise to you is that I will try my best to do the same for others.

Lee Moran, keep using your words to change the world, my friend.

Nico Pitney and NowThis, thank you for continuing to amplify voices of color.

Erik Kline, your original investment in me is one of the main reasons I will never stop working.

Dr. Marcus Tan (aka "The Don"), Dr. Daniel Barocas (aka "Scottie Pippen"), and the entire staff at Vanderbilt-Ingram Cancer Center. Thank you for literally saving my life.

To the Broken Frame fans, I'm so glad that you get to be a part of this story.

I'd like to acknowledge the haters for helping me fuel the fire that keeps me going. Y'all know who you are and I will never forget you.

To all of my Tyler Merritt Project peeps that have been with me from the ground floor; I can't thank you enough for believing in a vision that leads with love. Let's go change the world, shall we?

NOTES

CHAPTER 3

1. "Murder of Tupac Shakur," Wikipedia. https://en.wikipedia.org/wiki/Murder _of_Tupac_Shakur.
2. Chuck Philips, "Who Killed Tupac Shakur?" *Los Angeles Times*, September 6, 2002. https://www.latimes.com/archives/la-xpm-2002-sep-06-fi-tupac6-story .html.
3. Robert Sam Anson, "To Die Like a Gangsta," *Vanity Fair*, March 1997. https: //www.vanityfair.com/culture/1997/03/tupac-shakur-rap-death#.
4. Damon Hodge, "Gangster Turned Savior," Las Vegas Weekly, December 22, 2005. https://lasvegasweekly.com/news/archive/2005/dec/22/gangster-turned -savior/.
5. Towers Productions, "Sin City," *Gangland* (New York: A&E Television Networks, 2008). https://search.alexanderstreet.com/preview/work /bibliographic_entity%7Cvideo_work%7C1796620.
6. "Donna Street Crips," Unitedgangs.com. https://unitedgangs.com/donna-street -crips/.

CHAPTER 4

1. Henry Louis Gates Jr. "The Truth behind '40 Acres and a Mule,'" pbs.org. https://www.pbs.org/wnet/african-americans-many-rivers-to-cross/history /the-truth-behind-40-acres-and-a-mule/.
2. Christian G. Appy, *Working-Class War: American Combat Soldiers and Vietnam* (Chapel Hill: University of North Carolina Press, 1993), 27.
3. Marvin Gaye, "What's Going On." Genius Lyrics. https://genius.com/Marvin -gaye-whats-going-on-lyrics.
4. ASVAB, "History of Military Testing." https://www.officialasvab.com/history _res.htm.

CHAPTER 7

1. C. S. Lewis, *Mere Christianity* (New York: HarperCollins Publishers, 2001), 128 (section on "The Great Sin").

2. Brené Brown, "The Power of Vulnerability" (video). https://singjupost.com /power-vulnerability-brene-brown-transcript/.

3. Kelly McLaughlin, "A White Woman Who Called the Police on a Black Man Telling Her to Put Her Dog on a Leash Says She's 'Not a Racist,'" Insider, May 26, 2020. https://www.insider.com/central-park-woman-called-police-black -man-says-shes-not-racist-2020-5.

4. Eliott C. McLaughlin, "Ahmaud Arbery Was Hit with a Truck before He Died, and His Killer Allegedly Used a Racial Slur, Investigator Testifies," CNN, June 4, 2020. https://www.cnn.com/2020/06/04/us/mcmichaels-hearing-ahmaud -arbery/index.html.

5. Joanna Walters, "Georgia to Consider Charges in Killing of Unarmed Black Jogger as Video Emerges," *Guardian*, May 6, 2020. https://www.theguardian .com/us-news/2020/may/05/georgia-brunswick-shooting-ahmaud-arbery -grand-jury. Warning: this news article contains an embedded video which shows the footage of Arbery's killing. Viewer discretion is strongly advised.

6. David Morgan, "Bryan Stevenson: 'The North Won the Civil War, but the South Won the Narrative War' on the History of Racism," *CBS This Morning*, June 24, 2019. https://www.cbsnews.com/news/bryan-stevenson-we-are-all -complicit-in-our-countrys-history-of-racism/.

7. NPR, "Congress Apologizes for Slavery, Jim Crow," *Tell Me More*, July 30, 2008. https://www.npr.org/templates/story/story.php?storyId=93059465.

8. Journal of the Proceedings of the Constitutional Convention. https://babel .hathitrust.org/cgi/pt?id=uc2.ark:/13960/t7sn0dk7c&view=1up&seq=13.

9. Thanks to scholar and author Malcolm Foley for this succinct definition, given during this podcast. https://mereorthodoxy.com/lynchings-protests-unrest -racism-america-malcolm-foley/.

10. "Facts about Lynching," WashingtonPost.com, no date. https://www .washingtonpost.com/archive/local/2005/07/07/facts-about-lynching-38 /6cc4d6da-d7e5-4617-b571-6c87964dee60/.

11. Bryan Stevenson, *Lynching in America*. https://lynchinginamerica.eji.org /report/.

12. LifeWay Research, "The State of American Theology Study 2018,"

commissioned by Ligonier Ministries. http://lifewayresearch.com/wp-content
/uploads/2018/10/Ligonier-State-of-Theology-2018.pdf.

13. Eric Weiner, "Where Heaven and Earth Come Closer," *New York Times*, March 9, 2012. https://www.nytimes.com/2012/03/11/travel/thin-places-where-we -are-jolted-out-of-old-ways-of-seeing-the-world.html.

CHAPTER 8

1. "NAACP History: W. E. B. Du Bois." https://www.naacp.org/naacp-history -w-e-b-dubois/.

2. W. E. B. Du Bois, *The Souls of Black Folk* (New York, and Avenel, NJ: Gramercy Books, 1994).

CHAPTER 9

1. Erin Duffin, "College Enrollment in the United States from 1965 to 2018 and Projections Up to 2029 for Public and Private Colleges," Statistica, November 5, 2020. https://www.statista.com/statistics/183995/us-college-enrollment-and -projections-in-public-and-private-institutions/.

2. Dave Roos, "How the Cold War Space Race Led to U.S. Students Doing Tons of Homework," History.com, August 13, 2019. https://www.history.com/news /homework-cold-war-sputnik.

3. All data and charts on the following pages come from this NAEP report: https: //nces.ed.gov/pubs93/93442.pdf.

4. Jason A. Grissom, "Why Do Fewer Black Students Get Identified as Gifted?" Republished from The Conversation. https://digitalpromise.org/2018/09/18 /fewer-black-students-get-identified-gifted/.

5. A. W. Geiger, "America's Public School Teachers Are Far Less Racially and Ethnically Diverse than Their Students," Pew Research Center, August 27, 2018. https://www.pewresearch.org/fact-tank/2018/08/27/americas-public -school-teachers-are-far-less-racially-and-ethnically-diverse-than-their -students/.

6. Deirdre Oakley, Jacob Stowell, and John R. Logan, "The Impact of Desegregation on Black Teachers in the Metropolis, 1970–2000," *Ethnic and Racial Studies* 39(9) (2009): 1576–1598. https://www.ncbi.nlm.nih.gov/pmc /articles/PMC3769798/.

7. Oakley, "Impact of Desegregation on Black Teachers in the Metropolis."

8. Mallory Lutz, "The Hidden Cost of *Brown v. Board*: African American Educators' Resistance to Desegregating Schools," *Online Journal of Rural Research & Policy* 12(4) (2017). http://newprairiepress.org/ojrrp/vol12/iss4/2/.

9. EdBuild, "Nonwhite School Districts Get $23 Billion Less than White Districts Despite Serving the Same Number of Students." https://edbuild.org/content/23-billion.

10. EdBuild, "Nonwhite School Districts Get $23 Billion Less than White Districts."

11. Lauren Camera, "White Students Get More K–12 Funding than Students of Color: Report," *US News & World Report*, February 26, 2019. https://www.usnews.com/news/education-news/articles/2019-02-26/white-students-get-more-k-12-funding-than-students-of-color-report.

CHAPTER 10

1. Terry Mattingly, "On Religion: 'Nones' on the Rise," *Times Standard*, November 23, 2019. https://www.times-standard.com/2019/11/23/on-religion-nones-on-the-rise-2/.

CHAPTER 11

1. Kathryn Utke, "How *Rent* Revolutionized Modern Musical Theatre," The Learned Fangirl, no date. http://thelearnedfangirl.com/how-rent-revolutionized-modern-musical-theatre/.

2. Anthony Tommasini, "The Seven-Year Odyssey That Led to 'Rent,'" *New York Times*, March 17, 1996. https://www.nytimes.com/1996/03/17/theater/theather-the-seven-year-odyssey-that-led-to-rent.html.

3. "Lin-Manuel Miranda on 'In the Heights,'" video, YouTube, May 16, 2008. https://www.youtube.com/watch?v=EsY1QnahXdQ&feature=emb_logo.

CHAPTER 12

1. Deidre McPhillips, "How Racially and Ethnically Diverse Is Your City?" *US News & World Report*, January 22, 2020. https://www.usnews.com/news/cities/articles/2020-01-22/measuring-racial-and-ethnic-diversity-in-americas-cities.

2. Chinese Exclusion Act (1882). ourdocuments.gov. https://www.ourdocuments.gov/doc.php?flash=false&doc=47.

3. Olive Davis, *Stockton: Sunrise Port on the San Joaquin* (American Historical Press, 1998).

4. Javier Padilla, "Racism in Your Neighborhood," *Placeholder Magazine*, January 14, 2017. http://www.placeholdermag.com/culture/2017/01/14 /racisminyourneighborhood.html.

5. George Lipsitz, *The Possessive Investment in Whiteness: How White People Profit from Identity Politics* (Philadelphia: Temple University Press, 1998).

6. "Stockton (Detention Facility)." Densho Encyclopedia. https://encyclopedia .densho.org/Stockton_(detention_facility).

7. Emily Zentner, "What Happened to the Property of Sacramento's Japanese American Community Interned during World War II?" *Great Question*, CapRadio, June 4, 2019. https://www.capradio.org/articles/2019/06/04/what -happened-to-the-property-of-sacramentos-japanese-american-community -interned-during-world-war-ii/.

8. Gaby Galvin, "America's Most Diverse City Is Still Scarred by Its Past," *US News & World Report*, January 22, 2020. https://www.usnews.com/news /cities/articles/2020-01-22/stockton-california-americas-most-diverse-city-is -still-scarred-by-its-past.

9. Gwen Aviles, "An Ugly Legacy: Latino Couple Finds Racist Covenant in Housing Paperwork," NBC News, November 15, 2019. https://www.nbcnews .com/news/latino/ugly-legacy-latino-couple-finds-racist-covenant-housing -paperwork-n1082476.

10. "Mapping Inequality: Redlining in New Deal America," Digital Scholarship Lab, University of Richmond. https://dsl.richmond.edu/panorama /redlining/#loc=13/37.953/-121.331&city=stockton-ca&adview=full. This database of public maps is a searchable database that allows you to look for your city and see the prejudicial legal practices that codified racial and class segregation taken from official public records.

CHAPTER 13

1. United States Census. https://www.census.gov/quickfacts/fact/table/US /RHI125219#RHI125218.

2. Michael Gee, "Why Aren't Black Employees Getting More White-Collar Jobs?" *Harvard Business Review*, February 28, 2018. https://hbr.org/2018/02/why -arent-black-employees-getting-more-white-collar-jobs.

3. Phil Wahba, "There Are Now Just 4 Black CEOs in the Fortune 500 as Tapestry Boss Resigns," *Fortune*, July 21, 2020. https://fortune.com /2020/07/21/tapestry-black-ceos-fortune-500-jide-zeitlin/.

4. Phil Wahba, "The Number of Black CEOs in the Fortune 500 Remains Very Low," *Fortune*, June 1, 2020. https://fortune.com/2020/06/01/black-ceos -fortune-500-2020-african-american-business-leaders/.

5. History of the Fortune 500, *Fortune*. https://qlik.fortune.com/.

6. Clifton R. Wharton Jr. Profile. Blackentrepreneurprofile.com, June 28, 2016. https://www.blackentrepreneurprofile.com/people/person/clifton-r-wharton-jr.

7. "Black Chairman and CEO's of Fortune 500 Companies." Blackentrepreneurprofile.com, updated February 26, 2021. https://www .blackentrepreneurprofile.com/collections/black-fortune-500-ceos.

8. Wahba, "Number of Black CEOs."

9. Richard Zweigenhaft, "Diversity among CEOs and Corporate Directors: Has the Heyday Come and Gone?" Who Rules America. https://whorulesamerica .ucsc.edu/power/diversity_among_ceos.html.

10. Jeanne Sahadi, "After Years of Talking about Diversity, the Number of Black Leaders at US Companies Is Still Dismal," CNN Business, June 2, 2020. https://www.cnn.com/2020/06/02/success/diversity-and-black-leadership-in -corporate-america/index.html.

11. According to Stanford Corporate Governance Research Initiative.

12. Derek T. Dingle, "Power in the Boardroom: Blacks in Corporate Governance," *Black Enterprise*, October 9, 2019. https://www.blackenterprise.com/power-in -the-boardroom-corporate-governance/.

13. Julia Borstin, "Opportunity Missed: Why There Are No Black CEOs on This Year's Disruptor 50 List," CNBC, June 16, 2020. https://www.cnbc .com/2020/06/16/why-there-are-no-black-ceos-on-this-years-disruptor-50 -list.html.

14. Marlon Nichols et al., "Deconstructing the Pipeline Myth and the Case for More Diverse Fund Managers," MaC Venture Capital. https:// macventurecapital.com/in-the-news/deconstructing-the-pipeline-myth-and -the-case-for-more-diverse-fund-managers/.

15. Jessica Guynn and Brent Schrotenboer, "Why Are There Still So Few Black Executives in America?" USA Today Money, August 20, 2020. https://

www.usatoday.com/in-depth/money/business/2020/08/20/racism-black
-america-corporate-america-facebook-apple-netflix-nike-diversity
/5557003002/.

16. "All-Time #MLBRank: The 10 Greatest Second Basemen," ESPN.com,
July 11, 2016. https://www.espn.com/mlb/story/_/page/mlbrank100
_top10secondbasemen/ranking-top-10-second-basemen-ever.

17. "Jackie Robinson." National Baseball Hall of Fame and Museum. https://
baseballhall.org/hall-of-famers/robinson-jackie.

CHAPTER 14

1. "The Impeachment of Andrew Johnson (1868) President of the United States."
United States Senate, Art & History. https://www.senate.gov/artandhistory
/history/common/briefing/Impeachment_Johnson.htm.

2. History.com Editors, "14th Amendment," History.com, November 9, 2009,
updated January 12, 2021. https://www.history.com/topics/black-history
/fourteenth-amendment.

3. Allen W. Trelease, *White Terror: The Ku Klux Klan Conspiracy and Southern
Reconstruction* (Praeger, 1971).

4. Equal Justice Initiative, "Lynching in America." https://lynchinginamerica.eji
.org/report/.

5. History.com Editors, "Fort Pillow Massacre," History.com, November 9, 2009,
updated June 21, 2019. https://www.history.com/topics/american-civil-war
/fort-pillow-massacre.

6. History.com Editors, "Hundreds of Union Soldiers Killed in Fort Pillow
Massacre," This Day in History April 12, 1864, History.com. https://www
.history.com/this-day-in-history/the-fort-pillow-massacre.

7. United Nations Office on Genocide Prevention and the Responsibility to
Protect, "Definition: War Crimes." https://www.un.org/en/genocideprevention
/war-crimes.shtml.

8. Keisha N. Blain, "Made by History: Tennessee Just Showed That White
Supremacy Is Alive and Well," *Washington Post*, July 15, 2019. https://www
.washingtonpost.com/outlook/2019/07/15/tennessee-just-showed-that-white
-supremacy-is-alive-well/.

9. Joel Ebert, "Nathan Bedford Forrest Bust at the Tennessee Capitol: What You

Need to Know," *Tennessean*, August 18, 2017. https://www.tennessean.com/story/news/2017/08/18/nathan-bedford-forrest-bust-tennessee-capitol-what-you-need-know/578112001/.

10. Louise Davis, "Forrest in Bronze Immune to Time," *Tennessean*, October 29, 1978. https://www.newspapers.com/clip/13133466/the-tennessean/.

11. United States Census, "QuickFacts: Tennessee." https://www.census.gov/quickfacts/fact/table/TN,US/PST045219.

CHAPTER 16

1. "Selma, Alabama." Wikiwand. https://www.wikiwand.com/en/Selma,_Alabama.

2. Equal Justice Initiative, "Lynching in America." https://lynchinginamerica.eji.org/report/.

3. Richard Fausset, Richard Pérez-Peña, and Campbel Robertson, "Alton Sterling Shooting in Baton Rouge Prompts Justice Dept. Investigation," *New York Times*, July 6, 2016. https://www.nytimes.com/2016/07/06/us/alton-sterling-baton-rouge-shooting.html. Warning: this news article contains an embedded video which shows the footage of Sterling's killing. Viewer discretion is strongly advised.

4. Jamiles Lartey, "Alton Sterling Shooting: Two Police Officers Will Not Be Charged with Any Crime," *Guardian*, March 27, 2018. https://www.theguardian.com/us-news/2018/mar/27/alton-sterling-shooting-two-police-officers-will-not-be-charged-with-any.

5. Alex Johnson and Gabe Gutierrez, "Baton Rouge Store Owner Says His Video Shows Cops 'Murdered' Alton Sterling," NBC News, July 6, 2016. https://www.nbcnews.com/news/us-news/baton-rouge-store-owner-says-his-video-shows-cops-murdered-n604841. Warning: this news article contains an embedded video which shows the footage of Sterling's killing. Viewer discretion is strongly advised.

6. German Lopez, "Alton Sterling Shooting: Video from Baton Rouge Police's Cameras Released," Vox.com, updated March 30, 2018. https://www.vox.com/2016/7/6/12105380/alton-sterling-police-shooting-baton-rouge-louisiana. Warning: this news article contains an embedded video which shows the footage of Sterling's killing. Viewer discretion is strongly advised.

7. Fausset et al., "Alton Sterling Shooting."

8. Eric Levenson, "Baton Rouge Police Chief Apologizes for Hiring the Officer Who Killed Alton Sterling," CNN.com, August 1, 2019. https://www.cnn .com/2019/08/01/us/alton-sterling-baton-rouge-police/index.html.

9. "'Suspect Down': Video Footage, Dispatch Tape from Alton Sterling Police Shooting Released," RT.com, July 6, 2016. https://www.rt.com/usa/349787 -anton-sterling-video-dispatch/. Warning: this news article contains an embedded video which shows the footage of Sterling's killing. Viewer discretion is strongly advised.

10. Madison Park, "The 62-Second Encounter between Philando Castile and the Officer Who Killed Him," CNN.com, May 30, 2017. https://www.cnn .com/2017/05/30/us/philando-castile-shooting-officer-trial-timeline.

11. Todd Melby, "Jurors in Manslaughter Trial of Minnesota Cop Review Videos," Reuters, June 13, 2017. https://www.reuters.com/article/us-minnesota-police /jurors-in-manslaughter-trial-of-minnesota-cop-review-videos -idUSKBN1942JU.

12. Park, "62-Second Encounter."

13. Camila Domonoske, "Minnesota Gov. Calls Traffic Stop Shooting 'Absolutely Appalling at All Levels,'" NPR.org, July 7, 2016. https://www.npr.org/sections /thetwo-way/2016/07/07/485066807/police-stop-ends-in-black-mans-death -aftermath-is-livestreamed-online-video. Warning: this news article contains an embedded video which shows the footage of Castile's killing. Viewer discretion is strongly advised.

14. Tyler Merritt, "Before You Call the Cops," YouTube, June 5, 2018. https:// www.youtube.com/watch?v=wKeITMzMn7w.

CHAPTER 17

1. Brené Brown, "Shame v. Guilt." https://brenebrown.com/blog/2013/01/14 /shame-v-guilt/.

2. Not sure, but these ideas are in this message by John Ortberg, where I think I first heard this idea: https://www.faithgateway.com/think-great-thoughts /#.X67t8ZNKhTY.

3. Viktor E. Frankl, *Man's Search for Meaning* (Boston: Beacon Press, 2014), 105.

4. Tasneem Nashrulla, "Amy Cooper Is Facing Charges after She Called the Cops

on a Black Man Who Was Bird-Watching," Buzzfeed News, July 6, 2020. https://www.buzzfeednews.com/article/tasneemnashrulla/amy-cooper-christian -cooper-charges-bird-watcher.

5. "George Floyd: What Happened in the Final Moments of His Life," BBC News, July 16, 2020. https://www.bbc.com/news/world-us-canada-52861726.

6. Gillian Mohney, "Jimmy Kimmel Spotlights Son's Rare Heart Birth Defect," ABC News, May 2, 2017. https://abcnews.go.com/Health/jimmy-kimmel -spotlights-sons-rare-heart-birth-defect/story?id=47154245.

7. "Jimmy Kimmel Reveals Details of His Son's Birth & Heart Disease," Jimmy Kimmel Live, May 1, 2017. https://www.youtube.com/watch?v =MmWWoMcGmo0&t=3s.

8. "Jimmy Kimmel on George Floyd, Riots in Minneapolis & Trump's Violent Stupidity," Jimmy Kimmel Live, May 29, 2020. https://www.youtube.com /watch?v=j2pa-f7zqGU.

READING GROUP GUIDE

DISCUSSION QUESTIONS

1. In chapter 1, Tyler talks about how often people make snap judgments about him based solely on the color of his skin. Think of a time you were judged unfairly based on prejudice or misinformation. Why do you think people are so quick to make assumptions about people or situations they don't understand?

2. In chapter 1, Tyler writes: "It's not my job to try to make every human with fearful or racist thoughts feel comfortable." What does he mean by this? Where does the responsibility to lessen fearful or racist thoughts lie?

3. Tyler was raised in Las Vegas, Nevada, which, as a young child, had a significant impact on how he perceived himself in relation to the world. Where did you grow up? How did the culture of your hometown inform, whether positively or negatively, your understanding of the rest of the state, country, world?

4. When Tyler visits Eutaw in chapter 2, the first question he is asked by a neighborhood boy is whether he is kin. In chapter 3, Tyler struggles with possibly losing his blackness by not joining a gang. Both touch on the need within the black community to feel like family, but what is the difference for Tyler? Why is joining a gang considered solidifying Tyler's blackness?

5. In chapter 3, Tyler says, "If you're truly gifted at something... the black community will let you opt out of traditional roles and responsibilities...with the implicit agreement that you won't forget from whence you came." Discuss the idea of creativity and talent being a channel toward freedom.

6. Tyler talks about a black card as something that black people are born with but are constantly under threat of losing if they exhibit actions that are not considered black. What is your reaction to the term "black card"? Does the idea of a black card encourage black people to give reverence to their heritage and endurance as a people?

7. The desire for a parent's approval is inherent in all children—but the ramifications of that desire being unmet often bleed over into adulthood. How did this play out in Tyler's life? How did it play out in yours?

8. Discuss the Greek concept of *hamartia*, or, essentially, a person's fatal flaw. Why is it so easy to fall prey to behaviors that harm us? Do you think there's any way to avoid developing a *hamartia*?

9. In chapter 6, Tyler says, "There is something for you, something that the world really needs, and that only you can do. Only you. And it's not too late to do it." Can you relate to this statement? Do you have a *Sliding Doors* moment in your life?

10. How did the black church attempt to heal the wounds of its black congregants inflicted by oppression, prejudice, and violence? Discuss the correlation between black history and the fact that, still to this day, black Americans are the most devotedly religious demographic.

11. Merritt writes about the lack of contrition Southerners had toward the people they enslaved after the Civil War and how Southerners upheld the caste system that ensured the continuation of white superiority with lynchings. How do tragedies like the Ahmaud Arbery murder mirror this system in modern times?

12. What are some ways you've come to terms with your own double consciousness—be it race, religion, culture, or socioeconomic status?

13. Think about the quote "proximity breeds empathy." Do you agree with this sentiment? Why or why not?

14. In chapter 11, Tyler discusses the importance of his theater community in his overall personal development and maturation. Why is it so necessary that we invest in community? What lessons can we learn from those who are doing life alongside of us?

15. Tyler writes about Theater Central's love of *Rent* and says that, in the play, love is committing yourself to someone else's good, even if it costs you something. Is this a realistic depiction of love?

16. Consider the history of Stockton, California, the "most diverse city in the United States." Does diversity always equal inclusion? If not, what are some factors that cause distance between diversity and inclusion?

17. Did you have a significant adult influence in your life as a child, whether a parent, teacher, pastor, or coach? How did this person impact your development? Why is it so crucial for kids to have positive role models pouring into them?

18. Merritt describes two black impulses: the voice of Malcolm X, which encourages unflinching protection against violence and exploitation, and the voice of Martin Luther King Jr., which encourages unflinching optimism that freedom will come by resisting fear and hatred. What are the advantages and disadvantages of both?

19. After losing his job as a youth pastor, Merritt's mother advises him to not let someone define who he is. What is the best advice you've gotten after making a mistake? What would you like to hear from someone when you want to feel loved, even when they cannot empathize with you?

20. How can open, honest, intentional, non-judgmental dialogues between people with different cultural, racial, or socioeconomic backgrounds change the way we view those who are different from us? Why do we so often shy away from these types of discussions?

ABOUT THE AUTHOR

Tyler Merritt is an actor, musician, comedian, and activist behind the Tyler Merritt Project. Raised in Las Vegas, he has always had a passion for bringing laughter, grace, and love into any community that he is able to be a part of. For over twenty years now, he has spoken to audiences ranging from elementary school students to nursing home seniors. His television credits include ABC's *Kevin (Probably) Saves the World*, Netflix's *Messiah*, Netflix's *Outer Banks*, Disney/Marvel's *The Falcon and the Winter Soldier*, and Apple TV+'s upcoming series *Swagger*. Tyler's viral videos "Before You Call the Cops" and "Walking While Black" have been viewed by over 60 million people worldwide, with "Before You Call the Cops" voted the number one most powerful video of 2020 by NowThis Politics. He is a cancer survivor who lives in Nashville, Tennessee.

Twitter: @TTMProject · Instagram: @thetylermerrittproject
Facebook: TheTylerMerrittProject

DATE DUE

NOV 1 9 2021		
DEC 1 3 2021		
MAY 1 1 2022		

Demco, Inc. 38-293